393
CAR

Carlson, Lisa,
1938-

Caring for your own
dead.

$12.95

CARING FOR YOUR OWN DEAD

LISA CARLSON

UPPER ACCESS PUBLISHERS
HINESBURG, VERMONT
1987

Caring For Your Own Dead. Copyright © 1987 by Upper Access Publishers. All rights reserved. Printed in the United States of America. For information or to order, write or call:

Upper Access Publishers
One Upper Access Road
P.O. Box 457
Hinesburg, Vermont 05461
(802) 482-2988

Wood block illustrations by Mary Azarian

Library of Congress Catalog Card Number 87-50286

Library of Congress Cataloging-in-Publication Data

Carlson, Lisa, 1938-
    Caring for your own dead.

    Bibliography: p.
    1. Death--Handbooks, manuals, etc. 2. Funeral rites and ceremonies--United States--Handbooks, manuals, etc. 3. Burial law--United States.
    I. Title.
GT3202.C37 1987   393'.0973   87-50286

ISBN 0-942679-00-8

ISBN 0-942679-01-6 (pbk.)

First Edition -   2,3,4,5,6,7,8,9,10.

Contents

Contents

Part 3

To our children - Stuart, Josh, Joie, Shawn, and Rosalie - to whom the task of "final disposition" may fall.

CARING
FOR YOUR
OWN DEAD

Acknowledgements

Scores of people have provided information, insights, inspiration, and encouragement to make this a more detailed and useful book. To them I extend appreciation and gratitude.

I owe special thanks to Sally Cavanaugh. Her "How to Bury Your Own Dead in Vermont" (published by the **Vanguard Press**) was first shared in my writers' group. Because of that article, I had the details I needed just six months later when I had to use them. That information made all my ensuing experiences with death more meaningful, and was the germinating element behind the research for this book.

People in the funeral profession also provided help. Vermont funeral director James Meunier was on the other end of a telephone whenever I had an extra question. Jim Johnston, a member of the Vermont State Funeral Board, made his professional literature and directories available to me. As a result, I was able to call more than 500 crematories, many of which were affiliated with funeral homes. The idea of a family managing death was terribly new for almost all. Yet what I found in my conversations was that the vast majority in the funeral profession expresses caring and service-oriented views. Many listed in this book seemed far more interested in helping families in need than in protecting the "turf" of the funeral industry. And some, including those on state funeral boards, agreed to review the book for accuracy before we went to print.

Indeed, the accuracy and detail in this book would not have been possible without the time and effort of a great many experts in various fields. Patsy Santoro, as a highly respected crematory operator, was able to describe the cremation process in ways that would have been impossible for an outside researcher. Clayton Hewitt, a professional grief therapist and death educator, provided scholarly commentary in the "Afterword" on the value of caring for one's own dead as part of the grieving process. Professor Alexander Capron, widely acknowledged as the nation's foremost authority on the legal ramifications of death and dying, helped greatly to keep my proposals for statutory reform within realistic bounds.

I am indebted also to the various state's attorneys and state health department officials who have taken the time to correspond and review material before publication, to assure that the laws and regulations of each state are accurately represented.

It would be impossible to write about death and burial without acknowledging the classic volume, **Dealing Creatively with Death: A Manual of Death Education and Simple Burial,** by Ernest Morgan, now in its tenth edition. I had the pleasure of corresponding several times with Ernest Morgan during the long process or researching and writing this book. There is no way to quantify the value of the insights, advice, and encouragement that he provided.

Able and sensitive editing was shared with us by Sarah Seidman, Marielle Blais, Barbara Agnew, and Forrest Bowman. I was deeply honored when Mary Azarian, one of my favorite artists, agreed to create the cover.

Before she died, Mary Jane (see Chapter 3) had urged me to get on with my writing. The timely completion of this book, however, has been possible only because of the encouragement and help, in both writing and production, that her son (and my husband), Steve Carlson, has freely given. In many ways, this is his book, too.

Lisa Carlson
Hinesburg, Vermont

Introduction:

What you will learn from this book; and
Why I wrote it

After John died, there was a lot of publicity (with my permission) about the fact that I had handled my own "arrangements." Hardly a week went by in the following year without a telephone call or letter from someone else involved in the plans surrounding a death. I also was asked to speak to church groups and classes on "Death and Dying."

People were anxious for information, even if their choices might have been different from mine. Many expressed a desire to overcome feelings of helplessness or frustration in dealing with death. They expressed a need for more personal identity and control in the choices they made, similar to the decisions regarding "natural" childbirth and hospice.

One of the serious mistakes I made was to remove John's body before others - his mother and his children - had experienced his death first-hand. Over a year later, for example, when my son Shawn was four years old, he asked, "But where is my Daddy dead?" The need for involvement of the immediate family was echoed in the various groups with which I spoke. It became clear that all close friends and family should have the opportunity to participate, whenever possible, in ways that lend meaning to the person involved.

No one death is like any other. A family's choices must take into consideration religious, cultural, and personal beliefs, as well as the individual wishes of the deceased and the needs of surviving family and friends, often complicated by the circumstances at the time of death. But it is also difficult to make the most appropriate choices without first understanding the basic legal and practical considerations.

In important endeavors, we try to become educated consumers. Yet few of us learn the basics of planning for our own deaths or for the final act of friendship and dedication to a person we love. That is unfortunate and sometimes tragic. Death is among the most intimate and personal of human events. There is but one chance to honor the wishes of the deceased and meet the needs of grieving relatives and friends in each death experience.

I hope this book will encourage people to become more informed about the choices to be made and less afraid to deal with death. By dealing with the physical aspects of death, emotional needs may be handled effectively as well. For me and for many others with whom I have talked, personal involvement at a time of death was significant, meaningful, and even necessary in order to say goodbye to a loved one. Examples are shared in the first three chapters.

Each of those three chapters was written shortly after an experience with death. I have avoided the temptation to go back and edit them - even though the writing is inconsistent with the rest of the book. Rewriting would have dulled the emotional intensity that prompted the writing of this book. I hope that sharing those emotions will encourage others to become more actively involved in funeral arrangements.

The bulk of the book, however, is factual information. For those who choose to handle all of the arrangements without the help of a funeral director, I have described the available legal options and required procedures in each state. And for those who choose to work with a funeral director, the information here should help a family to make educated, well-considered decisions.

The book is designed to be used in two ways. It can be read for general information (to generate discussion and to help make funeral plans), or saved to use as a ready reference when specific details are needed quickly at a time of loss.

A side mission, important in its own right, developed during my research. No state currently has statutes which are complete or entirely appropriate regarding death. Some states are not clear or specific enough on procedures that are legitimately within the purview of a state's interest. Other states have restrictive statutes which have no place in a society that recognizes the diversity and worth of individuals.

Therefore, Chapter 10 of Part I contains recommendations for reforming state statutes. I have tried to make suggestions as comprehensive as possible, and I have borrowed from existing statutes where I could. While the rights of indivi- duals are my primary concern, I have tried to recognize all other legitimate needs as well. My hope is that private citizens and interested groups will urge their legislators to consider reform of their state's statutes. It is unfortunate that attention is usually drawn to these issues only at times of immediate need.

I expect to revise this book in subsequent printings and will welcome any correspondence that will help to make it more useful to others. I would be glad, too, to hear how this book has affected your experience with death.

Part One:
Caring For Your
Own Dead

WHY AND HOW: GENERAL INFORMATION

John

It was 2:30 a.m. when I woke up and found the empty space in our bed. John must have gone for a walk, and I wanted to be with him. There were intense, upsetting problems at the small Vermont school where he taught, and John had, for the most part, contained his anger at the situation, always hoping to be the peacemaker. As a result of that effort, he developed a serious stomach pain. He hated what the pain-relieving drugs did to him, and I knew he continued to be depressed. But just that night he'd taken me in his arms, as he so often did, and told me how much he loved me.

I threw on some clothes and tried following his footprints in the shallow March snow, quickly losing them. At the end of the driveway something made me stop. There was the bright red truck that was his pride and joy. I struggled with the icy door, unprepared for the shock . . . his still, cold body was there, his deer rifle beside him! My husband, my love, was dead! His note: "I'm sorry, I can't stand the pain any more."

In hysterical tears I ran to the house, made phone calls to close friends and to the police. The next few hours were a chaotic blur of anguish while I struggled to hold on to some control of what was happening and would happen. I had to answer questions only I could answer and make decisions that I wasn't prepared for but were mine to make. My anger at the school, John's pain, and my loss exploded over and over in sobbing. But there was a fierce need to protect John, to care for him as I never would again.

It was an intimate life John and I had shared, intimate with each other and with the world around us. We were married at home, and John had wanted to be buried at home. But since the ground was still frozen, cremation seemed the only alternative. I would select the simplest procedure.

Opening the Yellow Pages, I reluctantly called a funeral home and inquired about the price of cremation. (There was almost nothing in the bank, and I wasn't even sure if I could cash John's next paycheck. I was panic-stricken about my finances.) The man told me cremation would be $500 including the "required casket." But I didn't have that much money. I called the crematory in St. Johnsbury, 50 miles

away. It was very early in the morning, but the telephone
was answered, by a Mr. Pearl. He did request a box, but said
it could be of the simplest construction, even something I
made myself. And the price for cremation? $85. I thanked Mr.
Pearl and hung up. Did I have the energy in my despair to
build John's box? Probably not. My young children would be
up soon and they would need me now. So I tried another
funeral home.

"Well, the price for cremation, which includes everything,
is $700," said the funeral director.

Two more calls gave me total costs still above my bank
balance, but when I pressed for itemized prices, the amounts
quoted went as low as $50 for the box or for transportation.
Just in rough averages I thought my expenses should have
been well under $250 for the kind of service I requested,
without a viewing, calling hours, or other use of the funeral
home. I couldn't understand it.

Since there would be an autopsy, the police called a
funeral director to take John's body to Burlington. I plied
him, too, with my questions.

"How much is the simplest box for cremation?"

"$60."

"And how much is transporting the body to St. Johnsbury?"

"$50."

He saw me reaching a total of $195 on a scrap of paper as
I included the $85 for cremation. I was thinking with relief
that somehow I'd be able to manage that when he said, "But
you'll have to add a $325 service charge to that."

Someone offered me money. "Let him do it. Let him do it."

But a quiet realization made me answer, "No, I must do
this myself. I want to do it."

Only months before, a friend in my writers' group had
brought us her article, "How To Bury Your Own Dead in
Vermont." Its historical background had awakened an identity
with my own Vermont ancestors. The details faded in and out
of my consciousness now, and the task of grappling with
"arrangements" seemed enormous. I understood just how easy
it would be to let a funeral director take over as I drained
my body with tears. But I felt a strong need to express my
love and caring for John even in death.

I knew that under Vermont law I could transport the body
myself. I would need a permit to do so, and it would mean
asking for the help of a friend with a station wagon or
truck. But I suddenly knew that for me, and for John, my
decision would be the right one.

Would this funeral director be willing to sell just his box?
Yes. I asked if there would be a service charge to place the
body in his $60 box. There wouldn't. "Then call me when you

get back from the autopsy," I said, "and I will pick John up."

That the total cost would now be under $200 had become secondary. I needed to be a part of John's death as I was of his life. If I had had money, I would have lost that, given that away, in a moment of grief and confusion!

When our kids got up I told them everything, as truthfully as I could. We all cried. The house was full now, and their grandmother took them off to play. (It was months later that their grief and questions finally spilled and continued to flow.) But I went on weeping, for our five-year-old daughter whose father would not be there on her wedding day, and our three-year-old son who would learn to fish without his dad. I moved through that day in a haze, a Tilt-a-Whirl of emotion. And I had calls to make.

I worried about asking my friend Richard to make the drive with me to St. Johnsbury. A sensitive, older person who had lost his wife to cancer the year before, would he be uncomfortable on such a trip? It was not the way he had made his arrangements. But perhaps he'd understand. "Of course," he said, "John was my friend."

And so that snowy evening after the children had gone to bed, we drove to the funeral home to pick up John's body. The town secretary met us to sign the transit permit and share a hug. Then Richard and I left on the 50-mile trip, quietly crying, sometimes talking, sometimes silent. It seemed a long trip but one that should not be hurried.

Mr. Pearl had agreed to meet us at the crematory even though it was well after usual business hours. As we unloaded the box, I knew I had to see John one more time even if his body was now a lifeless one. Richard got a screwdriver from under the front seat of the truck. And as we lifted the cover, I wept for the tender, gentle man I had married, whose life I had shared with so much joy. Then I softly patted his face a final good-by. The person that I loved was living in my heart. I was ready to let the body go.

◙

John had been a rare and special person, not just for me but for the many children he had taught and for those whose lives he had touched. I became aware that others needed to express their love for John, to share his death as well.

In the obituary I asked the newspaper to announce an "Open House" in his memory two days later. It seemed like hundreds came. We heard John's favorite music from **Oliver**, the show his Children's Theater Group had done so well. And we were surrounded by flowers like the gardens he had loved. Our weeping and our laughing memories blended in a celebration of the gift his life had been to us.

14

Raphael

Chapter 2

There was no notice in the paper, no formal obituary. But on this early summer evening, the dirt road was lined with cars and trucks. We walked somberly toward the rustic country home. I took a bucket with blooming iris and my shovel. With me were my children - one a next year's kindergarten classmate of the boy now dead, the other slightly older - and Grandma on a cane.

Familiar people stood in quiet clusters around the yard, for the house was nearly full. I could hear a resonant voice though I did not recognize the reading, and as my children slipped inside I followed to be near. They found other children sitting on a stairway and moved close beside the dead child's sister, looking down. Their eyes were on the body in the small pine box. Lupines pink and purple in casual arrangements were all around. But my attention sought the sorrow-laden parents - the mother with the youngest daughter in her arms, her husband by her side. I was glad the poem continued on, for I needed the comfort of that metered voice and time to weep my silent tears.

Then the parents shared with us the joy they'd known in this, their only son, a child who had cared and understood their march for peace though he had stayed at home that day. Others offered, too, the happiness remembered - the boy who was so proud that his father walked on stilts, the boy who had picked a friend that he would marry when he grew up.

A final reading drew us to the task at hand. An uncle closed the box, secured the lid. In quiet reverence, four assumed the burden of the load and passed on through the door. The children ventured next and led our way, a winding path through fern and woods. A tiny bell his father carried called us, too.

The box was resting by the hole, a careful oblong in the earth beside a birch, and on the boulder at one end a candle burned. His mother read the Song of Mourning in a Hebrew chant that others joined. Then one by one, we laid our flower bouquets upon his box, to share the journey on ahead.

It was his father who made the final move, who tearfully beckoned help to gently guide the box, with ready strings, to rest below. He took a shovel in his hands and stabbed the pile of dirt, then lifted it and cast the dirt into the hole. The shovel soon changed hands, and all of us - the children, too - moved earth to rest upon the flowers and the box. And father hugged a sobbing daughter as we filled the hole, planted iris and a rose.

It was a gentle singing that grew among the many there: songs of God, of Heaven, a lullaby. And though we choked and wept, we sang again, of love and life in memory of this soul.

◉

Raphael, age 5, died sleeping in his mother's arms. He'd had pneumonia, though no one - even doctors - had known. His parents brought his body back from the New York grandparents they had been visiting at the time of the 1982 June peace march. His was a country burial on their own land in Middlesex, Vermont. (First printed in the **Vanguard Press**, September 1982)

woodcut by Sam Kerson

Mary Jane

by Steve Carlson   Chapter **3**

Although my mother was only 63 years old, her death was "expected," at least by the people who worked at the hospital. She had been terminally ill for some time, and her doctors were amazed she held on and remained productive as long as she did.

Yet when the time came for funeral arrangements, we were not well prepared. We had to learn and plan quickly at a time of great stress.

Our failure to plan ahead was not, I suspect, unusual.

Before she got sick, Ma was young and healthy, so there seemed to be little reason to discuss death.

Then, when she was stricken by a disease considered 100 percent fatal, she wasn't ready to die. As a teacher and writer, she had projects to complete and people who relied on her to help make meaning of their own lives. So she fought the disease.

Although she was given zero odds by the medical community, Ma was fighting to win. She said more than once she only wanted to be around people "who believe in miracles." Could we doubt her? Did John Henry's family ask him what they should do if the steam drill won?

We weren't just humoring her. Friends and family alike became convinced that if anybody could beat back an incurable disease, Mary Jane could. Funeral planning was a taboo subject which, if it had been brought up, would have hastened her death and ended her hopes of achieving more of her life's goals.

Her foe was the AIDS virus, but the situation would have been the same if she had been stricken by cancer, stroke, heart disease, or any other illness more commonly afflicting people my mother's age.

She did hedge her bets in the final weeks. Weak and bedridden, she asked her four sons to be with her, in shifts, 24 hours a day. In addition to caring for her physical needs, she wanted at least one of us there whenever she was able to summon up the energy to talk. She had things to tell us and, by implication, there was little time left.

It was a difficult time for all of us. My brothers and I had to juggle busy schedules and important commitments, but being with our mother took priority at this time of need.

At her request, on June 16, 1986, Ma was rushed to the hospital in extreme discomfort. She told her doctor she was now able to prepare for death, since she was satisfied that the more important aspects of her life's work would be continued. She said she needed three days of medical care, with her sons at her side, before going home to die. She repeated, for emphasis, her desire to die at home, not at the hospital.

During the three days, she summoned us as often as she was able, straining to speak. She commented on our shortcomings, specific tasks she wanted us to accomplish, political insights, and Biblical interpretations. It was not feasible for us to bring up other issues for discussion. She had only a few words left, which she had to reserve for subjects of her choosing.

She mentioned funeral arrangements only once. She said she wanted a simple burial, not cremation, and specified a location which had spiritual significance to her. The energy she consumed by making the brief request completely exhausted her.

Consistent with the schedule she had set, on June 19th the doctors agreed to send her home. She died a few hours later.

◙

Although none of us had experience with funeral arrangements, it didn't occur to us to delegate our final acts of love to outsiders.

In retrospect, that may have been partly because of our experiences when she was bedridden. Ma had preferred that her sheets be changed by family members, for example, even though trained nurses were far more skilled at replacing sheets on an occupied bed. That was because we took the time to rub her feet. She remarked more than once she needed her feet rubbed more than she needed the sheets changed. Yet nurses always seemed too busy to provide that extra attention.

When it came time for burial and tribute, the qualities of thoughtfulness, consideration, and love seemed far more important than professional expertise. Those qualities were abundant among Ma's family and friends.

All official acts had to await completion of a death certificate by my mother's doctor, who was out of state and wouldn't arrive until morning. In the meantime, it was up to us to notify friends and relatives.

Sitting in my mother's apartment, I telephoned as many close friends and relatives as I could. But the telephone calls were emotionally difficult, and I didn't personally know all of the people who should be informed.

My mother did, however, have an address book and a home computer. I was not familiar with her word processing program, and am not good at learning new computer languages. But somehow - I think with my mother's help, but I won't try to convince you of that - about 140 letters were written that night.

My wife and I spent the night on the couch in Ma's apartment. Was it just a body in the other room or were we there to be with her? I'm not sure, but we needed to be there.

In the morning, after the death certificate was filled out, I called in an obituary to the local newspaper. The reporter was accustomed to talking with funeral directors who dictate the information in the newspaper's standard format. But she was patient with me as I struggled to recall the maiden name of my mother's mother, the dates of her various leadership positions, and the precise numbers of nieces and nephews.

There was a sense of urgency about burial once the permits were in order. None of us knew how quickly bodies decompose, but we didn't want to leave Ma in her bed any longer than necessary.

The family had been inclined toward cremation, but Ma had specifically requested burial, so two of my brothers built a simple pine casket and brought it to the apartment. Another brother spent an hour with Ma, quietly saying goodbye. Then each of us joined him, lifting a corner of the sheet to place Ma's body in the box.

The burial site my mother had requested was unavailable, so we chose what we guessed would be an equally desirable location for her: a hilltop owned by her brother where she had spent many happy years.

We needed approval from the municipal clerks of the city where Ma died and the town where she was to be buried. Neither clerk was very familiar with the tasks, since the forms are usually filled out by funeral directors, who are deputized for that purpose.

Both clerks, however, were extremely responsive and helpful. After checking with health officers and other officials, they performed their duties with a minimum of delay.

My brothers and I transported the casket in my pickup truck, and spent the next eight hours digging the grave by hand. It was hard work, in clay soil with many large rocks. We were eager to meet all legal requirements, so we dug the grave six feet deep. We learned later that the law required only five feet, which would have saved us about an hour of hard labor, but complaints were minimal.

This task culminated weeks of shared work and shared emotions which brought the four of us closer together than anything else we could have possibly done. For many years we had been separated by distance, careers, and individual commitments. By working together at a time of great need we renewed and strengthened our family bonds. For my brothers and me, the private burial was the best way to say goodbye to our mother.

But others also needed a chance to pay their respects. (Although Ma was deeply religious, she was not a church member, so we had no prescribed procedure for honoring her.) We took the easiest route we could think of. We announced a memorial gathering a week after burial, brought a few jugs of cider, accepted offers by others to provide additional refreshments, and played it by ear.

Scores of people showed up, including some who drove great distances. None of us knew everybody else. The only thing we had in common was that Mary Jane had touched each of our lives in profound ways. But that was actually a lot to have in common, and gathering together, at least this one time, was important.

Lacking any formal rituals, we sat around the hillside grave site, saying and doing whatever seemed appropriate. Some spoke words of tribute, some recalled meaningful incidents and experiences, some sang songs, some planted flowers.

As far as I know, nobody felt uncomfortable, out of place, or unfulfilled. There were many comments about what a moving, special experience it was. Some of us remained long after the anticipated two or three hours, conversing and recalling our memories until sunset.

◙

It would be inaccurate to say there were no funeral costs. Wood and nails for the coffin were worth a few dollars, as were the cider and other refreshments. People who drove to the burial site had to fuel up their cars, and I'm sure some of the flowers people brought had been purchased. But overall financial costs were so minimal that nobody kept track of who spent what. We were able to earmark whatever was left of Mary Jane's checking account (after her bills were paid) for publication of a book of her final writings.

We are not a wealthy family, but if any of us had thought that spending two or three thousand dollars for a professional funeral would have made the experience more meaningful for anybody involved, we would have raised the money. We have no regrets over our decision to handle arrangements ourselves.

◎

We also handled probate ourselves, not a difficult task since there were few possessions and no disputes. The court clerk asked if the funeral director had been paid, and was astonished to learn we hadn't hired one. No questions were asked about bills due to health care providers, utilities, or other creditors. Those bills got paid, of course, but we found it ironic that funeral expenses were the only obligation not entrusted to the good will and honesty of the family.

◎

This experience with home burial is not offered as a blueprint for others. We were influenced by my mother's wishes, the needs of our family and friends, and the physical possibilities available to us. If Mary Jane's beliefs had been different, or if there hadn't been a rural hilltop that was appropriate for burial, the arrangements would have been far different. Perhaps, in other circumstances, help from a funeral director would have been desirable or necessary.

But since death is a common human experience, there are some general conclusions that may be of use to others. One is the importance of planning ahead if at all possible: in our case hard decisions were made harder because they were delayed until action became necessary. Another is that personal involvement in death arrangements is a way of fulfilling emotional needs that probably cannot be met in any other way.

Home Funerals:
A Historical Perspective

In early America, home funerals were the practice everywhere, and each community had a group of women who came in to help with the "laying out of the dead."

In some parts of the country, religious and ethnic groups have maintained the practice of caring for their own dead. American Indians, the Amish, Quakers, and some fundamentalist Christian congregations are notable examples of groups whose members often share in the duties of preparation and arrangements as well as support for the grieving family.

Many Hebrew congregations still maintain a "Hevra Kadisha" (Holy Society) to bathe and dress a deceased in the traditional simple linen garment, and lay the body in a plain pine box. Membership is considered a great honor, an opportunity to serve another with no thought or possibility of return.

With the increase of mobility and the onset of the Civil War, preservation of bodies through embalming came into widespread use for the convenience of distant relatives or the shipping of deceased. Undertaking became at least a part-time job in many towns. In Craftsbury Common, Vermont, the old sign used to read, "Hardware - Upholstery - Undertaking."

Along with the spread of wealth in this country, it became common to include a display of community position and status at the time of a person's funeral. One sociologist, quoted by the editors of **Consumer Reports** in the book **Funerals-Consumers' Last Rights***, states that ". . . because people increasingly lack both the ceremonial and social mechanisms and arrangements that once existed to help them cope with death, monetary expenditures have taken on added importance. . ." In large cities, this practice prompted sufficient business that undertakers could charge for keeping elaborate establishments available on a regular basis. Furthermore, crowded urban housing made home funerals more difficult. What once occurred at home was moved to funeral homes.

By the turn of the century, the term "funeral director" was considered preferable to undertaker (at least by those in the profession), and the newly formed National Funeral Directors Association was eagerly pressing its members to consider themselves "professionals", not tradesmen as the earlier coffin-makers had been. The regular use of embalming was encouraged, and the new professionals used this to suggest that they were keepers of the public health at a time when many diseases were prevalent.

As communities grew more diverse, funeral homes were established to serve ethnic or religious groups. According to some studies, there are now ten times the number of funeral establishments needed although there has been little change in the death rate. People seem willing to pay for service by "one of their own."

Certainly with the spread of the hospice movement and the popularity of Elisabeth Kubler-Ross's book **On Death and Dying**, families are again dealing with death in a more personal way. Some families are now choosing to handle their own death arrangements privately, without the use of a funeral director. Relatives who have done so share a feeling of spiritual and emotional fulfillment. For many, it has facilitated the grieving process by keeping the family involved at the time of death. Some have felt they were better able to "let go" when the time came. Personal fears of not being able to deal with a body have proved unfounded: "It was not as difficult as I thought it would be,". . ."I had to be close,". . ."I could not give his body to strangers."

The **Consumer Reports** book quotes the late Erich Lindemann, M.D., a Harvard psychiatrist, as saying that the most useful part of the funeral process is "the moment of truth that comes when living persons confront the fact of death by looking at the body." Funeral directors would choose this as a reason to suggest an open casket funeral. Family management of death is even more to the point.

In the conclusion of his scholarly work, **Inventing the American Way of Death, 1830-1920**, historian James Farrell writes:

Keeping death out of mind cuts people off from an important fact of their physical, mental, and spiritual existence. If knowing that we will die is part of what makes us human, then forgetting that we will die threatens our humanity. In the same way, the denial of death in American society also cuts people off from our **common** humanity, keeping them at such a distance from the deaths of others that they cannot grieve or mourn, except in the culturally prescribed "way." The paraphernalia of the American way of death keep such people at one remove from their own feelings. When they want to focus their mind and emotions on the loss in their lives, they find only a dead social convention designed to constrain and contain grief. This social convention developed historically, but it continues today, as Americans delegate control of death and the funerals to specialized funeral service personnel. Consequently, funerals are custom-made only in the same sense that automobiles are, and the price we pay for paying our last respects in the American way of death is the price of our personality, which we have purposely withheld from the funeral. By our passive role in directing our funerals, we have transformed an important rite of personal passage into an impersonal rite of impassivity. There have been costs as well as benefits from the American way of death.

Undoubtedly one factor that prompts people to care for their own dead is the financial saving. But of those who have described their experiences to me, all have felt - after the funeral - that caring for their own was ultimately more important than the dollar saving.

In **A Manual of Death Education and Simple Burial,** Ernest Morgan writes of his own experience with the Yellow Springs Friends Meeting Burial Committee, ". . . what I had anticipated to be a disagreeable chore turned out to be a meaningful privilege - serving one's friends at a time of profound need."

Cremation With Dignity

by Patsy Santoro with Peter Bilodeau   Chapter 5

History of Cremation

The use of fire to prepare the dead for memorialization is not new. Prehistoric people thought of fire as a miracle from their gods. Fire allowed them to cook and keep warm and was possibly used as a method to protect and honor their dead.

The Slavic tribes of the Dniester and Dnieper River valleys of Russia may have been the first to cremate, according to some literature. But the Babylonians ritualized their cremation ceremony. The Babylonians wrapped the bodies of deceased loved ones in a combustible material, then encased them in clay. The clay coffin was then placed on a brick form, and a funeral pyre was built around it and set ablaze.

People of ancient India also used the funeral pyre. They called it the "Sacred Flame" and displayed much of their artistic talents on the urns in which their loved ones' cremated remains were memorialized. The word "funeral" comes originally from a Sanskrit word of northern India which means "smoke."

Around the year 1000 B.C., the Greeks began to practice cremation to protect their war dead. Their enemies were known to take buried Greek soldiers' bodies from the ground and desecrate them. The Greeks, after getting wise to their enemies' tactics, cremated the remains of their soldiers and took the cremains back to Greece to be entombed with great ceremony and honor. Cremation of soldiers soon became a popular tradition of Greek culture, and the tradition spread throughout the country. Later, cremation became the most popular form of preparation of the dead for all Greeks.

The Bible, in I Samuel 31, reports the cremation of Saul:

(12) All the valiant men arose, and went all night, and took the body of Saul and the bodies of his sons from the wall of Beth'-Shan, and came to Ja'besh, and burnt them there.
(13) And they took their bones, and buried them under a tree at Ja'besh, and fasted seven days.

Romans, too, practiced cremation from 753 B.C. to 476 A.D. Ovid (43 B.C.-17 A.D.), the Roman poet, states that the body of Remus, one of the mythological founders of Rome, was cremated, as was that of Julius Caesar (100-49 B.C.). Remains were memorialized in elaborate urns built into the walls around Rome.

The extravagance of cremation during the later years of the Roman Republic made it difficult for the poor to practice it. The affluent of Rome spurned earth burial, preferring lavish funeral pyres and inurnment in beautiful gold and silver urns. Nero used more myrrh, incense, and fragrant oils to cremate his wife than were produced in all of Arabia that year.

The Vikings of the Bronze Age practiced a unique form of cremation. The leaders and dead warriors of the Viking fighting forces were placed into "fire ships," which were sent out to sea and ignited. Also, old German chronicles indicated that Attila, King of the Huns, was cremated fully armed and sitting on his horse.

Cremation, along with Buddhism, came into Japan in 552 A.D. The first recorded cremation in that country was 702 A.D., when a Buddhist priest was cremated. Jitro is considered the first Japanese emperor to be cremated.

Cremation was also the primary means of disposal of deceased persons in England from 787 A.D., when the Danes invaded, until 1066 A.D., when William the Conqueror had defeated Harold the Saxon at the Battle of Hastings. From that time, until 1840 or so, the practice of cremation faded.

The early 1800's brought a revival of cremation in Europe. The English poet Shelley drowned in the Mediterranean, and the Tuscan Quarantine Law stated that cremation was required in such cases to protect the populace from disease. His cremains were buried near Rome, close to the grave of another poet, Keats.

By 1869, the first modern crematory was constructed by an Italian scientist named Brunetti. After that, the International Medical Congress of Florence urged all nations to promote cremation. The Italian Congress viewed cremation as the most practical method of disposal of the dead. The Congress believed that open land should be for the living.

In England, between 1840 and 1870, people discovered that their country was rapidly becoming urbanized and that cemeteries were deteriorating. In 1874, Sir Henry Thompson formed the Cremation Society of England, with the first modern cremation being performed in that country in 1885. Thirty years hence, cremation became a subject for Parliamentary debate. Finally, the law-making body declared cremation a legal method of disposing of the dead.

Today, in both England and Japan, cremation is the most common form of disposition of the dead. Between half and three-quarters of those who die there are cremated.

A formal American crematory was established in Washington, Pennsylvania, by Dr. Francis Julius Le Moyne in 1876, but the first known cremation of an American colonist was the body of Colonel Henry Laurens in 1792. Laurens presided over the Continental Congress of 1777-78 and was a member of George Washington's military staff.

At least some American Indians preferred cremation to earth burial because they discovered that their deceased often were dug up by animals. In fact, two crude containers believed to be cremated remains of American Indians were discovered in Connecticut in 1974 and are now in the archives of the Connecticut state capital.

Traditional Jewish culture forbids cremation and the terrors of the Holocaust make cremation unacceptable to many Jews. The Catholic Church, however, has removed its ban on cremation.

In 1884 there were 41 cremations in the United States. By the turn of the century the total had risen to 13,281 a year. During the 19th century and into the early 20th century crematories were established throughout the country. From 26 crematories in 1900 the number grew to 585 in 1980, and the number is still growing rapidly, indicating a continuing increase in the choice of cremation for final disposition in America.

Contemporary Cremation Practices

Preparing the body for a wake or visitation hours and arranging church services are to be considered in a cremation, just as they are for earth burial or entombment.

When choosing a casket for cremation, most crematories simply require a rigid combustible container. Rosewood, mahogany, pine or cloth-covered caskets are suitable for cremation. Families who have wake or visitation hours generally are concerned with the appearance of the casket, and most handsome wood caskets are suitable for a cremation.

Few crematories will accept plastic or fiberglass caskets. The intense heat required for cremation will melt the container and interfere with proper cremation. Burning plastic also gives off lethal gases that have made some members of crematory staffs quite ill.

Caskets with polyvinyl chloride filler and lining are not allowed for cremation. The vinyl, when exposed to heat, releases particles of black, sooty, sticky material that pollute the environment. However, once that problem was brought to the attention of casket manufacturers, most of them stopped using the material. Although the increase in the number of cremations has hurt the casket industry, the manufacturers generally have cooperated by not using pollutants in their products. Many manufacturers have marked their caskets "suitable for cremation."

For those concerned with economy or simplicity, there are many types of boxes acceptable for cremation. Some funeral directors build their own cremation containers out of pine, plywood, pressboard, or other combustible material, but these are usually reserved for clients who choose not to have viewing hours. The lowest cost containers are usually labelled as "alternative containers," the expression used in the Federal Trade Commission's Funeral Rule. Many of these containers are made of heavy cardboard, and fulfill the crematory requirements.

If the family were to choose a non-combustible casket for viewing, the crematory would need a simple but sturdy combustible container for the cremation. In such situations, it is often possible to rent an attractive casket for viewing, at about half the cost of purchasing the casket.

When a cardboard cremation container is used, a thin piece of pine or plywood should be placed under the deceased to keep the container rigid. The board enables the deceased to be readily moved from a vehicle into a church, for example. Without the board, handling the deceased, particularly a heavy person, is difficult not only for the pallbearers but the staff at the crematory as well.

In fact, handling a body in an undignified manner has a psychological effect on the crematory staff. Pouches or body bags, often used to carry disaster victims from the scene of a tragedy, should be discarded and replaced by a rigid container prior to cremation.

Some crematories use a simple, uncovered cremation "tray," with sides about four to six inches high, if the body arrives with no other container. Other crematories require that the body be in a covered receptacle.

If handling the deceased becomes difficult for the crematory staff, much of the dignity and respect for the dead will be gone. In one unfortunate experience, a very large person was placed in a non-rigid container, and the sides of the container burst just as the deceased was being placed into the cremation chamber. It was unpleasant for the staff; dignity had vanished.

It is also important to remove a pacemaker from the deceased prior to cremation. The pacemakers with lithium-type batteries can explode and cause considerable damage to the cremation chamber. The explosion will pollute the environment. Usually a pacemaker is removed at the place of death, or a trained funeral director can be asked to remove one. The person delivering the body for cremation may be liable for any damage to a cremation chamber resulting from a pacemaker explosion.

When making cremation arrangements, you must remember to deal with the valuables that a deceased might have been wearing at the time of death. Too often, and too late, crematory staff members are asked what happened to a ring or other jewelry that was on the deceased at the time of cremation. One young widow managed to retrieve a wedding ring only because the crematory was shut down for the weekend. Cremators generally do not check the deceased for valuables.

With the fluctuating price in precious metals, many families ask what happens to the gold contained in a person's mouth. When the gold alloy is melted during the cremation process, it forms small BB-sized pellets. The pellets may possibly fall between the cracks of the fire brick lining in the retort (the cremation chamber). A family can ask that crematory staff check for this metal, but there is no certainty of retrieving it. At some high temperatures gold will vaporize. If saving the gold is important to a family, the metal should be removed from the body before the deceased is brought to the crematory. The services of a dentist might be arranged for this, but the cost would probably be greater than the value of the gold retrieved. Some dentists have refused such requests. Gold in dental work may be as little as 2% of the alloy. According to the Ney Company in Hartford, Connecticut, three gold crowns would yield only about $10 in gold value at current prices ($350 oz., July 1986). A 1979 study on dental gold done by the University of Minnesota in conjunction with the Minnesota Department of Health arrived at similar conclusions.

When the deceased is brought to the crematory, the legal transit documents, burial or cremation papers, and the crematory's authorization for cremation must be surrendered, along with the cremation fee. The documents are checked very carefully by the crematory staff to be sure the proper authorities have signed them. Signatures of a representative of the state's department of vital statistics or health agency, the medical examiner, the funeral director or whoever is administering the arrangements - usually family, but some-times a friend - are required. Many crematories require consent from all next of kin. A telegram will often suffice if a family member is not located in the area where the cremation will take place.

A very important element of the documentation is the time

of death. Many states require that a person must be deceased for 48 hours prior to cremation. This is a precaution to ensure that any investigation of the cause of death can be completed. Obviously, once cremation occurs, there is no way to determine the cause of death. If a person is buried conventionally, the body can be exhumed if further investigation is required. In some states, if a body is held for cremation beyond 24 hours, refrigeration or embalming may be required by state law.

When the necessary paperwork is completed, the deceased is given an identification number at the crematory. The tag, generally made of stainless steel, is placed in the cremation chamber during the process. Some crematories use a plastic identification tag and place it outside the chamber during the cremation. When the cremation is complete, the tag is placed with the cremains.

Many crematories have chapels. If a family wishes to have a service at the crematory, it is generally done prior to cremation. The casket or container is placed in the chapel as it would be in a funeral home or church. Flowers can be placed around the deceased, with prayers and reading as desired. Some crematory chapels have organs or can pipe in recorded music if the family wishes.

Some families will request to have someone stay in the crematory chapel or waiting room until the cremation is complete. On occasion, a member of the family may ask to see the casket being placed into the cremation chamber. On very few occasions, a family member may ask to view the entire cremation. Because of the way most cremation chambers are designed, it is impossible to view the cremation from the front of the chamber, and there may be other cremations already scheduled or in progress.

Most crematories will allow families to follow their religious beliefs and customs to the extent possible. For example, one family from India, whose loved one died in New Haven, Connecticut, had driven the deceased to the Evergreen Crematory there, stopping about 200 feet away. The family then carried the deceased to the crematory, since it was their custom to carry their loved ones to the funeral pyre. Inside the crematory, they held their religious service, and the cremation followed immediately. In this instance, the family was allowed to view the cremation. Another family from India chose to place branches on and beside the casket of their loved one as it was being placed into the cremation chamber.

Once the casket is placed into the cremation chamber, usually on wooden dowel rollers, the cremation process can begin. Most crematories use natural gas or oil to fuel the cremation. Others use propane gas or electricity as fuel. Many units are designed with flat surfaces, and burners are installed to cremate from two sides and the top. Newer units have burners that also cremate from below the casket.

The cremation chamber is lined with fire brick. These bricks can withstand heat up to 3,500 degrees Fahrenheit, but the units generally cremate at 1,800 degrees. If the chamber has been heated by a previous cremation, the temperature during the subsequent cremation may reach 2,400 degrees.

Cremation time varies with the type of container and the size of the deceased. Generally, a cremation can be completed in one or two hours, but some have taken up to three and one-half hours or so. Some of the newer units can cremate in less time because they are built more compactly and take less time to heat up. Many are on timers so they will shut off automatically after a given time. With automatic shut-off and other design features of the newer chambers, the cremains need not be handled extensively during the process.

All of the newer crematory units are constructed with after-burners and scrubbers to prevent air pollution. Crematory operators need to be careful about smoke and usually can control it by opening and closing drafts. In most states, crematories are inspected regularly, either by the Department of Health or an environmental agency.

When the cremation is complete and the burners in the chamber are shut off, the chamber must cool down before the cremains can be removed. In fact, the chamber is so hot that if you were to look at the hearth just after a cremation, the bricks would have a bright pink glow. Once cooled, the cremation chamber can be opened and the cremains, which are three to seven pounds of clean, white bone fragments, can be removed. The staff takes great care to retrieve every particle of the cremains and place them on a metal tray for processing.

Processing cremains begins by taking an electromagnet and withdrawing all the metal from the cremation container-nails, staples, and other small pieces of metal generally mixed with the cremains. Also, pieces of charcoal from the cremation process will be removed.

When all foreign matter is removed, the bone fragments will range in size from minute particles to four-inch-long pieces. They are then placed into a pulverizer, or some type of grinding machine, and converted to very small, unrecognizable fragments. Some machines can convert the cremains to the size of sugar crystals. The cremains then are placed in temporary containers, usually made of tin, plastic, or cardboard, and shipped to their destination.

Most cremains are sent or hand-delivered to local funeral

directors who are responsible for getting them to the family. Should the crematory have to hold the cremains for a short time, there usually is a fee for storage and insurance. When the cremains must be mailed, they are placed in a mailing carton. Generally cremains are shipped registered mail to ensure that they arrive at the appropriate destination. They are also insured and marked for special handling. As of this writing, cremains cannot be dispatched by United Parcel Service, according to UPS policy. In some states, Federal Express or Purolator Courier may be used for the delivery of cremains.

During the winter months when the ground is frozen in a large part of our country, immediate cremation may be preferable to waiting for a spring earth burial. Furthermore, it is not uncommon for one to die away from a final resting place. Some 8,000 Americans die abroad each year. When the remains must be transported over a great distance, cremation may be a convenient and desirable choice.

Memorialization

Cremains can be memorialized in almost every way imaginable, from traditional earth interment to placement in beautiful urns to rest in artistically designed columbariums. You may choose to scatter the cremains or bury them at sea.

Many cemeteries have been able to design lovely interment sites for cremains in portions of their property not suitable for traditional earth burial, such as shallow earth over ledges. This practice has enabled the cemeteries to utilize valuable land that would be wasted otherwise. Some cemeteries have "scatter gardens" landscaped with paths and planted with roses or other flowers.

There are many churches using their lawns and buildings to memorialize cremains from their congregations. This practice not only has brought needed revenue to the churches but also has encouraged families to return to church more frequently. A book of remembrance or a bronze plaque can be used to record those who are being memorialized there. Some churches have not realized the potential of using their facilities for dignified memorials.

In most states, cremains may be scattered if they are converted to unrecognizable skeletal remains. Now, many crematories provide the grinding or pulverization process as a standard service, but some may not. You should make sure that process is done before the cremains are scattered. There have been cases in which pieces of recognizable bone that were scattered as cremains have been discovered and reported to law enforcement authorities. The authorities then began investigating the incident, assuming foul play had taken place.

In one unpleasant incident in Connecticut, the family of a deceased person, whose cremains were supposed to have been scattered in Long Island Sound, was notified that a portion of the cremains had floated back to shore and were retrieved by local police. The persons charged with burying the cremains at sea had not scattered them nor poked holes in the container so it would sink. The cremains had been easily identified because the cremation identification tag was still attached, showing the crematory in which the cremation had occurred and a number identifying the deceased. The cremains were eventually disposed of again, properly.

If the deceased has made no plans for memorialization prior to death, cremains may be kept safely until the family completes its plans, unlike regular burials which should be done within a few days after death. Memorial observances can then be planned at the convenience of distant family and friends as well.

◙

Patsy Santoro is currently the Superintendent of the Evergreen Cemetery and Crematory in New Haven, Connecticut. He has been active for many years in various professional organizations and has spoken on cremation to a number of death education classes.

Peter Bilodeau is an editor for the Jackson Newspapers in New Haven, Connecticut.

Information used in this chapter was also provided by William S. Cook, formerly an operator of a funeral home and crematory in Columbus, Ohio. Resources include an article by Mr. Cook in the trade publication <u>Casket and Sunnyside</u>; and <u>Report on Dental Gold and Cremation</u>, Minnesota Department of Health, 1979.

Embalming: "Eternal Sleep," Family Convenience

Chapter 6

In the last century or so when death arrangements in the U.S. have been dominated by funeral professionals, embalming has become a widely accepted, and expected, practice.

Although it is usually part of a larger package of goods and services sold to a grieving family, there is no inherent contradiction between caring for one's own dead and embalming. It may be an appropriate choice in some instances. Embalming is a specific service - like cremation - that must be contracted to professionals, but families may handle many or all of the other arrangements themselves.

One example of this was described to me by a funeral director in Bend, Oregon, who provided the service of embalming for a young American Indian girl. When the embalming was complete, two grandmothers led a procession to the reservation, one riding in the funeral van. The funeral director was asked to drive his van around the Long House three times, then was left to wait until all was ready. The body was finally carried in and circled three times around the inside of the Long House before being placed on a woven mat in the center of the room. The body was clad only in the undergarments supplied by the family. Women of the tribe then began the Dressing Ceremony, clothing the young woman in "gorgeous buckskins." Beside her was a box lined with 15 to 20 blankets that had been woven and dyed by hand. Traditional rituals and ceremonies, including viewing, continued through the night.

History of Embalming

The Egyptians began embalming the bodies of wealthy and important people sometime before 4,000 B.C., and the practice spread to other ancient cultures. Generally, the bodies were soaked in a carbonate of soda, and the viscera and brains were removed. Herbs, salts, and aromatic substances were packed into the body cavities. Then the bodies were wrapped in cloth that had been soaked with preservatives. Variations of these procedures were employed as embalming spread to other cultures: for example, Alexander the Great was reportedly embalmed with wax and honey.

Knowledge of embalming moved to parts of Europe about

500 A.D., but was not widespread, although the bodies of several well-known historical figures (including King Canute and William the Conqueror) were preserved.

In the 19th century, Italian and French scientists developed techniques to inject preservatives into veins and arteries. The practice reached the U.S. during the Civil War, when it was used in a few instances to preserve the bodies of war victims for transportation and burial. When President Lincoln was assassinated, his body was embalmed to allow public viewing in locations throughout the nation. It was considered an unusual step to take, in an unusual period of national sorrow.

In his book **Inventing the American Way of Death, 1830-1920**, James J. Farrell comments: "Before 1880 people viewed embalming only as a historical phenomenon, an exotic custom of the ancient Egyptians." He notes that with organized encouragement from a rapidly emerging funeral industry, "by 1920, almost all dead bodies were embalmed, not just those intended for transport."

As an example of how sophisticated the practice had become in those four decades, Farrell cites a 1920 advertisement by a Boston undertaker:

For composing the features, $1.
For giving the features a look of quiet resignation, $2.
For giving the features the appearance of Christian
  hope and contentment, $5.

The Reverend William L. Coleman, in his book **It's Your Funeral**, notes that, "The science of embalming had largely been abandoned for 1,500 years," and its sudden re-emergence in the late 19th and early 20th centuries aroused considerable controversy. "Both Christians and humanitarians often objected strenuously," Coleman writes. "They had visions of bodies being severely mutilated. Ministers denounced it as a desecration of 'the temple of God'." That view continues to be held by some religions, including Orthodox Judaism.

Yet despite such objections, embalming became - and has remained - an expected part of the majority of death arrangement packages offered by U.S. funeral directors. Why? What are the benefits that have come into demand in North America but seem less important to the rest of the world?

Almost all sources agree that embalming meets one real need: by postponing decomposition it allows bodies to be transported and viewed by family members in circumstances which delay funeral services and final disposition.

Embalming was also promoted early on as a means of preventing premature burial, a horror which had been verified in several instances in the late 19th and early 20th centuries.

Farrell quotes the Portland, Oregon, city attorney in an address to the 1910 convention of the National Funeral Directors' Association as saying: "There is consolation in the thought that when a man's undertaker is finished with him he can be reasonably sure he is not in a trance." That seems a harsher form of "consolation" than the practice of some religious groups which delay body disposition for three days, to allow time for the exit of the spirit.

Sanitation was another - and perhaps the most emphatic-argument made by the funeral industry in its early promotion of embalming. The idea put forth was that embalming served to disinfect bodies, preventing the spread of infectious and communicable diseases, although there has been no scientific evidence to support this premise. (At best, funeral-type embalming merely delays the decaying process for a few days in a warm, moist climate.)

Encyclopedia Britannica (1978 Edition) notes that the popularity of embalming in the U.S. received much encouragement from requirements imposed by government. It says:

In the United States, embalming is standard practice as a result of the government support it has received, and is mandatory when bodies are being transported by common carrier, and, in many states, usually when there is an interval of more than 48 hours between death and burial. In Europe, however, embalming is rarely practiced. In many countries permits are required; in most it is performed only by medical practitioners, and the costs are relatively high.

By all accounts, the funeral industry, emerging between 1880 and 1920, successfully convinced the public (through the efforts of the newly formed NFDA) that professional services were necessary for proper care of the dead. Embalming was the centerpiece of that effort: families could place a body on ice to slow its deterioration, but only an experienced professional could embalm. The **Encyclopedia Britannica** points out that "Embalming remains the only specific skill required in the undertaking business."

The Myth of Sanitation

The belief that embalming prevents the spread of disease is still widely held, but public health as a reason for embalming has been refuted by the few limited studies on the subject.

The **Consumer Reports*** book on funerals notes that disease does not run rampant in countries where bodies are seldom embalmed. Furthermore, studies show that embalming does not affect certain bacteria or viruses: tuberculosis, smallpox, anthrax, tetanus, and AIDS have all been found in embalmed bodies shortly after death. Almost no research exists on the effects of funeral-type embalming beyond 24-48 hours. (Since funeral embalming is for short-term preservation only, bodies thus embalmed can be expected to begin the decomposition process within the week.)

This same book quotes a British Columbia deputy health minister as saying: "It is our view that the process of embalming serves no useful purpose in preventing the transmission of communicable disease. In those few cases where a person dies of a highly infectious disease, a far better procedure would be to wrap and securely seal the body in heavy plastic sheeting before removing it from the room where death occurred." Similar assertions have been made in the U.S. by at least one funeral director in the 1980 hearings on the FTC "Funeral Rule."

In 1986 telephone conversations with several people at the Center for Disease Control (CDC) in Atlanta, Georgia (in the Biosafety Department and the AIDS Unit) I was unable to find a single official who felt that embalming protects public health. Among the notes I took: "Embalming certainly isn't . . . relevant to AIDS. I see no reason for embalming for public protection in any circumstances."

The most convincing evidence against the sanitation argument for embalming is provided by a current practice of U.S. medical schools. They all solicit donations of bodies, and many have urgent need for additional donations. Although all cadavers are embalmed (with a far more complete process than that used by funeral directors) bequests are routinely refused if the donor has died of an infectious disease. According to one medical school, the bacteria or viruses, including AIDS, become "encapsulated" in the dormant stage and are not destroyed during the embalming process.

The sanitation argument is still widely believed, however. In ten states the statutes require embalming of people who die of specific diseases, a holdover from the turn-of-the-century efforts of the funeral profession to set itself up as guardian of the public health. In other states, embalming may be required at the discretion of the medical examiner or health department.

Many funeral directors I interviewed have privately questioned these statutes as they relate to AIDS. Older embalmers are worried for their sons and daughters who carry on the business. Others seem confident, however, that the same precautions used when embalming a Hepatitis B deceased will be sufficient protection for all staff. (The procedures recommended by CDC are usually used.)

CDC has found no spread of AIDS in health care or

mortuary workers, but the topic has consumed recent funeral convention issues. At least a few in the profession have suggested requiring immediate disposition of AIDS deceased without embalming. Many others have argued against such a proposal, noting it would probably encourage cremation and less expensive funerals. Still others seem very willing to follow the CDC guidelines for protection during embalming (which seem very effective so far) if embalming is desired by the family. There is clearly mixed reaction within the profession regarding AIDS and embalming.

Modern Embalming Practices

The major differences between current funeral practices and those used by the Egyptians are the use of modern chemicals and equipment, and an emphasis on temporary cosmetic restoration rather than preservation of mummies.

The process consists of both arterial embalming (draining the blood and filling the veins and arteries with preservatives) and cavity embalming (emptying fluids from the chest and abdomen, replacing them with preservatives).

The job is performed on an embalming table, which is surrounded by a conduit to catch body fluids and route them to a special container or the sewer system.

First, the limbs and joints are massaged to counter the effects of rigor mortis so that the body can be positioned. The face is then restored, with the use of plastic cusps to hold the eyelids together, and wires to close the jaws.

Arterial embalming then begins. The embalmer chooses one of three (or in some cases all three) locations in which a major artery and vein are in close proximity - the armpits, the neck, and/or the groin - and makes a small incision. An injection needle is placed into the artery and a drainage forceps into the vein to allow blood to flow into the table trough. An injection machine pumps a chemical solution (dyed for the proper effect on body color) into the artery while body parts are massaged to assist the flow.

The next step is cavity embalming. A "trocar" (a large-bore hollow needle) is connected to an electric aspirator (a pump that removes wastes from abdominal and chest cavities). The trocar is inserted near the naval, and blood and waste are pumped out. The cavities are then filled with a formalin solution to kill microorganisms and preserve the viscera.

In most cases, the body is then cosmetically restored. The extent of this depends upon the condition of the corpse and the wishes of the family. Sometimes a little rouge, face cream, and hair styling will do. But if the body is severely mutilated or decayed, the embalmer will do whatever it takes to restore the body to recognizable form, with wax, plaster of Paris, and additional make-up.

The embalming procedures used by medical schools, which require longer-term preservation, are different from those of funeral directors. This subject is covered in Chapter 8.

Embalming Costs

While embalming fees vary greatly, the national average at this writing is in the neighborhood of $200 for "preservation and restoration." In any establishment, the price depends on the amount of restoration that is needed or requested.

This strikes me as an extremely modest fee for a service that requires significant professional expertise and overhead expense. On the other hand, embalming is usually performed as part of a larger package that includes other items with higher mark-ups. When embalming is done, families are more likely to choose open-casket funerals with expensive coffins, for example. The mark-up on some coffins is 300 percent or more. If it became common practice to contract for embalming only, the price would probably rise.

(During the 1980 hearings on the FTC "Funeral Rule," funeral directors objected to itemizing costs because their practice had been to recover their overhead by charging less per item on "economy" funerals, and charging more on the elaborate ones. Without the ability to do this under current regulations, all people must pay the same rate for each service used, such as embalming or body transportation. This leaves the coffin as the major variable expense.)

A Perspective On Embalming

Clearly, there are some instances in which embalming is beneficial. If you donate your body to a medical school, you can expect it to be embalmed, although the procedures are different from those of funeral directors. Schools generally keep bodies for six months to two years, and there is no other practical way to keep a body intact for that long.

The most common argument for embalming today is that friends and family have an emotional need to see the body one last time before final disposition. If people are unable to gather for a week or longer, embalming may help to fill that need. That is a fairly credible argument.

But having spoken with a great many people on the subject, I have heard that viewing a restored corpse did not always fulfill that need. In some cases, the body was made to appear so lifelike that it became even harder to say goodbye. In other cases, it looked like nothing more than a statue or mannequin, a caricature of the departed friend or relative.

A common complaint has been that funeral directors assume that embalming is part of their task, with little or no discussion with the family, even in situations where there is no open-casket funeral or any other particular reason for embalming. Instances were cited in the FTC hearings of bodies being embalmed just before delivery for cremation, unknown to the families until they were billed for the service. The FTC Funeral Rule now prohibits that practice. Funeral directors are now required to note on their price lists that embalming is not a legal requirement (except in the relatively rare cases where it is required by state law, for example if body disposal is delayed for, say, 24 or 48 hours). Because of the FTC Rule, most conscientious funeral directors now request the permission of the family in writing before they proceed with embalming.

Even in cases where bodies must be preserved for viewing, refrigeration is usually an available and legally acceptable alternative to embalming. In the past, people stored bodies on ice, for long periods because it sometimes took relatives a week or more to arrive.

Refrigeration technology has advanced greatly since the 1800's, and because the population has become more mobile, most funerals can be held within three or four days after death. (Refrigeration is also a service that can be contracted out, at a cost usually lower than embalming.)

My own feeling is that most families are able to gather quickly and that it is far more emotionally fulfilling to participate actively in the funeral arrangements than merely to let a funeral director arrange a viewing. There is much that families can do: helping to build a box and transport it to the grave site or crematory; participating in digging the grave or scattering of "ashes;" helping to comfort survivors and notify other friends and relatives; helping with the filing of death certificates and transit permits.

Seeing the body one last time may well occur - either by choice or necessity - while performing many of those tasks. Friends have commented that seeing a body which was obviously dead made it easier to let go: that the spirit may well endure, but not in physical remains that are devoid of color. Actively participating in the final acts of friendship can be a meaningful way to say goodbye. Holding on to the memory of a beautifully restored body in "eternal sleep" may ultimately prove to be a denial, rather than acceptance of death.

*Funerals: Consumers' Last Rights Copyright 1977 by Consumers Union Of United States, Inc., Mount Vernon, NY 10553. Excerpted by permission from Consumer Report Books, 1977.

Burial: Public, Religious, and Family Cemeteries

Chapter 7

Someone once said to me that it's a good thing we have cemeteries - they may be the only open land left in the future. In many countries, including England and Japan, cemetery space is already at a premium.

Body Burial in Established Cemeteries

Cemeteries are usually administered by a superintendent, the person with whom all cemetery arrangements must be made. Arrangements for the time of interment or burial must be scheduled. For example, the city cemeteries in Burlington, Vermont, allow no burials on Sunday, in order to keep one day totally free for visitations. Other visitation hours are set by these cemeteries as well.

Most established cemeteries require that excavation be handled by cemetery personnel only. This may be true even for the simple excavation needed to bury cremains. On the other hand, it is possible that cemetery workers would agree to oversee a family's personal by-hand excavation in some instances. Filling in a grave by hand is often possible, with cemetery supervision. The cemetery persons with whom I have spoken understand a family's need to participate.

Usually cemeteries require a grave liner (made of concrete slabs assembled at the site) or a coffin vault (a one-piece unit, also made of concrete, metal or fiberglass). A grave liner is about half the price of a coffin vault, but many funeral directors and cemeteries choose to stock the coffin vault only. Either item must be lowered into the hole by machine. Both serve the purpose of keeping the earth from settling after burial, thus reducing maintenance of the grounds after excess soil is carted away. Claims of added preservation are sometimes made for the vault, but this is unlikely in an area with any ground water or in a warm humid climate. Arlington National Cemetery in Virginia does not require grave liners or vaults. Nearly three-quarters of the remaining national cemeteries, however, require some sort of grave liner. Some cemeteries require that such an item be purchased from them only. On the other hand, a liner

purchased from a cemetery may be cheaper than one purchased through a funeral home. The average price for a liner
is about $200; vaults cost considerably more.

If the ground is frozen, remains often are placed in a
holding chamber until spring. Bodies of those who have died
from a contagious disease, however, may be rejected, at least
according to printed policies of some cemeteries.

Specifications for monuments, markers, and planting around
graves as well as restrictions on other embellishments such
as paths or fencing are described in the policies of most
cemeteries. Some cemeteries require that monuments be
purchased only through them.

Some cemeteries bill families annually for upkeep of grave
sites. Most cemeteries continue care, even when next-of-kin
have passed away without making further maintenance
provisions, but one cemetery commissioner remarked that "the
place ought to look like an asparagus patch if you count
everyone who hasn't paid his bill." "Perpetual care" may be
arranged by the payment of a larger lump sum or may be
included in the sale price of the cemetery lot.

Many cemeteries are in churchyards for use by members of
the congregation, and larger cemeteries exist for people of
specific religious faiths. For many, burial in a religious
cemetery is important, and indeed, a church can provide a
logical support group for a family dealing with death. At one
time family members not of the same faith were refused
burial in such cemeteries, but current policies tend to be
more accepting.

With the sale of lots as part of a pre-need package, many
cemeteries are now considered big business and are being
purchased or established by corporations desiring access to
the pre-need money for investment purposes. The price of a
single lot in a small town municipal cemetery can be as low
as $100, including care. Some large, commercial cemeteries,
however, charge $300 - $500 for a single lot, with perpetual
care extra. In all instances, there will be additional charges
for opening grave sites, making total cemetery costs as much
as $800 without the marker. Grave diggers expect a tip in
many areas.

Burial of Cremains

Few states have any restrictions on the final resting place
of cremains, which may be buried in any yard or garden or
scattered from a country mountain top if a cemetery location
has not been chosen. Therefore, when it is consistent with
personal and religious beliefs, cremation is a practical choice
of many who handle their own death arrangements, especially

in urban or suburban areas.

There seems to be a strong feeling on the West Coast that scattering is less satisfying to families than burial of the cremains in a specific location. One mortician told me of a mother who, at the urging of friends, had agreed to ocean scattering because her teenage son had loved surfing. At the time it seemed appropriate. A year or so later, at a social gathering, the mother confided to this mortician her feeling of emptiness in not having "a place" by which to remember her son. The funeral director suggested that she purchase a columbarium space and choose some of the son's personal belongings to put into it. The mother gratefully did so, with a certain sense of relief at having a spot that was "his." (It is my belief that part of that relief was gained because the mother took an active role in the "burial" this time.)

Some companies offer a scattering service, often by air or at sea. On the West Coast a scandal developed in 1984 involving a company which merely dumped the cremains in a nearby location instead of providing the service that was contracted. This prompted a new statute in California which limits disposition of cremains and requires such contracts to be honored. Wisconsin requires that final disposition of cremains be accomplished within 60 days.

Home Burial

Families considering home burial must examine local zoning ordinances. For those with land in rural or semi-rural areas, home burials are usually possible.

Body burial sites must be some distance from any water supply. The slope of the land and the soil conditions must also be taken into account, especially where the earth is shallow over ledge, or clay. Power lines are to be avoided, since overhead power may be replaced with buried cable at some future time.

There is strong historical precedent in the establishment of a family burial plot, but a family should consider the long-range implications on land value in doing so because a graveyard becomes a permanent easement on the property in many states. In a 1959 Oklahoma case, Heiligman vs. Chambers, a grandson sued to keep the new landowner from moving family bodies to a town cemetery. The court decision upheld the right to permanency created by any such family burial ground, at least in that state. Other states have provisions for moving the graves from "abandoned" burial sites.

A family must realize, too, that someone else, in future years, may not maintain a family cemetery after ownership changes. And while visitation rights may be protected by the Oklahoma precedent, how will people feel returning to land no longer in the family?

For many of us, the deterrents are minimal compared to the satisfaction and personal identity that a home burial offers. No one else sets visitation hours, and plantings or markers can be appropriate to the family or individual.

In my case, I found a rough piece of slate, one too large to be moved easily, but one that I could manage. I used a Boy Scout jackknife and a screwdriver to carve John's name and date on the one flat surface. Acid rain will probably fade the writing in 50 years, but perhaps it won't matter by then. Because John was cremated, I was free to pick the garden site I wanted for his spot, without a permit. But because this is not registered in the town clerk's office as an official home burial site, there will be no guarantee of permanency in preserving recognition there. The slate marker may stay, but then again it may get moved. I sold the house five years ago, and it has been sold once again since then. Perhaps we have been lucky, but a recent visit showed the spot to be well tended.

Body and Organ Donation

Chapter 8

"Let the Dead Teach the Living"
- Columbia University, et al

The above quotation is frequently used by medical schools in their appeals to the public for body donations. The eye banks, kidney foundations, and other organizations that facilitate organ donations might say just as appropriately, "Let the dead heal the living."

All major religions approve of body and organ donations for medical and dental teaching, research, and transplants. According to public opinion polls, most people believe that such donations are desirable. Death provides many of us with a one-time-only chance to make a valuable gift to humanity.

If all of us followed through on our convictions, there would be no medical schools in urgent need of cadavers, and no one vainly waiting for the donation of kidneys, eyes, or other desperately needed gifts of life.

Tragically, that is not yet the case.

Organ Donations

Many medical schools request that a Uniform Donor Card be filled out as part of the process of making a bequest. Such cards can also be obtained from many other sources, including kidney foundations, eye banks, and Memorial Societies. The card is pictured below.

UNIFORM DONOR CARD

OF_____

Print or type name of donor

In the hope that I may help others, I hereby make this anatomical gift, if medically acceptable, to take effect upon my death. The words and marks below indicate my desires.

I give: (a) _____ any needed organs or parts

(b) _____ only the following organs or parts

_____

Specify the organ(s) or part(s)

for the purposes of transplantation, therapy, medical research or education;

(c) _____ my body for anatomical study if needed.

Limitations or
special wishes, if any :_____

Line (a) identifies "any needed organs or parts." That is, if any organs or other body parts are needed by another living human being, organ donation is to be considered first even if line (c), total body donation, is also checked. It should be remembered that donation of a major organ may preclude body donation to a medical school. Line (b) has a space to identify "only the following organs or parts." This could be "eyes" for example, if donation "for anatomical study" - line (c) - is the primary intent of a donor.

Your signature, on the back, must be witnessed by two other people. The Uniform Donor Card incorporates language which is consistent with the Anatomical Gifts Acts adopted by nearly all states.

If there are some organs you are willing to donate, but not others, you can specify your desires. If there is only one medical school to which you are willing to entrust your body, you can say that. Medical schools and organizations which facilitate organ transplants are extremely conscious of the need to honor the wishes of the deceased. If there is any doubt, they will err on the side of not accepting the donation.

In most states, there is also a check-off on a driver's license to determine whether or not you are an "organ donor." States expect, however, that an additional wallet card, such as the Uniform Donor Card, will be carried, establishing the specifics and restrictions regarding that offer.

Most organ donations are now handled with complete privacy, without identifying either the donor or the recipient to the other. Emotional excesses on the part of both donor families and those receiving an organ have made such anonymity necessary. For example, excessive gratitude caused one family to constantly foist itself on the bereaved father of the son whose kidney had been given to their son. The father became sorry that he had made the gesture. Donor families have also intruded into the lives of those now carrying a bit of "my son Johnny," unable to let go. In some unpleasant instances, money has apparently been requested. All hospitals now handle organ transplants discreetly.

At this writing, there is a particular need for corneas and kidneys. The numbers fluctuate, but there are thousands of people waiting for donations of those valuable organs. For any of them, a donation can make the difference between sight and blindness, or life and death. But medical science is advancing rapidly. There are laboratory studies being done with the transplanting of the islets of Langerhans, the small cells in the pancreas which produce insulin. If islet transplants become the "cure" for diabetes, another million people would be added to the waiting list for organ donations.

Funeral directors are being trained to enucleate eyes, but the conditions necessary for organ donation - removal of the organ shortly after death in a sterile environment - can be met for the most part only if death occurs in a hospital. Indeed, according to funeral industry sources, 70 percent of all deaths occur (or are confirmed) at hospitals.

Next-of-kin should be aware of the desire for donation or bequest. Family members should be sure the intent is known to medical personnel as well and is included on the patient's hospital chart.

Medical and Dental Schools

To satisfy the increase in research and education, body donations must continue in all states. I knew that bodies were needed for medical study, but until the research for this book, I did not realize that dental schools use an entire cadaver in their required anatomy courses. Dental interests are therefore covered in my use of the word "medical."

Some medical schools, either routinely or with permission, will share donations with other schools. Others do not. I found it unfortunate, for instance, that Dartmouth College in Hanover, New Hampshire, says it rejects a body if program needs are currently met, when less than 150 miles away the University of New England College of Osteopathic Medicine has an urgent need for body donation and will assume costs of transportation for "several hundred miles." In many medical schools, especially the osteopathic and chiropractic schools, over-enrollment of body donors has never occurred.

All schools and state boards of anatomy prefer to receive an enrolled donor - a person who had filed a "bequest" during his or her lifetime. In some states, a bequest can legally take precedence over the wishes of surviving family members, but few medical schools are willing to accept a body if there are objections. For that reason, most bequests must be witnessed, preferably by family members. A bequest may be cancelled at any time.

The body donor information I surveyed ranged widely in quality of presentation and depth of information. One New England medical school sent a single mimeographed information sheet that covered only the most basic of facts, plus a body donation form. From a midwestern medical college I received a many-paged, purple-covered folder in a plastic case. This attractive pamphlet listed, as other schools have, the "Frequently Asked Questions About Body Donation." Almost all medical schools are grateful for such a gift, and assure the donor that the body will be treated with respect.

Most schools issue a donor card that can be carried in a wallet, although a few I saw were too large for a wallet, and several failed to include the necessary telephone numbers or information regarding the procedure to follow at the time of death. It also occurs to me that a conspicuous failing on all such cards is the lack of a place to indicate whether donation may be to the nearest medical school at the time of death or whether a bequest to a specific medical college must be honored (with transportation costs borne by the estate even if a person died in Europe, for example).

In some situations, the next-of-kin may donate a body without prior enrollment, but policies on this vary greatly. Schools that are beginning to receive sufficient donors often restrict donation to those previously enrolled or in "ideal" condition, but a check of other near-by schools, especially the chiropractic and osteopathic, will usually reveal a need.

Almost all medical schools also receive bodies from the state - persons who have died in institutions or alone with no known relatives.

There is no remuneration for body donation. No medical school buys bodies. Some medical schools may pay for all or part of body transportation at the time of death. Most pay for body preservation and almost all pay for final disposition. In short, body donation is likely to alleviate, but not eliminate, cost to the family.

Often a medical school will have a contract with a certain funeral establishment for body transportation, and many funeral directors will accept less than the usual rate as a commitment to the public good. These practices are not always clear, however. One friend, dealing with the imminent death of her grandfather, contacted a particular medical school about body donation at the suggestion of a neighbor who was also a funeral director. She was told by the school that it would handle all transportation costs. When her grandfather finally died, she called the same funeral director again. He moved the body from the hospital to his establishment two and a half miles away and filed the death certificate. In the meantime, she notified the medical school. As a result, there were some quick changes in arrangements. The first funeral director was not willing to complete the trip for the rate the medical school normally paid, so another funeral director was sent to pick up the body. My friend later received a bill of $175 from the first funeral director. As can be seen from this example, it is important to ask not only what costs the medical school covers but also how those costs are handled.

A health history is often requested by a medical school, as well as death certificate information if the medical school is to complete the filing. Families may not request a report of medical findings from the school's examination of the body.

The donor's family is encouraged to consider a memorial service (a service without the physical presence of the body) so that the body can be removed for preservation as soon after death as possible. In some cases, if embalming is done under the direction of the anatomy department, body delivery can be delayed, but this must be arranged in advance with the medical school.

Medical schools do not assume the responsibility of filing an obituary.

Medical Embalming

Medical embalming procedures are considerably different from and far more complex than those used in the funeral industry. Each school of anatomy has developed its own system according to the interests and specialties of the school and staff involved. The thorough embalming needed for long-term preservation requires stronger chemicals, and can take as long as three days to complete.

It is important that the methods be as non-disruptive to the body as possible. Blood is not routinely drained from the body since only the arterial system is injected with preserving fluid, allowing the blood to "pool" on the venous side of the system. Any swelling is minimal and not a cosmetic consideration for medical study. Through the arterial system all capillary "beds" can still be reached. Organs that would not be affected by the arterial system alone including, for example, the brain, must be separately and carefully perfused with preservatives with a great deal of attention paid to detail. It is necessary to maintain the integrity of the body as a whole, and of entire systems within it. For instance, the circulatory routes can be filled with dyed latex as a marker. However, this is not attempted until body preservation is complete. At least some medical schools use refrigeration in addition to embalming for preservation.

Most bodies are used within a two-year period. Many medical schools cremate the remains when study is finished and offer a simple memorial service, interring or scattering cremains in a plot reserved for this purpose. If the school is notified at the time of body donation or delivery, remains or cremains can be returned to the family, although this option is not available at all schools. A family member expecting remains should notify the school if there is a change of address.

Enrolled body donors should make alternative disposition plans since bodies may be rejected for a variety of reasons.

The University of South Alabama, the State Anatomy Board of Maryland, the University of South Dakota, and South-western Medical School in Texas will dispose of all enrolled donors regardless of condition, in fulfillment of their contract with a donor. All other schools, however, reserve the right to refuse donations.

Although some schools share their donors with other schools, usually within the same state, over-enrollment may become a reason for body rejection if donations become more numerous. Skin and eye donations may be considered and are encouraged by most schools, but other organ donations make a body unacceptable for teaching use. Autopsy makes a body unacceptable for all but a few medical schools. In addition to autopsy, other common reasons for body rejection include:

▸ missing body parts - extremities, thoracic organs;
▸ age - 76 is too old at one school; below 21, 18, 15, "infant" or "fetal" are too young at others;
▸ severe burn victim - preservation is not readily accomplished if there is extreme tissue damage;
▸ decomposition;
▸ emaciation;
▸ trauma or mutilation;
▸ surgery at or near the time of death;
▸ obesity - not only difficult to preserve, but difficult to handle and use;
▸ size - over six feet tall (only a few schools), because of limitations in storage facilities;
▸ contagious or diseased - sepsis, TB, hepatitis, AIDS, meningitis, Creutzfeldt-Jakob, Alzheimer's, systemic cancer, and others at the discretion of the institution.

National Anatomical Service

Since 1975 the National Anatomical Service has been in the business of procuring and transporting cadavers to various medical schools in need. No medical school buys a cadaver, but this company does make money from the transportation of cadavers, as do most funeral directors.

If next-of-kin desire to make a body donation and cannot locate a nearby medical school in need, National Anatomical Service can be called. The Service has headquarters in New York (718-948-2401) and St. Louis (314-726-9079) with 24-hour phone coverage. Arrangements for refrigeration will be made by the Service with a local funeral director until transportation is provided. In some cases, a receiving medical school will pay for the refrigeration and transportation costs.

In other cases, the family may be asked to pay $150-$600, depending on the distance to be shipped. In either case, the National Anatomical Service is aware of medical schools with great need and will try to locate the nearest one. This could be helpful to persons in Alaska, Delaware, Idaho, Montana, and Wyoming where there are no medical schools or in states where all medical schools require prior enrollment - Arizona, Nebraska, Nevada, South Carolina, and Wisconsin. Most medical schools will return cremains to a family if requested.

In Case of Death Abroad

The need in some foreign countries is even greater than in the U.S. In Argentina, for example, 200 medical students must share one cadaver. Since international shipping of scientific cadavers is not allowed (although a private body may be), anatomy classes from an Italian medical school have travelled to Israel for study. If death were to occur abroad, perhaps inquiry as to local need would fulfill the intent of someone who has made an anatomical bequest, either for organs or whole body donation.

◙

Dr. William Worden, director of Project Omega, a Harvard study of terminal illness and suicide, has written in **Personal Death Awareness** of the depression of those whose lives will quickly end when no medical intervention is in sight. In one of the examples he cites, a young man - father of two- waiting for a third kidney transplant "began to sit in the hospital hallway and watch the elevator in the hope that an anonymous donor would appear. . . . Finally he realized the donor would never arrive." In making his final preparations for death, the young man's poignant remark was: "I want you to be sure my eyes are donated to people who need them. I lived a little longer because of two kidney transplants, and I want some other people to have the same break I did."

Managing Death –
Necessary Information

Chapter 9

Important!

Persons who choose to handle death privately must take great care to follow all state and local regulations! Several in the funeral profession have already experienced unpleasant situations with family management.

One crematory, for example, was sued for rejecting a body sent by a family. The case was thrown out of court, of course, because the family had merely hired someone to deliver the body, without a death certificate, transit permit, or authorization from next-of-kin for cremation. Another crematory will no longer accept bodies from a family because in one particular case the family had assumed that medical personnel would know how to fill out the forms properly. Unfortunately, the cause of death as stated by the medical examiner on the permit to cremate was not written exactly as it had been on the death certificate, and the state later made an issue of it.

Death Certificate

A death certificate signed by a doctor or local health officer stating the cause of death must be filed; usually in the county or district where death occurs, or where a body is found, or where a body is removed from a public conveyance or vehicle.

The wording for the cause of death should follow national guidelines as summarized in Appendix I, and any family member acting as a funeral director should check carefully for this. If a doctor felt rushed when signing the form, the wording may not be acceptable or the doctor may have signed the form on the wrong line. These are common complaints of many registrars and funeral directors in almost every state. Any such errors will necessarily cause a delay in obtaining the final permits for disposition.

If complicated laboratory work is necessary to accurately determine the exact cause of death, the physician or medical examiner may write "pending" or a similar phrase for the cause of death and release the body for disposition. In those few cases, a "delayed" or corrected death certificate will be sent to the state registrar by the physician when the cause is known.

The death certificate information must be typed or written LEGIBLY in black ink (in some states, "blue-black" ink is permissible). In addition to the medical portion, facts such as "mother's maiden name" must be provided by the family. Unless the signature of a licensed funeral director is required by state statute, the family or church member who is handling arrangements must sign the death certificate in the space marked "funeral director," followed by his or her relationship to the deceased, immediately after the signature. (A copy of the national standard death certificate is also included in the Appendix.)

States vary in the time required for filing the death certificate with the local registrar, but this must usually be accomplished before other permits are granted and before final disposition.

Fetal deaths (miscarriages)

A special death certificate, or fetal death report, is required in all but two states for fetal deaths (miscarriages). Eleven states seem to require registration of **all** fetal deaths.

In a majority of states, a fetal death must be registered if it occurs after 20 weeks of pregnancy. In Hawaii, the requirement goes into effect after 24 weeks of gestation.

Some statutes gauge pregnancy duration by fetal weight, i.e., 350 grams (12.5 oz.), and since any unattended death- including fetal death - could require a coroner's investigation, a physician should be called in any event.

Even if there is uncertainty as to whether reporting requirements are applicable, in some situations reporting of a fetal death may be helpful in obtaining insurance benefits.

Dealing with a coroner/medical examiner's office - autopsy

Autopsies are generally required when cause of death is violent, unexpected, uncertain, or "unusual," including suicide. For this reason, the police should be called when death occurs outside a hospital or nursing home and is "unattended" by a physician. If an ambulance service has been called first, the medics may notify authorities for you.

Death from a contagious disease may also necessitate involvement with a coroner or local health officer.

When body donation to a medical school has been planned, a family should request that no autopsy be done. The decision will depend on the circumstances surrounding death.

The practices in coroners' offices vary widely. In California, it is legal for medical examiners to amputate fingers for identification, and remove tissue and organs for study. One woman discovered that her father had been buried without his heart when she arrived at a workman's compensation hearing and saw the heart presented as evidence.

An Alaskan funeral director was concerned that I would suggest family involvement since 45% of the deaths in his state are autopsied. The bodies are not usually closed by the medical examiners there, and he felt this experience would be traumatic for a family.

According to one California mortician, bodies picked up from the Los Angeles county morgue are rarely cleaned up and barely tacked back together, whereas other area coroners (and those in most states or cities) try to restore bodies to intact condition. This mortician cautioned that relatives choosing to handle arrangements when a coroner's office is involved may be treated indifferently and without compassion, as well as kept waiting for what may seem an unreasonable amount of time. There have been instances when such a delay stretched for days, and the body was released only after legal and political maneuvers. In any state, press and public pressure might help to improve state health department regulations and enforcement of them in such situations.

Generally, the funeral director a family has chosen picks up an autopsied body from the coroner's office. Nevertheless, in California and several other states, the state is obligated to cover all costs of returning a body to a family if asked to do so. My request for return was honored here in Vermont. Perhaps if families routinely requested direct return of a body at state expense, even if a funeral director is to be involved later, more care might be taken with the condition in which a body is returned.

The term "medical examiner" is usually reserved for those with medical training and the person in such a position is often appointed by the department of health. In a few states the word "coroner" is used interchangeably with medical examiner. Generally, however, the term coroner implies an elected position. In California a medical degree is required to run for coroner. In other states, however, anyone may run for the office, with or without medical training.

A coroner may have a direct relationship with a funeral home, either as a practicing funeral director in that funeral home or by agreement. To avoid any appearance of impropriety, a coroner or medical examiner will usually rotate pick-up calls among all funeral homes within his or her jurisdiction, but, according to my research, this is not always the case. No family should feel obliged to continue a relationship with a funeral home just because a body arrived at that destination under state aegis!

Routine handling of dead bodies may harden the sensibilities of some of the people who work in the fields of pathology and forensic medicine. That does not excuse certain behavior. I believe that any state government should be obligated to assure that the dead are treated with dignity and that families are treated with courtesy and consideration.

Home Death

With hospice support, many persons are able to die at home in familiar surroundings, near familiar faces. In some states, an "expected" death can be certified by an attending Registered Nurse under such circumstances.

A home death can allow the family additional time to obtain permits and make necessary arrangements. Turning off the heat in a room or turning on an air-conditioner can make it reasonable to contain a body without further action for 24 hours or more, depending on the weather.

There appears to be some therapeutic value to keeping the body at home for at least a brief period, allowing the family a chance to congregate and deal with the death, as often occurred in the front parlor two generations ago.

Nursing Home Death

When death has occurred in a nursing home, it will be important to work out your plans with the nursing home staff ahead of time. If the deceased has had only a semi-private room, for example, the nursing home may have no other location for placement of a body while permits are obtained. Staff members are accustomed to calling a funeral director, regardless of the time, and having the removal within an hour or so of death. Out of consideration for other residents, it may not be feasible for the nursing home personnel to allow a long delay while permits, a container, and vehicle are obtained.

Hospital Death

Disposition of a fetal or infant death can be handled entirely by the hospital as a courtesy if a family so chooses. (Many funeral homes or crematories charge little if anything for an infant death, depending on the arrangements.)

When other deaths occur in a hospital, the relative on hand should ask nursing staff to remove any life-support articles such as catheters, I.V. needles, and feeding or breathing tubes. A catheter, for example, is held in place by a "balloon" and is not as simple to remove as an I.V. needle.

Some of the nasal tubes appear especially disfiguring after death and may be of concern to other family members who are expected later to help with the death arrangements. Most hospitals will probably cooperate with this request, although not all are accustomed to doing so.

Some hospitals may be reluctant to release a body directly to a family without the use of a funeral director. If the death involved is an "expected" death, advising the hospital ahead of time of your intentions may be helpful. If hospital personnel are confused or misinformed about their obligations, a telephone call from your lawyer may be in order.

It is important for families to recognize the legitimate needs of hospitals. Some hospitals may have no storage facilities for dead bodies while permits are obtained and may insist on calling a funeral director for immediate removal after death if they feel there is to be any significant delay.

Body and Organ Donation

Donation of eyes and organs must be done under sterile conditions, and usually within a short time after death. Since organ donor cards are not usually immediately available to hospital personnel, next-of-kin should make this decision known to attending staff at the earliest time possible.

Hospital employees are often reluctant to approach a grieving, distressed family. Anyone who can find emotional healing in a gift of life or sight is encouraged to take the initiative in making such an offer even if the time of death is uncertain. The corneas of elderly persons can usually be used, and eyes and skin may be donated even if total body donation to a medical school is subsequently planned.

With the increasing success of organ transplants, persons and families must consider whether organ donation takes priority over body donation. There may develop a competition between those needing body parts and those who need whole bodies. Loss of a major organ involving a thoracic incision usually makes a body unacceptable for a teaching donation because of the difficulty in embalming a system interrupted by recent surgery. My husband and I have written in on the body donation cards we carry that organ donation is to be considered first. If organ donation is not needed, only then should our bodies be considered for body donation. But this is our personal preference.

Body donation to a medical school may be an option even if the deceased has not enrolled in such a program. Check Chapter 8 as well as the particular requirements for the medical schools in your state. Also check that chapter for cautions about transportation reimbursements if you are not planning to deliver the body.

Embalming

No state requires routine embalming of all bodies. Special circumstances, such as an extended time between death and disposal, may make it necessary. Interstate transportation by a common carrier may also necessitate embalming. Refrigeration can take the place of embalming in many instances. In some states, embalming may be required if the person has died of a communicable disease.

Moving A Body

Never move a body without a permit (or medical permission)!

Always call ahead before moving a body even if you have a permit. A medical school or crematory staff member who is unprepared, or a town clerk who just isn't sure about family burial plots, may need some time and help in doing his or her job. By calling first to make arrangements at the destination you will be expected and prepared! ·

The use of a simple covered box allows some dignity for all involved in the handling and moving of a body, regardless of final disposition.

If a family chooses to make the container for delivery of a body for cremation, the size should be considered. A standard cremation chamber opening is 38 inches wide and 30 inches high. A container two feet wide and 18 inches deep is usually sufficient for most bodies, however. One crematory mentioned that most home-made boxes tend to be too large. Ernest Morgan, in his **Manual For A Simple Burial,** includes directions and measurements for a plywood container.

Simple cardboard containers can be purchased from most funeral homes. In the crematory listings for each state, I have noted those which have such containers in stock. Some boxes are conspicuously more expensive than others because of construction. There are those which are paraffin-coated, others plastic lined, and some have plywood bottoms.

The length of the box for transporting a body should be considered in choosing the vehicle for transportation.

Most states require a permit for transportation or disposition. The death certificate must usually be completed first and often a permit to cremate is also needed. In most states funeral directors serve as deputy registrars. If death occurs during an evening, weekend, or holiday, when local municipal offices are closed, a funeral director may be needed to furnish or sign the disposition or transit permit.

As a deputy of the state in this function, there should be no charge unless such a charge is already set by the state.

Body Fluids

After death, the blood in a body settles to the lowest points, leaving the upper portions pale and waxy with purple coloring below. Some parts of the body may swell a little.

Fluids may be discharged from body orifices. It will be helpful to use absorbent material, such as towels or newspaper, under the deceased. A sheet is convenient for wrapping and moving the dead person. If the person has died from a contagious disease, it will be important to take all health precautions with any discharge and in handling of the body. Your state may require the use of a funeral director in such an instance. Consult your family doctor for instructions if the information for your state is not specific.

When an autopsy has been performed or death occurs from trauma, the body may have to be wrapped in a vinyl body bag, available from a funeral director, to prevent additional leakage or seepage of body fluids. A plastic, zippered mattress cover might work as well, but such materials should be avoided whenever possible if cremation is contemplated.

Out-of-state Disposition

All states honor the properly acquired permits of other states when a body is to be moved from one state to another. There may be local regulations with regard to disposition, however, which should be checked by telephone before setting out for the destination.

Burial

If burial is chosen, Chapter 7 will be helpful. In some states, when burial will be outside the county or town where death occurred, you will need an additional permit to inter (whether on private land or in a cemetery) from the local registrar in that town.

In those states that have such statutes or regulations, I have included depth requirements for burial. Standard practice in many states places the top of the coffin at least three feet beneath the natural surface of the earth.

Cremation

When cremation is chosen, an additional permit is often required from the local coroner or medical examiner. A modest fee is generally charged for this. In addition, an authorization from next-of-kin is required by most crematories. Usually this can be obtained by Western Union or overnight mail if family members live out of state.

Next-of-kin is determined in this order (although it varies slightly from state to state):
(1) surviving spouse;
(2) all adult sons and daughters;
(3) parents (both if they are both alive);
(4) all adult siblings;
(5) guardian or "person in charge".

That is, if there is a surviving spouse, his or her permission is all that is required. If there is no surviving spouse but several children, all adult sons and daughters may be required to grant permission for disposition by cremation. Adult siblings must assume responsibility if no spouse, off-spring, or parents survive.

A pacemaker must be removed before cremation. The services of an attending physician, the medical examiner, or a funeral director can be requested for this. On the other hand, one funeral director told me, "Anyone can do it." A pacemaker is about the size of a silver dollar embedded just under the skin, usually near the neck or lower on the rib cage. It is attached to wires which should be snipped. If a pacemaker is not removed and explodes during the cremation process, damages may possibly be the liability of the person delivering the body. One crematory operator in Washington state claims to cremate pacemakers routinely with no problem. All others I spoke with, however, said failure to remove a pacemaker can cause significant damage.

Selecting a Crematory

I have chosen to list crematories in the state sections not because I prefer cremation but because most people don't know where the crematories are.   Furthermore, I felt you ought to know "which doors it was okay to knock on."
I am told that there are about 800 crematories in the U. S. at this time. However, I had access to only 600 using the directory of the Cremation Association of North America (CANA) and the National Directory of Morticians. (I obtained a few others by word-of-mouth.) Please check your local yellow pages or any other source of information for possible others in your area.
The prices and policies quoted were obtained in late 1986 and early 1987 and may be altered by the time you read this

book. Therefore, while I hope the listings in this book are a useful guide, some changes can be expected.

If you know of additional crematories that should be listed, or find that the policies of any establishment are different from those quoted, please let me know so that corrections or additions can be made in the next edition of this book.

Obituary

When a person dies, it is almost impossible to notify personally everybody who knew or cared about the deceased. Close friends and relatives, of course, should be informed by a telephone call or letter before they read the news in the newspaper, if at all possible. But an obituary may help assure that the news reaches a wider circle of acquaintances in a timely manner.

It will be the responsibility of a family managing death privately to arrange for an obituary if one is desired. Some newspapers charge for obituaries, while others print them as a public service. Big city newspapers generally print obituaries only if the deceased is considered well-known or influential. Most small-to-medium circulation newspapers will accept obituaries if the deceased lived or was known within their circulation areas.

It should be emphasized that the policies of newspapers on this issue vary greatly. Some newspapers, for example, consider obituaries to be "advertising" for funeral homes, and will charge a high price if a funeral home is mentioned. On the other hand, it may run the obituary free of charge if there is no funeral establishment named. It is a good idea to telephone your local newspaper, to learn its policies and any costs, before writing the obituary.

Your local paper may have a standard format for obituary information. If so, that will be apparent in the notices published on any given day. By checking other obituaries before contacting your newspaper, you will be more likely to have at hand all the necessary information.

Generally, you can either telephone in an obituary or deliver one in writing. In either case, unless you have faithfully followed the newspaper's format, you can expect some editing and should be prepared for questions if additional information is needed.

If burial or cremation is to occur at the convenience of the immediate family, don't overlook the obituary as a logical place to announce a memorial gathering which might occur a bit later.

Miscellaneous, but still important

It is not uncommon for family members to forget to remove jewelry at the time of death!

◉

If your family needs additional services to manage a death, you should expect additional charges. A family using the time of funeral professionals for advice should find it reasonable to pay a consultant's fee.

If any memorial services are held at a funeral home, you should expect to pay for use of the facilities.

Going back to the crematory to view the body again is expecting an additional service, too, if that is even possible. If there is a waiting period before cremation, or a long wait until the usual business hours of a crematory, there may be additional charges for refrigerated storage. Some crematories will arrange a weekend cremation for an extra charge.

If a person who works in a funeral home or crematory offers to file a death certificate, he or she would be performing a "professional service" for which the funeral home may legitimately charge.

◉

Some crematories expect to be paid at the time a body is delivered even if the family expects to receive insurance or other death benefits. Some have a 30-day billing period. Other crematories are able to work with the family to manage the bill, and the designation "negotiable" is used in those listings. Individual circumstances for local families are usually taken into account.

◉

When private death arrangements are made in an area of the country where the practice is not already established, you can expect some hesitancy on the part of involved persons such as registrars and town clerks. Some hospitals may even be reluctant to release a body to a family.

I have tried to include in each state section relevant legal citations enabling family disposition. People in authority, accustomed to delegating their duties to funeral directors, may have to be informed of their responsibilities. That can be frustrating, particularly when you are enduring a time of loss and grief. Please remember that the majority of these people will probably be concerned with performing their duties appropriately. Few will want to hinder your choice if you have followed all required procedures and if you seem well informed.

Important Legal Issues
Regarding Death

Chapter 10

Watch For Change

An increase in personal disposition of bodies may precipitate an effort by funeral directors or others to change state and local laws. (In Vermont, the newspaper article, "How To Bury Your Own Dead in Vermont," prompted one state legislator to submit a restrictive bill on the issue, although it died in committee.) It will be important to watch the legislative action in your state or request that a Memorial Society do so.

While it is wise to be wary of changes proposed by interest groups, the statutes in virtually all states need some revision. And for those who desire to effect change in the states where personal body disposition is not possible, I have cited the limiting statutes or regulations.

At the end of this chapter are some suggested model statutes concerning death, most of which are borrowed from existing statutes in several states.

Why Change Is Needed

After conducting the research for this book - accumulating personal death experiences as well as reviewing legal concerns and statutes - it is my conviction that:

A state's legitimate interests in regulating the procedures to use at a time of death lie in the areas of "public interest," namely: vital statistics, public health, criminality, and protecting the rights of individuals-dying, deceased, or as survivors.

Testing that conclusion, I contacted the legal expert widely considered to be the nation's foremost authority on laws relating to death and dying, Professor Alexander Capron of The Law Center at the University of Southern California. Professor Capron expressed "basic agreement" with my conclusions, which he rephrased, in more proper legal language, as "interests in the accuracy of statistics, in protecting public health, and in preventing crime and ensuring the availability of necessary evidence for legal proceedings (i.e. autopsies and inquests)."

He emphasized, however, that, "Little seems to have been written on the subject of a family's legal rights regarding a dead relative. The major concern of the law has been with the obligations of the next-of-kin, not their rights vis-a-vis the state."

He noted that if the rights of the family are "fundamental rights," the state could restrict them only when the state's interests are "compelling." In this regard, public health is certainly a "compelling" issue with which I take no exception.

Professor Capron added that while, in his own judgment, a family's interest is most often "fundamental," there is little case law on that issue. If rights are not "fundamental," a state needs only to show that its restrictions have a "rational basis." He adds, "When the courts apply the 'rational basis' standard, they generally give the state wide leeway and often accept minimal evidence as sufficient to prove rationality."

In other words, if you were to argue before the Supreme Court that states are exceeding their authority when they require that a funeral director sign a death certificate or that a body be transported only in a hearse, you could expect a long hard fight. The legal ground on those issues has not yet been tested.

Personally, I would prefer to appeal to state legislators to examine their statutes to see if they fulfill the legitimate interests of the state. Legislators, unlike courts, have the power to define "rational" the way you or I might. Most state legislators I have met are reasonable people. And I think, after reviewing the sum total of death laws that have accumulated - that there is much room for improvement.

To be candid, I found that many state laws were excessive, incomplete, or unclear. Some seemed too wordy, some too brief. Mississippi, for example, does not have a Vital Statistics statute that requires the registration of all deaths occurring in the state. There are, however, comprehensive Health Department regulations which make this necessary. This is inconsistent with the generally accepted principle of establishing weighty policy issues by statute, and specific procedures for implementing those policies by regulation.

While Mississippi's Health Department seems to have done an excellent job with its regulations, the health departments in some states leave all such related issues to the supervision of the state funeral boards or coroners. In Riverside County, California, the local coroner decided that all AIDS deceased should be embalmed. Even though local funeral directors suggested that this was unnecessary when direct cremation

was to take place, the coroner ordered all AIDS cases sent
to the coroner's office for embalming. A new coroner has
been elected (for 1987) so the policy may change. But what
about the effect on the families whose loved ones may have
been embalmed without regard to religious or moral conviction? And on what scientific basis was such an order made?
Here is an instance of a regulation being promulgated without
a formal procedure, on the authority of a single person.

The states which prohibit disposition by anyone other than
a funeral director should be challenged. In Louisiana,
Massachusetts, Michigan, and Nebraska, the prohibition does
not appear in the public health statutes. Instead, it is found
in the statutes or regulations controlling licensing of
professional funeral directors. Those sections of statute were
almost certainly drafted by people in the profession, to
protect the profession rather than to meet legitimate needs
of the state. In three other states - New Hampshire, New
Jersey, and New York - where the statutes are pervaded by a
reliance upon the funeral profession, I can only conclude that
the lobbying efforts of the funeral profession, coupled with
the lack of information on the part of legislators, allowed
such statutes to pass without much consideration.

(For most professions, licensing standards are applied only
to those who hire out their services. In setting standards for
plumbers, electricians, doctors, and lawyers, legislators and
regulators routinely seek out the expertise of those who are
accomplished in those professions. But the licensing requirements do not restrict those who wish to change a faucet
washer or electrical switch in their own homes, diagnose
their own children's colds, or even represent themselves in a
court of law, so long as all other laws are followed and no
commercial transaction has taken place.)

In Indiana, a somewhat restrictive state which requires the
signature of a funeral director on the death certificate, I am
told there is a strong funeral lobby. However, I believe every
state has an obligation to protect the rights of individuals
who are not, in all cases, organized into lobby groups.

Dealing With Death From AIDS And Communicable Diseases

In ten or more states embalming is required by state
statute for death from a contagious or communicable disease,
and in some states embalming may be at the discretion of a
health department official. Yet according to many sources,
including testimony presented to a hearing on the Federal
Trade Commission "Funeral Rule" in 1980, the Consumer
Reports book **Funerals: Consumers Last Rights,** and recent
conversations with people at CDC and medical schools - **there**

is no public health purpose served by embalming. Embalming may help to meet the needs and desires of a family but embalming should not be required!

Statutes and regulations may describe elaborate precautions for the handling of a body with a contagious disease, but the disposition of blood and other fluids flushed in the embalming process is rarely controlled. The West Virginia Department of Health guidelines include "incineration" of body fluids for AIDS and Hepatitis B.   However, almost without exception embalmers admit, "Oh, sure. It all goes down the drain," meningitis, hepatitis, rabies, and measles included. One person in the Biosafety Department at CDC felt there was no public health danger in this.

In talking with more than 500 funeral directors and crematory operators, I learned that a concern about AIDS has consumed the industry. In all parts of the country, there are some funeral directors who have refused to pick up AIDS deceased. (A New York court has ruled against such discrimi- nation.) On the other hand, at least one mortician has charged that some hospitals and doctors fail to include any reference to the AIDS virus on death certificates. This mortician said that in one specific instance, he later gained the knowledge from the family. While he is frankly more concerned about Hepatitis B, he feels he should be informed in every case so that reasonable precautions will be taken.

In the model statutes at the end of this chapter, death from contagious or communicable disease is cause for immediate burial or cremation without embalming. This statute is meant to consider the well-being of those in the funeral industry as well as to protect the environment. Most personal and religious choices can still be made within that context and allow a death to be handled with meaning and dignity.

State Funeral Boards

I have included in my model statutes a requirement that the majority of the State Funeral Board in any state be comprised of consumer representatives, as is now the case in California.

The president of the California board, himself one of the minority of funeral directors, commented to me, "That's the way it should be. We shouldn't be governed by the people we're trying to govern."

I would also suggest that funeral boards encourage funeral directors to advertise their services as "funeral consultants." This idea seems to have the support of many in the profes- sion. As consultants, funeral directors could provide to families whatever amount of professional help they desire or need and be paid on an hourly basis. Families handling most of the arrangements themselves should not expect to get free advice or help from a professional, but neither should they have to pay an inflated price for a coffin. Most other professionals, such as lawyers and accountants, are available as consultants who can be paid by the hour. The same should be true for funeral directors.

Model Statutes

In seeking to compile model statutes, I have borrowed from existing statutes wherever possible. In some cases I have left out small portions of the language. I have also suggested additions: these are identified with parentheses and underlining. Suggested statutory language is in boldface, while explanatory material is in normal typeface.

I - Death Registration

Several states do not have a vital statistics statute requiring registration of all deaths occurring within the state. While this requirement may be covered in fact by regulations or by bits and pieces of other statutes, such omission is inconsistent with the laws of the majority of states. The federal government requires each state to keep vital statistics for all births, deaths and marriages within that state.

In order to be complete, a death registration statute should give not only the time in which a physician must certify the cause of death, but also where the death certificate must be filed, by whom, and how soon. The deaths requiring investigation should be specified.

Oklahoma 63, sec.1-317(a). Death certificate - Filing-Contents

A death certificate for each death (and fetal death) which occurs in this state shall be filed with the local registrar of the district in which the death occurred, within three (3) days after such death and prior to burial or removal of the body; provided that,
  (1) if the place of death is unknown, a death certificate shall be filed in the registration district in which a dead body is found, within three (3) days after such occurrence; and
  (2) if death occurs in a moving conveyance, a death certificate shall be filed in the registration district in which the dead body was first removed from such

conveyance.

Alaska Sec. 18.50.230(c). Death registration.

The medical certification shall be completed and signed within twenty-four hours after death by the physician in charge of the patient's care for the illness or condition which resulted in death except when an official inquiry or inquest is required and except as provided by regulation in special problem cases.

Mississippi State Board of Health Rules Governing the Registration and Certification of Vital Events - Rule 36.

The medical examiner shall certify cause in deaths affecting the public interest. A death affecting the public interest. . . includes, but is not limited to, any of the following:
(1) Violent death, including homicidal, suicidal or accidental death.
(2) Death caused by thermal, chemical, electrical or radiation injury.
(3) Death caused by criminal abortion, including self-induced abortion, or abortion related to or by sexual abuse.
(4) Deaths related to disease thought to be virulent or contagious which may constitute a public hazard.
(5) Death that has occurred unexpectedly or from an unexplained cause.
(6) Death of a person confined in a prison, jail or correctional institution.
(7) Death of a person where a physician was not in attendance within thirty-six hours preceding death, or in pre-diagnosed terminal or bedfast cases, within twenty days preceding death.
(8) Death of a person where the body is not claimed by a relative or a friend.
(9) Death of a person where the identity of the deceased is unknown.
(10) Death of a child under the age of two years where the death results from an unknown cause or where the circumstances surrounding the death indicate that sudden infant death syndrome may be the cause of death.
(11) Where a body is brought into this state for disposal and there is reason to believe either that the death was not investigated properly or that there is not an adequate certificate of death.

West Virginia 16-5-19(e). Death registration.

When death occurs in a manner subject to investigation, the coroner or other officer charged with the legal duty of making such investigation shall investigate the cause of death and shall complete and sign the medical certification within twenty-four hours after making determination of the cause of death.

Oklahoma 63, Sec. 1-317(b)

The funeral director or person acting as such who first assumes custody of a dead body shall file the death certificate. He shall obtain the personal data from the next of kin or the best qualified person or source available. . .

II - Fetal Death Registration

Some states do not have statutes regarding fetal deaths; a few others appear to require a fetal death report for all miscarriages.

West Virginia 16-5-20(a). Fetal death registration.

A fetal death certificate for each fetal death which occurs in this State after a gestation period of twenty completed weeks shall be filed with the local registrar of the registration district in which the delivery occurs. . . (All other procedures apply.)

III - Disposition Permit

Statutes regarding disposition should state who grants such a permit, with reference to after usual business hours, and where it must be filed as well as when. When disposition is made within a district other than the district issuing the permit, it seems important to obtain an additional signature from the registrar in the district of disposition before burial and to record a cremation with the registrar of that district. A number of states require no medical examiner's permit before cremation. Some of these states require a waiting period which by itself does not seem to serve a significant purpose. Because of the finality of cremation, a second medical involvement is a sound practice. Requiring the consent of all next-of-kin for cremation is another important consideration.

Regulations proposed by the Alaska Health and Social Services -
7 AAC 35.090(a). Care of Human Remains.

All human remains shall be treated in a respectful manner.

Vermont T.18, Sec. 5201(a). Permits; removal of bodies.

A dead body of a person shall not be buried, entombed or removed from a town, or otherwise disposed of, except as hereinafter provided, without a burial-transit or removal permit issued and signed by the town clerk or his deputy.

The town clerk of the town or city shall provide for registering deaths that occur in the town and for issuing burial-transit permits at a time when town clerks' offices are closed.

Author:

(The permit for disposition shall be returned to the issuing registrar after removal, certifying final disposition, whether in-state or out-of-state, within ten days.)

Oklahoma 63, Sec. 1-319(c).

A burial transit permit issued under the laws of another state which accompanies a dead body or fetus brought into this state shall be authority for final disposition of the body or fetus in this state, (but subject to registration in the local district of disposition).

IV - Burial

Connecticut 7-65. Burial permits.

No deceased person shall be buried in the town . . . until a burial permit, specifying the place of burial and stating that the death certificate and any other certificate required by law have been. . . recorded, has been issued by the registrar of vital statistics.

Oklahoma 63, Sec. 1-319(d).

No person in charge of any premises on which interments are made shall inter or permit the interment of any body

unless it is accompanied by a burial, removal or transit
permit duly issued and signed . . . Such person shall
endorse upon the permit over his signature the date of
interment, and the name and location of the place of
interment, and return such permit to the local registrar
of vital statistics. (If the disposition permit originated
out of district, the local registrar will forward the
permit to the issuing registrar within ten days.)

Washington State Regulations 86-14-008 (8).

All dead human bodies to be disposed of by earth burial
in the state of Washington shall be buried in the ground
at least three feet: (top of casket to surface of ground).

Michigan 128.111, 128.112. Private burial grounds.

Sec. 1. That it shall be lawful for any person or persons
in this state to lay out. . . any tract of land not
included within the corporate limits of any city or
village which may be owned by such person or persons,
as a private burial ground for the use of their families
or descendants for purposes of interment of members of
such families and descendants, and for no other purpose,
not exceeding in quantity 1 acre of land. . . and shall be
recorded in the county where such land shall lie.

Sec. 2. Such land so laid out . . . , when recorded in the
register's office of the county where such land lies, shall
operate as a grant forever of the land described . . . to
. . . their successors forever, for the purposes described
. . . , and no sale, judgment, or decree shall be made
which shall have the effect to divert the same from the
objects of said grant. . .

V - Cremation or Burial at Sea

West Virginia 61-12-9. Permits required for cremation (with
author's additions for burial at sea).

It shall be the duty of any person cremating, or causing
or requesting the cremation of, the body of any dead
person . . . (or before burial at sea), to secure a permit
for such cremation (or sea burial) from the chief medical
examiner, or from the medical examiner of the county
wherein such death occurred. . .

Oklahoma 63, Sec. 1-330. Certificate of cremation.

After cremation (or sea burial) of the body of a deceased person within the State of Oklahoma, the special permit therefore shall be returned to the local registrar . . . with a certificate thereon, signed by the person in charge of the crematory (or sea burial) which performed the service, showing the date thereof and (, in the case of cremation,) the name of the person or persons to whom the residue resulting from such cremation was delivered, or showing such other disposition as may have been made thereof. Each crematory shall keep a complete record of each cremation performed by it. . .

Author:

(Authorization from all next-of-kin must be received prior to cremation.)

Delaware 16, Sec. 3165. Witnesses at cremation.

A representative of the family or some individual accredited to act as representative of the family of the individual being cremated may be present at the time the cremation is being carried out.

VI - Death From a Communicable Disease

There are no studies to show that embalming serves any public health purpose. In fact, the CDC and funeral industry guidelines for dealing with any death of a communicable disease, urge funeral personnel to use, among other things, heat or incineration to deal with contaminated items and waste. Controls for disposition of funeral home waste are rarely enforced by the state or city. Although it is my belief that cremation is the most suitable method for disposition under these circumstances, the following statute should allow for almost all religious convictions regarding body disposition.

Ohio 3707.19. Disposal of body of person who died of a communicable disease.

The body of a person who has died of a communicable disease declared by the department of health to require immediate disposal for the protection of others shall be buried (in a non-biodegradable pouch) or cremated within twenty-four hours after death (without embalming.)

VII - State Funeral Board

California Funeral Directors and Embalmers Law, Article 1(7601).

There is in the Department of Consumer Affairs a State Board of Funeral Directors and Embalmers which consists of eight members appointed by the Governor, three of whom shall be licentiates of the board, and five of whom shall be public members.

◙

Other Provisions That Should Appear In State Statutes

There are at least three other legislative issues which should be examined by anyone who is concerned with protection of the death rights of individuals and families: the Living Will; Durable Power of Attorney; and consumer protection for pre-need funeral contracts.

While in-depth treatment of these issues is outside the immediate scope of this book, they are so important that I would be negligent if I failed to mention them at least briefly here.

▸ **Living Will.** A Living Will is a legal document specifically recognized by the statutes in 39 states. In some states, the statutes refer to it by another name, such as "Terminal Care Document." By signing it (with proper witnessing and other legal requirements which may be imposed by your state), you may indicate that no "heroic" or extraordinary measures should be provided if you are terminally ill and close to death. In most states that recognize the Living Will, you can sign it at any time if you are of sound mind and at least 18 years old.

▸ **Durable Power Of Attorney.** Many individuals and legal authorities prefer the Durable Power of Attorney to the Living Will because it is much more flexible. It is recognized in many, but not all, states. Signed when you are of sound mind, this document designates another person to make health care decisions for you if you become unable to make them yourself. The person, of course, should be someone who is intimately familiar with your wishes, and who would, therefore, make the same decisions you would make if you were able to. By law, the person designated must be "mentally competent" at the time of signing. In signing this document, you can include any guidelines, contingencies, and statements of intent you feel are appropriate.

Examples of the Living Will and Durable Power of Attorney are provided in the Appendix. If you desire information on the laws of your (or any other) state regarding the Living Will and Durable Power of Attorney, a good source to contact is: Society for the Right to Die; 250 West 57th Street; New York, New York 10107 (Telephone 212-246-6973).

▸ **Consumer Protection for Pre-Need Sales.** My personal advice to anyone approached by a Pre-Need salesman is to just say no. The Reverend James Cunningham, a Toledo pastoral counselor, has been quoted in the **Funeral Service Insider** (Nov. 17, 1986) as saying, "Funerals are for the living. Isn't it possible that the pre-arrangement of one's funeral service later may deprive families and individuals of their planning and participation experience in the service for the person they have lost? An experience that is a valuable part of resolving grief stress?" But Pre-Need has become a huge business throughout the nation in recent years. Legislation is desperately needed in many states to protect the interests of the many individuals who do sign Pre-Need contracts. The issues involved are discussed briefly in a **Wall Street Journal** article reprinted in Appendix III.

Part Two:
Caring For Your
Own Dead In . . .

LAWS, REGULATIONS, AND SERVICES IN EACH STATE

In Alabama

Please refer to Chapter 9 as you use this section.

Persons in Alabama may care for their own dead. The legal authority to do so is found in:

> Title 22-9-70: . . .The funeral director or other person in charge of interment shall be responsible for obtaining and filing the certificate of death. . .

There are no other statutes or regulations which might require you to use a funeral director when no embalming is desired. A 1986 letter from John Wible, General Counsel, Alabama Department of Health verifies this interpretation.

▸ **Death Certificate**

The family doctor or a local medical examiner will supply and sign the death certificate within three days stating the cause of death. The remaining information must be supplied, typewritten or in permanent ink. The death certificate must be filed with the local registrar within five days and prior to cremation or removal.

▸ **Fetal Death**

A fetal death report is required after 20 weeks of gestation. All other procedures apply if disposition is handled by the family.

▸ **Transporting and Disposition**

A receipt for burial, removal or other disposition must be obtained from the county health department. (Someone should be available - on call - even on weekends and holidays.) This receipt must be obtained prior to the release of a body from a hospital or nursing home since one copy must be left with that institution. Another copy must be delivered to or mailed to the local registrar within seventy-two hours. The remaining copy must stay with the body to its final destination. If disposition is planned in another state make sure to ask for the out-of-state form which is slightly different from the one used for local disposition.

▶ **Burial**

Check with the county or town registrar for local zoning laws regarding home burial. There are no state burial statutes or regulations with regard to depth.

The receipt for burial must be signed by the person in charge and filed within three days with the registrar of the district where interment occurred.

▶ **Cremation**

A permit for cremation must be signed by a local medical examiner. If no medical examiner is available, the county sheriff will secure a licensed physician for this purpose. Most crematories insist that a pacemaker be removed, and authorization by next-of-kin usually is required. The crematory will return the burial-transit permit to the registrar.

▶ **Other Requirements**

Alabama has no requirements controlling the time schedule for the disposition of unembalmed bodies. Weather and reasonable planning should be considered.

If the person died of a contagious or communicable disease, the doctor in attendance should be consulted.

Embalming or cremation is required before removing a body from the state.

▶ **Crematories**

Pine Crest Cemetery Co.
1939 Dauphin Island Pkwy.
P.O. Box 5347
Mobile, AL 36605
205-478-5227
Independent
Available 8-5 M-F, 8-12 Sat.,
  or by arrangement.

Cost of cremation only: $180
Body container requirements:
  rigid combustible
Cardboard casket: $40
Cost of mailing cremains: $15
Payment: at time of delivery

The crematory in Birmingham was uncomfortable with my request for information.

There may be additional crematories that are not on the lists

I used for this research.

▸ **Body Donation**

Alabama Anatomical Board
Department of Anatomy
College of Medicine
University of South Alabama
Mobile, AL 36688
205-460-6490, 8-5 M-F only
(Check hospital holding
facility or use a local funeral
director on weekends and
holidays.)

Cost to family: transportation
  unless from U.S.A. Medical
  Center; embalming if
  weekend or holiday death
Prior enrollment: not required
Disposition: cremation;
  cremains returned by
  request
Body rejection: none for
  prior enrollees

(Also serves University of Alabama in Birmingham)

▸ **State Funeral Board**

The Alabama Funeral Board has seven members. There are no
consumer representatives.

(This section was reviewed by the attorney for the Alabama
Department of Health.)

In Alaska

Please refer to Chapter 9 as you use this section.

No Alaskan statute requires the use of a funeral director for
body disposition. Indeed, in AS 08.42.020 (c), unlicensed
persons may be granted a permit to dispose of the dead if no
embalming is required.

▸ **Death Certificate**

The family doctor or a local medical examiner will supply and
sign the death certificate within 24 hours stating the cause
of death. The remaining information must be supplied,
typewritten or in black ink. The death certificate must be
filed with the local registrar or subregistrar within three
days and prior to disposition.

► **Fetal Death**

A fetal death report is required after 20 weeks of gestation. A physician must sign the fetal death certificate except in special problem cases handled by the Department of Health.

► **Transporting and Disposition Permit**

The local registrar or subregistrar will issue a burial-transit permit. The death certificate must be obtained first.

► **Burial**

Check with the county or town registrar for local zoning laws regarding home burial. There are no state burial statutes or regulations with regard to depth.

If the death occurred outside the district where burial will take place, the burial-transit permit must be filed with a magistrate of the court in that district.

► **Cremation**

Approval for cremation must be granted by a local medical examiner or magistrate. Most crematories insist that a pacemaker be removed, and authorization by next-of-kin usually is required.

► **Other Requirements**

When the body will not reach its destination within 24 hours after death embalming is required.

Human remains shipped into or out of Alaska must first be embalmed. If body donation to a medical school is considered, have a funeral director check with the medical school first regarding acceptable procedures.

When death occurs from smallpox, plague, anthrax, diphtheria, meningococcal meningitis, cholera, epidemic typhus, or any unusual and highly communicable disease, the body shall be embalmed. A physician shall advise appropriate precautionary measures in other deaths from a communicable disease.

The rate of autopsied deaths runs close to 45% in Alaska. According to the Health Department regulations now being considered, a medical examiner is not required "to make the head, face and hands of the deceased presentable. . . " after autopsy. Indeed, according to a funeral director in one area, the body may not even be closed after autopsy. Any family choosing to handle a death personally under such circumstances may wish to ask for the assistance of a funeral director to at least place the body in a covered container.

▶ **Crematories**

Forestlawn Memorial Crematory
Box 1127 South Station
Anchorage, AK 99511
907-344-1497
Funeral Home
Available: 24 hours

Cost of cremation only: $235
Body container requirements: rigid combustible
Cardboard casket: available
Cost of mailing cremains: postage
Payment: negotiable

Witzleben Funeral Home
P.O. Box 2351
Anchorage, AK 99511
907-274-7576
Available: 24 hours

Cost of cremation only: $260
Body container requirements: rigid combustible
Cardboard casket: $60
Cost of mailing cremains: $50 (approximate)
Payment: negotiable

Northern Lights Mortuary
S.R. Box 20055
Fairbanks, AK 99701
Funeral Home
907-479-2545
Available: 24 hours

Cost of cremation only: $365
Body container requirements: rigid combustible
Cardboard casket: $125
Cost of mailing cremains: included
Payment: at time of delivery, negotiable

Beaverloot Funeral Home and Crematory
P.O. Box 5065
Kenai, AK 99611
907-283-9644
Available: 24 hours

Cost of cremation only: $365
Body container requirements: rigid combustible
Cardboard casket: $125
Cost of mailing cremains: included
Payment: at time of delivery, negotiable

Spenard Heights Mortuary
3804 Spenard Rd.
Spenard, AK 99503
907-279-3741
Funeral Home
Available: 24 hours

Cost of cremation only: $330
Body container requirements:
 rigid combustible
Cardboard casket: $48
Cost of mailing cremains:$12
Payment: at time of delivery

There may be additional crematories that are not on the lists I used for this research.

▶ **Body Donation**

There are no medical schools in Alaska. Check the nearest states although the time required for transportation must be considered. A body shipped out of state must be embalmed which may make the body unacceptable to a medical school if the school's procedures are not followed. Preliminary embalming may be at the expense of the family.

▶ **State Funeral Board**

Alaska has no state funeral board. The Department of Commerce issues the license to a funeral director.

(This section was reviewed by the Alaska Department of Health and Social Services, Division of Public Health.)

In Arizona

Please refer to Chapter 9 as you use this section.

Persons in Arizona may care for their own dead. The legal authority to do so is found in:

Rule 9-19-102 (9): "Person acting as a funeral director" means a person other than a licensed funeral director who has assumed the responsibility for the disposition of a dead human body.

Rule 9-19-324: Persons who are not licensed funeral directors may transport a body within the State by private conveyance for burial on privately owned or noncommercial property provided the elapsed time between the issuance of the burial transit permit and the time of disposition does not exceed 36 hours.

There are no other statutes or regulations which might require you to use a funeral director when no embalming is desired.

▶ **Death Certificate**

The family doctor or a local medical examiner will supply and sign the death certificate within 72 hours stating the cause of death. The remaining information must be supplied, typewritten or in black ink. The death certificate must be filed with the local registrar within three days and prior to cremation or removal.

If death has occurred without medical attendance on an Indian reservation and if no medical examiner is available, tribal law enforcement authority may certify as to the cause of death.

▶ **Fetal Death**

A fetal death report is required after 20 weeks of gestation or when the weight is 350 grams or more. If there is no family physician involved, the local medical examiner must sign the fetal death certificate. All other procedures apply if disposition is handled by the family.

▶ **Transporting and Disposition**

The local registrar will issue a burial-transit permit. If the death has occurred after usual business hours, a funeral director may be asked to supply the permit. The death certificate must be obtained first.

The "State copy" must be mailed immediately to the State registrar as a notification of death. After disposition, the original page of the burial-transit permit must be signed and returned to the clerk of the county where it was issued or to the State registrar within 10 days of disposition.

▶ **Burial**

Check with the county registrar for local zoning laws regarding home burial. Title 36-333 reads, "Any person who inters dead human remains in a burial ground where there is no person in charge shall endorse, sign and file the permit and write across the face of the permit the words No person in charge.'" There are no state burial statutes or regulations regarding depth.

▸ **Cremation**

When cremation is chosen, the permit for cremation must be obtained from a local medical examiner before the burial-transit permit can be issued. If no medical examiner is available, the county sheriff shall secure a licensed physician for this purpose. A fee may be charged for this. Most crematories insist that a pacemaker be removed, and authorization by next-of-kin usually is required.

▸ **Other Requirements**

If disposition does not occur within 24 hours, the body must be embalmed or refrigerated.

The body of a person who died from smallpox, asiatic cholera, plague, typhus, yellow fever, glanders, anthrax, meningitis, or Hansen's disease must be embalmed. If the person died of any other contagious or communicable disease, the doctor in attendance should be consulted.

▸ **Crematories**

Beller-Sutton Crematory
P.O. Box 4027
2215 Northern Ave.
Kingman, AZ 86401
602-757-4022
Tucker Funeral Home
    757-3111
Available: 24 hours

Cost of cremation only: $110
Body container requirements:
    rigid combustible
Cardboard casket: available
Cost of mailing cremains:
    postage
Payment: at time of delivery,
    negotiable

East Valley Crematory
33 N. Sirrine
Mesa, AZ 85201
602-964-8686
Bunker Funeral Home
Available: 24 hours

Cost of cremation only: $100
Body container requirements:
  rigid combustible
Cardboard casket: $40
Cost of mailing cremains: $25
Payment: at time of delivery,
  negotiable

Valley of the Sun Crematory
348 W. Chandler Heights Rd.
Phoenix, AZ 85061
602-249-1100
Funeral home affiliated
Crematory hours: 8-5 M-F

Cost of cremation only: $135
Body container requirements:
  rigid combustible
Cardboard casket: available
Cost of mailing cremains:$190
Payment: at time of delivery,
  negotiable

Greenwood Memorial Park
2300 W. Van Buren
Phoenix, AZ 85009
602-254-8491
Independent
Available: 8-4:30 M-F,
  8-12 Sat.

Cost of cremation only: $110
Body container requirements:
  rigid combustible
Cardboard casket: not carried
Cost of mailing cremains: $35
Payment: at time of delivery,
  negotiable

Mountain View Cemetery
1051 Willow Creek Rd.
P.O. Box 2016
Prescott, AZ 86302
602-445-4990
Independent
Available: 8-5 M-Sat.

Cost of cremation only: $150
Body container requirements:
  rigid combustible
Cardboard casket: not carried
Cost of mailing cremains: $25
Payment: negotiable

Green Acres Crematory
401 N. Hayden Rd.
Scottsdale, AZ 85257
602-945-2654
Funeral home affiliated
Available: 24 hours

Cost of cremation only: $100
Body container requirements:
  rigid combustible
Cardboard casket: available
Cost of mailing cremains: $35
Payment: at time of delivery,
  negotiable

Sedona Funeral Home
701 W. Highway 39A
P.O. Box 3267
Sedona, AZ 86340
602-282-3253
Crematory hours: 8-5 M-F, 8-12 Sat., 24-hour phone

Cost of cremation only: $125
Body container requirements: rigid combustible
Cardboard casket: available
Cost of mailing cremains: $30
Payment: at time of delivery

Sunland Memorial Park
15826 N. Del Webb
Sun City, AZ 85351
602-933-0161
Funeral home affiliated
Available: 24 hours

Cost of cremation only: $100
Body container requirements: rigid combustible
Cardboard casket: $75
Cost of mailing cremains: postage
Payment: negotiable, 60 days

Bring's Crematory
236 S. Scott Ave.
Tucson, AZ 85701
602-623-4718
Funeral home affiliated
Available: 24 hours

Cost of cremation only: $110
Body container requirements: rigid combustible
Cardboard casket: $30
Cost of mailing cremains:$40
Payment: negotiable

Adair Funeral Home
1050 N. Dodge Blvd.
Tucson, AZ 85716
602-326-4343
Crematory hours: sunrise to sunset M-F, weekends by special arrangement

Cost of cremation only: $112
Body container requirements: rigid combustible
Cardboard casket: $55
Cost of mailing cremains:$50
Payment: time of delivery, negotiable

Evergreen Memorial Park
3015 N. Oracle
Tucson, AZ 85705
602-888-7470
Funeral home affiliated
Available: 8-5 daily

Cost of cremation only: $110
Body container requirements: rigid combustible
Cardboard casket: $32
Cost of mailing cremains: $40
Payment: at time of delivery

Tucson Memorial Park
P.O. Box 11157
Tucson, AZ 85706
602-294-2603
Funeral home affiliated
Available: 24 hours

Cost of cremation only: $110
Body container requirements: rigid combustible
Cardboard casket: $25
Cost of mailing cremains: $45
Payment: negotiable

Hudgel's Swan Funeral Home
1335 S. Swan Rd.
Tucson, AZ 85711
602-747-2525
Available: 24 hours

Cost of cremation only: $110
Body container requirements:
  rigid combustible
Cardboard casket: $25
Cost of mailing cremains: $35
Payment: negotiable

Ryzek Yuma Crematory
16th St. at 6th Ave.
P.O. Box 590
Yuma, AZ 85364
602-783-9503
Funeral home affiliated
Available: 24 hours

Cost of cremation only: $160
Body container requirements:
  rigid combustible
Cardboard casket: not carried
Cost of mailing cremains: $25
Payment: negotiable

Desert Lawn Memorial Park
1415 1st St.
Yuma, AZ 85364
602-782-1633
Funeral home to be added in
  1987, Available 24 hours.
  Until then, 8-5 M-F

Cost of cremation only: $150
Body container requirements:
  rigid combustible
Cardboard casket: available
Cost of mailing cremains: $35
Payment: negotiable

One crematory in Mesa declined to accept a body from other than a funeral director. The gentleman said he was "uncomfortable with the whole idea."

There may be additional crematories that are not on the lists I used for this research.

▶ **Body Donation**

University of Arizona
College of Medicine
Department of Anatomy
1501 N. Campbell Ave.
Tucson, AZ 85724
602-626-6084
    626-6443 after 5 & page

Cost to family: transportation
  outside 35-mile radius
Prior enrollment: required
Over-enrollment: not shared
Disposition: cremation, no
  return of cremains
Body rejection: standard*,
  under 18, previous embalming, obesity, systemic
  cancer

*autopsy, decomposition, mutilation, severe burn victim, meningitis, hepatitis, AIDS

▸ **State Funeral Board**

The Arizona State Funeral Board has seven members. There are three consumer representatives.

(This section was sent to the Arizona Department of Health for review, but no response was received by the time of publication.)

In Arkansas

Please refer to Chapter 9 as you use this section.

Persons in Arkansas may care for their own dead. The legal authority to do so is found in:

Title 82-513 (b): The funeral director or person acting as such who first assumes custody of the dead body shall file the death certificate.

There are no other statutes or regulations which might require you to use a funeral director when embalming is not desired.

▸ **Death Certificate**

The family doctor or a local medical examiner will sign the death certificate within 48 hours stating the cause of death. The remaining information must be supplied, typewritten or in black, unfading ink. The death certificate must be filed with the local registrar within 10 days and before final disposition.

▸ **Fetal Death**

A fetal death report is required after 20 weeks of gestation or when the weight is 500 grams or more. The certificate may be prepared by the physician or other person in attendance or the father or mother. However, when gestation has reached a period of 28 completed weeks, the cause of death must be certified by a physician. The fetal death certificate must be filed within five days. All other procedures apply if disposition is handled by the family.

▶ **Transporting and Disposition Permit**

A body may be moved with the consent of a physician, medical examiner or county coroner. A burial-transit permit, obtained from the local registrar or deputy registrar, is required when a body is transported into or out of the state or for cremation. No burial-transit permit is required for burial within the state.

▶ **Burial**

Family graveyards are exempt from taxation and must be registered with the county clerk before burial. There are no state burial statutes or regulations with regard to depth.

▶ **Cremation**

A permit for cremation must be obtained from the county health department. There may be a fee for this. If the death was unattended, there is a 72 hour wait before cremation. This waiting period may be waived when the death certificate has been signed by a physician or coroner and the cause of death is not accident, homicide or suicide. Most crematories insist that a pacemaker be removed, and authorization by next-of-kin usually is required.

▶ **Other Requirements**

When disposition has not occurred within 72 hours, the body must be embalmed or refrigerated.

A body to be shipped by common carrier must be embalmed.

If the person died of a contagious or communicable disease, the doctor in attendance should be consulted.

▶ **Crematories**

Crestlawn Crematory
8th Ave. & Vine St.
Conway, AR 72032
501-327-7727
McNutt Funeral Home
Crematory Hours: 8-5 M-F

Cost of cremation only: $140
Body container requirements:
  rigid combustible
Cardboard casket: $25
Cost of mailing cremains: $15
Payment: at time of delivery

Caruth Funeral Home
655 Park Ave.
P.O. Box 876
Hot Springs, AR 71902
501-623-2533
Available: 24 hours

Cost of cremation only: $170
Body container requirements:
  rigid combustible
Cardboard casket: $50
Cost of mailing cremains:
  included
Payment: negotiable

Benton County Crematory
Route 11, Box 83
Rogers, AR 72756
501-636-2412
Available: 24 hours
3 funeral homes affiliated
Callison-Lough in Rogers,
Bentonville, and Gravette

Cost of cremation only: $140
Body container requirements:
  rigid combustible
Cardboard casket: $65
Cost of mailing cremains: $15
Payment: at time of delivery

Three crematories, one each in Fayetteville, Little Rock, and
Mountain Home, declined to accept a body from other than a
funeral director. Their concerns were "too risky," "liability,"
and "loss of other business."

There may be additional crematories that are not on the lists
I used for this research.

▶ **Body Donation**

University of Arkansas
Department of Anatomy
School of Medicine
Little Rock, AR 72205-7199
501-661-5180
  661-5000 other times

Cost to family: transportation
  outside the state
Prior enrollment: preferred
Over-enrollment: sharing can
  be arranged
Disposition: cremation
Body rejection: autopsy, burn
  victim, decomposition,
  missing body parts, obesity,
  destruction of internal
  organs

▸ **State Funeral Board**

The Arkansas State Board of Embalmers and Funeral Directors has seven members. There are two consumer representatives, including one Senior Citizen representative.

(This section was reviewed by the Director and State Registrar, Division of Vital Records for Arkansas.)

In California

Please refer to Chapter 9 as you use this section.

In California persons may care for their own dead. Legal authority to do so is stated in the California statutes, Chapter 3, section 7100-1003:

> The right to control the disposition of the remains of a deceased person, unless other directions have been given by the decedent, vest in, . . . (a) the surviving spouse, (b) the surviving child or children of the decedent, (c) the surviving parent or parents of the decedent, (d) the person or persons respectively in the next degree of kindred. . .

There are no other statutes or regulations which might require you to use a funeral director when no embalming is desired.

▸ **Death Certificate**

The family doctor will supply and sign the death certificate stating the cause of death within 15 hours. A coroner will supply a death certificate within three days. The remaining information must be completed, typewritten or in black ink. The death certificate must be filed with the local registrar within five days and before final disposition.

(Many funeral personnel in California complained of inaccurate and slow completion of death certificates by doctors.

Check the Appendix for death certificate guidelines.)

▶ **Fetal Death**

A fetal death report is required after 20 weeks of gestation. If there is no family physician involved, the local medical examiner must sign the fetal death certificate. All other procedures apply if disposition is handled by the family.

▶ **Transporting and Disposition Permit**

Upon presentation of a completed death certificate, the local registrar in the county health department will issue the permit for disposition. This must specify the cemetery, burial at sea, or crematory with final resting place for cremains. One copy must be filed with the registrar of the county where disposition takes place and one must be returned to the issuing registrar within 10 days. The charge for this permit is $3. After usual business hours, the charge is $6 if the county provides after-hour service. This service may not be available in all counties. Therefore, a family trying to make arrangements when death occurs during a weekend may find the process difficult. (Funeral directors seem to be given some latitude in dealing with such requirements in that situation.) Temporary removal of a body with medical permission will probably be permitted (without the permit for disposition) in a community where you are known. Certainly refrigeration or embalming must be considered if there is to be a delay in final disposition.

▶ **Burial**

Check with the county registrar for local zoning laws regarding home burial. In most situations, burial must be in an established cemetery. There are no state burial statutes or regulations with regard to depth.

▶ **Cremation**

Most crematories insist that a pacemaker be removed, and authorization by next-of-kin usually is required.

Cremains, having been removed from any container, may be scattered at sea. A verified statement must be filed with the local registrar nearest the point where scattering occurred. Otherwise, cremated remains may be interred, but not scattered, on land; or they may be kept in the dwelling of the person having the right to control disposition.

▶ **Other Requirements**

California has no other requirements controlling the time schedule for the disposition of unembalmed bodies. Weather and reasonable planning should be considered.

If the person died of a contagious or communicable disease, the doctor in attendance should be consulted. In Riverside County, all AIDS deceased must be embalmed - as of this writing, and the coroner in each county may have control of disposition.

▶ **Crematories**

Mt. View Cemetery
2400 N. Fairbanks Ave.
P.O. Box M
Altadena, CA 91001
818-794-7133
Funeral home affiliated
Available: 24-hour phone

Cost of cremation only: $95
Body container requirements:
  rigid combustible
Cardboard casket: included
Cost of mailing cremains: $25
Payment: at time of delivery,
  negotiable

Cremar Crematory
2303 S. Manchester
Anaheim, CA 92802
714-634-3836
Independent
Available: 8-4 M-F, 10-1 Sat.
  24-hour phone

Cost of cremation only: $50
Body container requirements:
  rigid combustible
Cardboard casket: $10
Cost of mailing cremains:
  postage
Payment: at time of delivery,
  negotiable

Humboldt Cremation Co.
1070 H Street
Arcata, CA 95521
707-822-1314
Pierce Mortuary Chapels
Available: 24 hours

Cost of cremation only: $165
Body container requirements:
  rigid combustible
Cardboard casket: $40
Cost of mailing cremains: $35
Payment: negotiable

Mish Funeral Home/Crematory
120 Minner Ave.
Bakersfield, CA 93308
805-399-9391
So. Cal. 1-800-222-9391
Available: 24 hours

Cost of cremation only: $150
Handling charge: $75
Body container requirements:
  particle board/plywood
Wood box: $75
Cost of mailing cremains: $35
Payment: at time of delivery

Weaver Mortuary/Crematory
690 Euclid Ave.
Beaumont, CA 92223
714-845-1141
Crematory Hours: 8-5 M-F

Cost of cremation only: $125
Body container requirements:
rigid combustible
Cardboard casket: $24
Cost of mailing cremains:
postage
Payment: at time of delivery,
negotiable

Sunset View Cemetery
101 Colusa
Berkeley, CA 94707
415-525-5111
Funeral home affiliated
Available: 24 hours

Cost of cremation only: $150
Body container requirements:
rigid combustible
Cardboard casket: $50
Cost of mailing cremains: $30
Payment: negotiable

Frye Crematory
799 S. Highway 86
P.O. Box 1325
Brawley, CA 92227
619-344-1414
Funeral home affiliated
Available: 24 hours

Cost of cremation only: $150
Body container requirements:
rigid combustible
Cardboard casket: $45
Cost of mailing cremains: $25
Payment: at time of delivery

Memory Garden Memorial
Park and Mortuary
455 W. Central
Brea, CA 92621
714-529-3961
Available: 8-5 daily,
24 hour phone

Cost of cremation only: $100
Body container requirements:
rigid combustible
Cardboard casket: $25
Cost of mailing cremains: $25
Payment: at time of delivery,
negotiable

Desert Lawn Park
11251 Desert Lawn Drive
P.O. Box 485
Calimesa, CA 92320
714-795-2451
Funeral home affiliated
Available: 8-5 M-F,
24 hour phone

Cost of cremation only: $125
Body container requirements:
cardboard only
Cardboard casket: included
Cost of mailing cremains: $26
Payment: at time of delivery,
negotiable

Oakwood Memorial Park
22601 Lassen
Chatsworth, CA 91311
818-341-0344
Independent
Available: 8:30-5 M-F,
weekends by arrangement

Cost of cremation only: $90
Body container requirements:
rigid combustible
Cardboard casket: not carried
Cost of mailing cremains:
postage
Payment: at time of delivery

Chico Cemetery Association
700 Camellia Way
P.O. Box 893
Chico, CA 95927
916-345-7243
Hall-Van Hook Funeral Home
916-342-4291
Crematory hours: 8-4:30 M-F

Cost of cremation only: $140
Body container requirements:
  rigid combustible
Cardboard casket: not carried
Cost of mailing cremains: $45
Payment: at time of delivery,
  negotiable

Olivet Memorial Park
1601 Hillside
Colma, CA 94014
415-755-0322
Independent
Available: 8-5 M-F,
  9-4:30 Sat.

Cost of cremation only: $125
Body container requirements:
  rigid combustible
Cardboard casket: not carried
Cost of mailing cremains: $65
Payment: negotiable

Woodlawn Cemetery
P.O. Box 307
Colma, CA 94014
415-755-1727
Independent
Available: 9-4:30 M-F

Cost of cremation only: $125
Body container requirements:
  rigid combustible
Cardboard casket: not carried
Cost of mailing cremains: $30
Payment: at time of delivery,
  negotiable

Harbor Lawn Mt. Olive
1625 Gisler Ave.
Costa Mesa, CA 92626
714-540-5554
Available: 24 hours

Cost of cremation only: $75
Body container requirements:
  rigid combustible
Cardboard casket: $25
Cost of mailing cremains: $35
Payment: negotiable

Ocean View Cemetery and
  Sunset Memorial Park
P.O. Box 998
Eureka, CA 95501
707-445-3188
Chapel of the Ferns Funeral
Home, 707-443-1641
Crematory Hours: 8-5 M-F

Cost of cremation only: $160
Body container requirements:
  rigid combustible
Cardboard casket: $25
Cost of mailing cremains: $35
Payment: at time of delivery,
  negotiable 30 days

Fairmont Memorial Park
1900 Union Ave.
P.O. Box 7
Fairfield, CA 94533
707-425-4697
Bryan Braker Funeral Home
Available: 24 hours

Cost of cremation only: $150
Body container requirements:
  rigid combustible
Cardboard casket: $45
Cost of mailing cremains: $35
Payment: at time of delivery

Cedar Lawn Memorial Park
Scott Creek Road
Fremont, CA 94538
415-656-5565
Lima Family-Milpitas-Fremont
  Mortuary
Available: 24 hours

Cost of cremation only: $100
Body container requirements:
  rigid combustible
Cardboard casket: $40
Cost of mailing cremains: $35
Payment: at time of delivery,
  negotiable

Irvington Memorial Cemetery
41001 Chapel
Fremont, CA 94538
415-656-5800
Independent
Available: 8-5 M-F,
  weekends by arrangement

Cost of cremation only: $107
Body container requirements:
  rigid combustible
Cardboard casket: not carried
Cost of mailing cremains:
  postage
Payment: at time of delivery,
  negotiable

Belmont Memorial Park
201 N. Tielman Ave.
Fresno, CA 93728
209-237-6185
Stephens & Bean Chapel
Available: 8:30-5 M-F,
  8:30-2 Sat.

Cost of cremation only: $100
Body container requirements:
  rigid combustible
Cardboard casket: not carried
Cost of mailing cremains: $40
Payment: negotiable

Chapel of the Light
1620 W. Belmont
Fresno, CA 93728
209-233-6254
Funeral home affiliated
Available: 24 hours

Cost of cremation only: $100
Body container requirements:
  rigid combustible
Cardboard casket: $25
Cost of mailing cremains: $40
Payment: at time of delivery

Dimond Service Corp.
10630 Chapman Ave.
Garden Grove, CA 92640
714-537-1038
Funeral home affiliated
Available: 24 hours

Cost of cremation only: $60
Body container requirements:
  rigid combustible
Cardboard casket: $84
Cost of mailing cremains: $15
Payment: negotiable

Roosevelt Memorial Park
18255 S. Vermont Ave.
Gardena, CA 90247
213-321-0482
Funeral home affiliated
Available: 24 hours
Crematory hours: 8-4 M-F

Cost of cremation only: $57
  cardboard; $100 wood
Body container requirements:
  rigid combustible
Cardboard casket: $10
Cost of mailing cremains: $95
Payment: at time of delivery

Forest Lawn Memorial Park
1712 Glendale Ave.
Glendale, CA 91209
213-254-3131
Funeral home affiliated
Available: 24 hours

Cost of cremation only: $95
Body container requirements:
  rigid combustible
Cardboard casket: $29
Cost of mailing cremains: $25
Payment: negotiable

Grand View Memorial Park
1341 Glenwood Road
Glendale, CA 91201
818-242-2697
Independent
Available: 8:30-5 M-F,
  8:30-4 Sat.

Cost of cremation only: $60
Body container requirements:
  rigid combustible
Cardboard casket: $11
Cost of mailing cremains: $28
Payment: at time of delivery

Chapel of the Chimes
  Memorial Park
32992 Mission
Hayward, CA 94544
415-538-3131
Funeral home affiliated
Crematory Hours:8-4:30 M-F
24-hour phone

Cost of cremation only: $115
Body container requirements:
  rigid combustible
Cardboard casket: $26.50
Cost of mailing cremains: $55
Payment: negotiable

Inglewood Park Cemetery
720 E. Florence
Inglewood, CA 90307
213-678-1251
Independent
Available: 8-4:30 M-Sat.

Cost of cremation only: $90
Body container requirements:
  rigid combustible
Cardboard casket: not carried
Cost of mailing cremains:
  postage
Payment: at time of delivery

Jones Mortuary
115 S. Main St.
Lakeport, CA 95453
707-263-5389
Available: 24 hours phone

Cost of cremation only: $125
Body container requirements:
  rigid combustible
·Cardboard casket: available
Cost of mailing cremains:
  postage
Payment: at time of delivery,
  negotiable

Oakmont Memorial Park and
  Mortuary
2099 Reliez Valley Rd.
P.O. Box 417
Lancaster, CA 94549
415-935-3311
Available: 24 hours

Cost of cremation only: $125
Body container requirements:
  rigid combustible
Cardboard casket: $25
Cost of mailing cremains: $25
Payment: at time of delivery,
  negotiable 90 days

Cherokee Memorial Park
Highway 99 at Harney
Lodi, CA 95240
209-334-9613
Independent
Available: 8-4:30 M-F

Cost of cremation only: $100
Body container requirements:
rigid combustible
Cardboard casket: not carried
Cost of mailing cremains:
postage
Payment: at time of delivery

Dilday-Mottell Crematory
1250 Pacific
Long Beach, CA 90813
213-436-9024
Funeral home affiliated
Available: 24 hours

Cost of cremation only: $125
Body container requirements:
rigid combustible
Cardboard casket: $30
Cost of mailing cremains: $35
Payment: at time of delivery,
negotiable

Long Beach Crematory
1952 Long Beach Blvd.
Long Beach, CA 90806
213-426-3365
Stricklin/Snively affiliated
Available: 8-5 M-F,
24 hour phone

Cost of cremation only: $95
Body container requirements:
rigid combustible
Cardboard casket: $20
Cost of mailing cremains: $15
Payment: at time of delivery

L.A. Odd Fellows Cemetery
3640 Whittier Blvd.
Los Angeles, CA 90023
213-261-6156
Independent
Available: 8:30-4:30 M-F

Cost of cremation only: $90
Body container requirements:
rigid combustible
Cardboard casket: $10
Cost of mailing cremains: $20
Payment: at time of delivery

Pierce Bros. - Chapel of the
Pines
1605 S. Catalina St.
Los Angeles, CA 90060
213-731-5179
Funeral home affiliated
Available: 8-5

Cost of cremation only: $100
Body container requirements:
rigid combustible
Cardboard casket: $20
Cost of mailing cremains: $35
Payment: at time of delivery,
negotiable

Rosedale Mortuary and
Cemetery
1831 W. Washington Blvd.
Los Angeles, CA 90007
213-734-3155
Available: 24 hour phone

Cost of cremation only: $50
Body container requirements:
rigid combustible
Cardboard casket: $16
Cost of mailing cremains: $35
Payment: at time of delivery,
negotiable

Sierra View Memorial Park
Highway 65 S
P.O. Box 126
Marysville, CA 95901
916-742-6957
Funeral home affiliated
Available: 24 hour phone

Cost of cremation only: $125
Body container requirements:
  rigid combustible
Pressboard casket: $50
Cost of mailing cremains:
  included
Payment: at time of delivery

Evergreen Memorial Park
1480 B Street
Merced, CA 95340
209-383-7489
Independent
Available: 8-5 M-F,
  Sat. by arrangement

Cost of cremation only: $140
Body container requirements:
  rigid combustible
Cardboard casket: not carried
Cost of mailing cremains: $15
Payment: negotiable

Lakewood Memorial Park
P.O. Box 1666
Modesto, CA 95354
209-883-4465
Funeral home affiliated
Available: 8:30-5 M-Sat.

Cost of cremation only: $125
Body container requirements:
  rigid combustible
Cardboard casket: included
Cost of mailing cremains: $12
Payment: at time of delivery

Benedict-Rettey Crematory
1401 Quintana Rd.
Morro Bay, CA 93442
805-772-7382
Funeral home affiliated
Available: 24 hours

Cost of cremation only: $125
Body container requirements:
  rigid combustible
Cardboard casket: $30
Cost of mailing cremains:
  postage
Payment: at time of delivery,
  negotiable

Pacific View Memorial Park
3500 Pacific View
Newport Beach, CA 92663
714-644-2700
Funeral home affiliated
Available: 24 hours

Cost of cremation only: $100
Body container requirements:
  rigid combustible
Cardboard casket: $20
Cost of mailing cremains: $35
Payment: negotiable

Evergreen Cemetery and
  Crematory
6450 Camden Street
Oakland, CA 94605
415-632-1602
Available: 8-4 M-F
Nautilus Society affiliated
415-638-6943

Cost of cremation only: $95
Body container requirements:
  rigid combustible
Cardboard casket: not carried
Cost of mailing cremains: $48
Payment: at time of delivery

Mountain View
5000 Piedmont
Oakland, CA 94611
415-658-2588
Independent
Available: 8-4:30 M-F

Cost of cremation only: $100
Body container requirements:
  rigid combustible
Cardboard casket: not carried
Cost of mailing cremains: $55
Payment: negotiable 30 days

Eternal Hills Memorial Park
  and Mortuary
199 El Camino Real
P.O. Box 510
Oceanside, CA 92054
619-757-2020
Available: 24 hours

Cost of cremation only: $85
Body container requirements:
  rigid combustible
Cardboard casket: $10
Cost of mailing cremains: $35
Payment: at time of delivery,
  negotiable

Little Chapel by the Sea
Asilomar and Lighthouse
Pacific Grove, CA 93950
408-375-4191
The Paul Mortuary
Available: 24 hours

Cost of cremation only: $125
Body container requirements:
  rigid combustible
Cardboard casket: $47
Cost of mailing cremains: $45
Payment: negotiable 30 days

Wiefels and Son Mortuary
666 Vella Road
Palm Springs, CA 92264
619-327-1257
Available: 24 hours

Cost of cremation only: $65
Body container requirements:
  rigid combustible
Cardboard casket: $15
Cost of mailing cremains: $20
Payment: at time of delivery

Alta Mesa Memorial Park
695 Atascadero
Palo Alto, CA 94306
415-493-1041
Independent
Available 8-4:30 M-F,
  9-4 Sat. and Sun.

Cost of cremation only: $140
Body container requirements:
  rigid combustible
Cardboard casket: not carried
Cost of mailing cremains: $45
Payment: negotiable

Paradise Chapel of the Pines
5691 Almond St.
P.O. Box 194
Paradise, CA 95969
916-877-4991
Funeral home affiliated
Available: 24 hours

Cost of cremation only: $140
Body container requirements:
  rigid combustible
Cardboard casket: $25
Cost of mailing cremains: $30
Payment: negotiable

Rose Chapel Mortuary and
  Crematory
6382 Clark Rd.
Paradise, CA 95969
916-877-4923
Available: 24-hour phone
Crematory Hours: 8-5

Cost of cremation only: $140
Body container requirements:
  rigid combustible
Cardboard casket: $30
Cost of mailing cremains: $35
Payment: at time of delivery

Cypress Hill
430 Magnolia Ave.
Petaluma, CA 94952
707-762-6683
Independent
Available: 8-4:30 M-F

Cost of cremation only: $90
Body container requirements:
  rigid combustible
Cardboard casket: available
Cost of mailing cremains: $40
Payment: at time of delivery

Pomona Cemetery/Crematory
502 E. Franklin Ave.
Pomona, CA 91767
714-622-2029
Independent
Available: 8-4:30 M-F,
  or by special arrangement

Cost of cremation only: $100
Body container requirements:
  rigid combustible
Cardboard casket: not carried
Cost of mailing cremains: $25
Payment: at time of delivery

Redding Cemetery/Crematory
Continental at Eureka Way
Redding, CA 96001
916-241-2256
McDonald's Chapel affiliated
Crematory hours: 8-5 M-F

Cost of cremation only: $140
Body container requirements:
  rigid combustible
Cardboard casket: not carried
Cost of mailing cremains: $25
Payment: at time of delivery

Pacific Crest Cemetery Co.
2701 182nd
Redondo Beach, CA 90278
213-370-5891
Funeral homes affiliated
Crematory hours: 8-5 M-Sat.

Cost of cremation only: $85
Body container requirements:
  rigid combustible
Cardboard casket: $9
Cost of mailing cremains: $60
Payment: at time of delivery

Pierce Bros. Crestlawn
Memorial Park and Mortuary
11500 Arlington Ave.
Riverside, CA 92504
714-689-1441
California 1-800-762-7200
Out of state 1-800-345-7447
Available: 24 hour phone
Crematory hours: 8:30-5 daily

Cost of cremation only: $100
Body container requirements:
  rigid combustible
Cardboard casket: included
Cost of mailing cremains: $35
Payment: at time of delivery,
  negotiable

Evergreen Cemetery
4414 14th Street
Riverside, CA 92501
714-683-1840
Independent
Available: 8-4 M-F

Cost of cremation only: $100
Body container requirements:
  rigid combustible
Cardboard casket: included
Cost of mailing cremains: $10
Payment: at time of delivery

Camellia Memorial Lawn
10221 Jackson Road
P.O. Box 7008
Sacramento, CA 95826
916-363-9431
Independent
Available: 8:30-5 M-F,
  9-12 Sat.

Cost of cremation only: $95
Body container requirements:
  rigid combustible
Cardboard casket: not carried
Cost of mailing cremains: $20
Payment: at time of delivery

East Lawn Memorial Park
43rd and Folsom Blvd.
Sacramento, CA 95819
916-455-3033
Funeral home affiliated
Available: 8-5 daily

Cost of cremation only: $125
Body container requirements:
  rigid combustible
Cardboard casket: $60
Cost of mailing cremains: $55
Payment: negotiable

Mt. Vernon Memorial Park
8201 Greenback
Sacramento, CA 95628
916-969-1251
Funeral home affiliated
Available: 24 hours

Cost of cremation only: $95
Body container requirements:
  rigid combustible
Cardboard casket: $45
Cost of mailing cremains: $25
Payment: at time of delivery,
  negotiable

North Sacramento Memorial
  Crematory
725 El Camino Ave.
Sacramento, CA 95815
916-922-9668
No. Sacramento Funeral Home
Available: 24 hours

Cost of cremation only: $95
Body container requirements:
  rigid combustible
Cardboard casket: $50
Cost of mailing cremains: $25
Payment: at time of delivery

Sacramento Memorial Lawn
506 "O" Street
Sacramento, CA 95814
916-421-1171
Funeral home affiliated
Available: 9-6 daily

Cost of cremation only: $85
Body container requirements:
  rigid combustible
Cardboard casket: $20
Cost of mailing cremains: $25
Payment: at time of delivery

Mt. View Cemetery of San
  Bernardino
302 E. Highland Ave.
San Bernardino, CA 92406
714-882-2943
Independent
Available: 8-5 M-Th, 8-12
  Fri., 9-4 office other times

Cost of cremation only: $125
Body container requirements:
  rigid combustible
Cardboard casket: $10.60
Cost of mailing cremains: $10
Payment: at time of delivery

Cypress View Mausoleum &
  Crematory
3953 Imperial Ave.
San Diego, CA 92113
619-264-3168
Bonham Bros. Funeral Home
Available: 24 hour phone
Crematory hours: 8-5 M-F

Cost of cremation only: $100
Body container requirements:
  rigid combustible
Cardboard casket: $10
Cost of mailing cremains: $80
Payment: at time of delivery

Greenwood Memorial Park
  and Mortuary
Market and 43rd Streets
San Diego, CA 92112
619-264-3131
Available: 24 hours

Cost of cremation only: $100
Body container requirements:
  rigid combustible
Cardboard casket: $10
Cost of mailing cremains: $35
Payment: at time of delivery

Los Gatos Memorial Park
2255 Los Gatos-Almaden
San Jose, CA 95124
408-356-4151
Darling Fischer Mortuaries
Crematory hrs: 8-4:30 M-Sat.

Cost of cremation only: $100
Body container requirements:
  rigid combustible
Cardboard casket: not carried
Cost of mailing cremains: $35
Payment: at time of delivery

Oakhill Memorial Park
300 Curtner
San Jose, CA 95103
408-297-2447
Oakhill Funeral Home
Available: 24 hours

Cost of cremation only: $85
Body container requirements:
  rigid combustible
Cardboard casket: not carried
Cost of mailing cremains: $35
Payment: at time of delivery

Los Osos Valley Memorial
  Park
2260 Los Osos Valley Road
San Luis Obispo, CA 93402
805-528-1500
Funeral home affiliated
Available: 8:30-5 M-F,
  8:30-12 Sat.

Cost of cremation only: $125
Body container requirements:
  rigid combustible
Cardboard casket: available
Cost of mailing cremains: $25
Payment: at time of delivery

Skylawn Memorial Park
Skyline and Half Moon Bay
San Mateo, CA 94402
415-349-4411
Independent
Available: 9-5 daily

Cost of cremation only: $97
Body container requirements:
 rigid combustible
Cardboard casket: not carried
Cost of mailing cremains: $35
Payment: negotiable

IOOF Cemetery and Crema-
 tory
1927 Ocean Street
Santa Cruz, CA 95060
408-426-1601
Independent
Available: 8-5 M-Sat.

Cost of cremation only: $120
Body container requirements:
 rigid combustible
Cardboard casket: not carried
Cost of mailing cremains:
 postage
Payment: at time of delivery,
 negotiable

Dudley-Hoffman Mortuary
1003 E. Stowell Rd.
Santa Maria, CA 93456
805-922-8463
Available: 24 hours

Cost of cremation only: $110
Body container requirements:
 rigid combustible
Cardboard casket: $25
Cost of mailing cremains: $25
Payment: at time of delivery,
 negotiable

Chapel of the Chimes
 Crematory
2601 Santa Rosa Ave.
Santa Rosa, CA 95401
707-545-0196
Neptune Society affiliated
415-771-1701
Available: 24 hours

Cost of cremation only: $115
Body container requirements:
 rigid combustible
Cardboard casket: $65
Cost of mailing cremains: $52
Payment: at time of delivery,
 negotiable

Santa Rosa Memorial Park
Franklin Ave. and Poppy Dr.
Santa Rosa, CA 95402
707-542-1580
Independent
Available: 8-5 M-Sat.
 except holidays

Cost of cremation only: $105
Body container requirements:
 rigid combustible
Cardboard casket: not carried
Cost of mailing cremains: $30
Payment: at time of delivery

Pleasant Hill Crematory
Pleasant Hill at Watertrough
Sebastopol, CA 95492
707-823-5042
Pleasant Hill-Analy-O'Leary
Available: 24 hours

Cost of cremation only: $100
Body container requirements:
 rigid combustible
Cardboard casket: $24
Cost of mailing cremains: $25
Payment: at time of delivery

Soquel Crematory
P.O. Box 655
Soquel, CA 95073
408-476-2888
Funeral homes affiliated
Crematory hours 8-4 M-F

Cost of cremation only: $120
Body container requirements:
  rigid combustible
Cardboard casket: not carried
Cost of mailing cremains:
  postage
Payment: at time of delivery,
  negotiable

Allen Mortuary and Crematory
247 N. Broadway
Turlock, CA 95380
209-634-5829
Available: 24 hours

Cost of cremation only: $125
Body container requirements:
  rigid combustible
Cardboard casket: included
Cost of mailing cremains: $40
Payment: negotiable

Turlock Memorial Park
P.O. Box 1666
575 N. Sodorquist
Turlock, CA 95380
209-632-1018
Independent
Available: 8-5 M-F

Cost of cremation only: $125
Body container requirements:
  rigid combustible
Cardboard casket: not carried
Cost of mailing cremains: $20
Payment: at time of delivery,
  negotiable

Evergreen Memorial Garden
141 Low Gap Rd.
Ukiah, CA 95482
707-462-2206
Eversole Mortuary
Available: 24-hour phone
Crematory hours: 9-5 M-Sat.

Cost of cremation only: $120
Body container requirements:
  rigid combustible
Cardboard casket: $25
Cost of mailing cremains: $35
Payment: negotiable

Skyview Memorial Lawn
200 Rollingwood Drive
Vallejo, CA 94590
707-644-7474
Funeral home affiliated
Available: 24 hours

Cost of cremation only: $100
Body container requirements:
  rigid combustible
Cardboard casket: not carried
Cost of mailing cremains: $25
Payment: at time of delivery

Ventura Crematory
3150 Loma Vista Rd.
Ventura, CA 93003
805-643-9977
Ted Mayr Funeral Home
Available: 8-5 daily,
  24-hour phone

Cost of cremation only: $220
Body container requirements:
  rigid combustible
Cardboard casket: $16
Cost of mailing cremains: $25
Payment: at time of delivery,
  negotiable

Victor Valley Memorial Park
17150 "C" Street
Victorville, CA 92392
619-245-7664
Independent
Available: 7:30-4:30 M-F,
  weekends by arrangement

Cost of cremation only: $125
Body container requirements:
  rigid combustible
Cardboard casket: $15
Cost of mailing cremains: $18
Payment: at time of delivery

Miller Memorial Chapel
1120 W. Goshen Ave.
P.O. Box 430
Visalia, CA 93279
209-732-8371
Funeral home affiliated
Available: 24 hours

Cost of cremation only: $100
Body container requirements:
  rigid combustible
Cardboard casket: $35
Cost of mailing cremains: $35
Payment: at time of delivery,
  negotiable

Hull's Walnut Creek Crematory
1139 Saranap Ave.
Walnut Creek, CA 94595
415-934-5400
Funeral home affiliate
Available: 24 hours

Cost of cremation only: $100
Body container requirements:
  rigid combustible
Cardboard casket: $25
Cost of mailing cremains: $35
Payment: negotiable

Peek Family Crematory
7801 Bolsa Ave.
Westminster, CA 92683
714-893-3525
Funeral home affiliated
Available: 8-4:30 daily,
  24 hour phone

Cost of cremation only: $85
Body container requirements:
  rigid combustible
Cardboard casket: $40
Cost of mailing cremains:
  postage
Payment: at time of delivery,
  negotiable

Westminster Memorial Park
  and Mortuary
14801 Beach Blvd.
Westminster, CA 92683
714-893-2421
Available: 24 hours

Cost of cremation only: $60
Body container requirements:
  rigid combustible
Cardboard casket: $53
Cost of mailing cremains: $10
Payment: at time of delivery,
  negotiable

Ullrey Funeral Home
P.O. Box Q
Yuba City, CA 95992
916-673-9542
Available: 24 hours

Cost of cremation only: $125
Body container requirements:
  rigid combustible
Cardboard casket: $50
Cost of mailing cremains:
  postage
Payment: at time of delivery,
  negotiable

Fifteen crematories in California declined to accept a body
from other than a funeral director, two in Stockton and one
each in Atascadero, Colma, Compton, El Cajon, Laguna Beach,
Livermore, Pasadena, Rancho Palos Verde, San Diego, San
Pedro, Santa Barbara, Whittier, and Willits. Their concerns
included, "The stress level would be a tad much for a family.
. . leave it to those who are trained.". . . "This is a small-
town situation and the funeral directors wouldn't like it.". . .
"We're not here to answer questions like that. . . I don't
think we really care.". . . "Call somebody in Vermont, we're
not interested.". . . "Not feasible or appropriate. . . I
wouldn't do it to a relative.". . . "Legal reasons.". . .
"Accuracy of permits.". . . "I don't want to be misquoted.". .
. "What you're suggesting is awkward."

There may be additional crematories that are not on the lists
I used for this research.

▸ **Body Donation**

University of California
Department of Human
  Anatomy
Davis, CA 95616
916-752-2100

Cost to family: transportation
  beyond 30-mile radius
Prior enrollment: required
Over-enrollment: never
  occurred
Disposition: cremation,
  no return of cremains
Body rejection: standard*,
  Kuru, Alzheimer, MLS,
  Kruetsfeldt-Jakob, ALS,
  previous embalming, over-
  enrollment

University of California
School of Medicine
Irvine, CA 92717

Repeated requests for
information have not been
returned from this school.

University of California,
 San Diego
School of Medicine
La Jolla, CA 92093
619-534-4536

Cost to family: transportation
 outside San Diego Co.
Prior enrollment: required
Over-enrollment: shared
Disposition: cremation,
 return upon request at
 expense of family
Body rejection: autopsy,
 previous embalming

Loma Linda University
School of Medicine
Loma Linda, CA 92354

Repeated requests for
information have not been
returned from this school.

University of California
Department of Anatomy
Los Angeles, CA 90024
213-825-9563

Cost to family: transportation
 beyond 50 miles
Prior enrollment: not required
Over-enrollment: shared
Disposition: cremation,
 no return of cremains
Body rejection: standard*,
 previous embalming

University of So. Calif.
School of Medicine
1333 San Pablo St.
Los Angeles, CA 90033
213-222-0231

Cost to family: transportation
 beyond 50 miles
Prior enrollment: not required
Over-enrollment: shared
Disposition: cremation,
 return upon request at
 expense of family
Body rejection: standard*

California State Polytechnic
 University
Pomona, CA 91768

Repeated requests for
information have not been
returned from this school.

College of Osteopathic
Medicine of the Pacific
309 Pomona Mall E.
Pomona, CA 91766
714-623-6116
 433-5717 evenings
 and weekends

Cost to family: transportation
 beyond 75 miles
Prior enrollment: not required
Over-enrollment: not shared
Disposition: cremation; return
 of cremains by request
Body rejection: standard*

University of California
School of Medicine
San Francisco, CA 94143

Repeated requests for
information have not been
returned from this school.

Stanford University
School of Medicine
Division of Human Anatomy
Stanford, CA 94305
415-723-2404
after 5, 723-2300

Cost to family: transportation
  beyond 50 mile radius
Prior enrollment: required
Over-enrollment: never
  occurred
Disposition: cremation
Body rejection:standard*,
  missing body parts

Los Angeles College of
  Chiropractic
16200 East Amber Valley Dr.
P.O. Box 1166
Whittier, CA 90609
213-947-8755 ext.252,221
home phone 422-0338

Cost to family: transportation
  beyond 50-mile radius
Prior enrollment: not required
Disposition: cremation
Body rejection: standard*, 10
  or younger, bilateral
  amputee, severe internal
  hemorrhage

*autopsy, decomposition, mutilation, severe burn victim, meningitis, hepatitis, AIDS

▶ **State Funeral Board**

The California Board of Funeral Directors and Embalmers has five members. Three of these are consumer representatives.

(This section was reviewed by telephone with the Chief of the Health Data and Statistics for the State of California. It was also submitted to the Chairman of the California Funeral Board.)

In Colorado

Please refer to Chapter 9 as you use this section.

The Funeral Board for the State of Colorado no longer exists, and no other state agency has been assigned the task of licensing and regulating funeral directors or embalmers. Therefore, anyone may make funeral arrangements in Colorado.

Furthermore, there is a specific statute which remains in the laws permitting religious groups in Colorado to care for their own dead:

Title 12-54-118 (2) This part 1 (re funeral directors) shall not apply to, nor in any way interfere with, any custom or rite of any religious sect in the burial of its dead, and the members and followers of such religious sect may continue to care for, prepare, and bury the bodies of deceased members of such religious sect, free from any term or condition, or any provision of this part 1, and the persons caring for and preparing for disposal of such bodies need not be licensed. . .

▶ **Death Certificate**

The family doctor or a local medical examiner will supply and sign the death certificate within 48 hours stating the cause of death. The remaining information must be supplied, typewritten or in black ink. The death certificate must be filed with the local registrar within five days and prior to disposition.

▶ **Fetal Death**

Each fetal death in Colorado must be reported. A "Report of Spontaneous or Induced Abortion" is used when gestation is less than 20 weeks. A "Certificate of Fetal Death" is used in any case where gestation has been more than 20 weeks. A physician's signature is required.

▶ **Transporting and Disposition**

The county registrar or coroner will issue a disposition permit. The death certificate must be obtained first. The permit must be endorsed by the sexton or crematory and returned within five days to the person authorizing disposition.

▶ **Burial**

Check with the county registrar for local zoning laws regarding home burial. There are no state burial statutes or regulations with regard to depth.

▶ **Cremation**

The disposition permit serves as the permit to cremate. No additional permit is required. Most crematories insist that a pacemaker be removed, and authorization from next-of-kin usually is required.

▶ **Other Requirements**

If disposition will not take place within 24 hours of death, the body must be embalmed or refrigerated.

If the person died of a contagious or communicable disease, the person acting as the funeral director must consult with the local or state health officer concerning disposition.

▶ **Crematories**

Hold-Dixon Funeral Home
806 Macon Ave.
Canyon City, CO 81212
303-275-4113
Available: 24 hours

Cost of cremation only: $125
Body container requirements:
  rigid combustible
Cardboard casket: $15
Cost of mailing cremains: $15
Payment: at time of delivery,
  negotiable

Colorado Springs Crematory
  Corporation
225 N. Weber St.
Colorado Springs, CO 80903
303-632-7600
Funeral home affiliated
Available: 24 hours

Cost of cremation only: $110
Body container requirements:
  rigid combustible
Cardboard casket: $50
Cost of mailing cremains: $20
Payment: at time of delivery

Evergreen Shrine of Rest
1730 E. Fountain
Colorado Springs, CO 80910
303-634-1597
Funeral home affiliated
Available: 24-hour phone

Cost of cremation only: $125
Body container requirements:
  rigid combustible
Cardboard casket: $12
Cost of mailing cremains: $40
Payment: at time of delivery

Hamden Memorial Park
Clarkson & 17th Ave.
Denver, CO 80218
303-832-7832
Funeral home affiliated
Available: 7:30-3:30 M-F,
  weekends by arrangement

Cost of cremation only: $140
Body container requirements:
  rigid combustible
Cardboard casket: available
Payment: at time of delivery,
  negotiable

Denver Crematory
6425 W. Alameda Ave.
Denver, CO 80226
303-232-0139
Funeral home affiliated
Available: 24 hours

Cost of cremation only: $150
Body container requirements:
  rigid combustible
Cardboard casket: $40
Cost of mailing cremains:
  postage
Payment: at time of delivery,
  negotiable

Fairmont Cemetery Assn.
E. Alameda & Quebec
Denver, CO 80231
303-399-0692
Independent
Available: 8-4 M-F,
  24-hour phone

Cost of cremation only: $185
Body container requirements:
  rigid combustible
Cardboard casket: $40
Cost of mailing cremains:
  postage
Payment: negotiable

Englewood Crematory
1375 E. Hampden Ave.
Englewood, CO 80110
303-789-2535
Bullock Mortuary affiliated
Available: 8-5 M-Sat.,
  24-hour phone

Cost of cremation only: $150
Body container requirements:
  rigid combustible
Cardboard casket: not carried
Cost of mailing cremains:
  postage
Payment: at time of delivery,
  negotiable

Western Slope Crematory
P.O. Box 45
Glenwood Springs, CO 81601
303-945-6468
Hold-Dixon Funeral Home
Available: 24 hours

Cost of cremation only: $150
Body container requirements:
  rigid combustible
Cardboard casket: $125
Cost of mailing cremains: $15
Payment: negotiable

Martin's Crematory
550 North Ave.
Grand Jct., CO 81501
303-243-1538
Funeral home affiliated
Available: 24 hours

Cost of cremation only: $150
Body container requirements:
  rigid combustible
Cardboard casket: $35
Cost of mailing cremains:
  included
Payment: negotiable

Northern Colorado Crematory
  Inc.
700 8th St.
Greeley, CO 80631
303-351-0130
Independent
Available: 24-hour phone

Cost of cremation only: $115
Body container requirements:
  rigid combustible
Cardboard casket: $15
Cost of mailing cremains:
  postage
Payment: at time of delivery

Aspen Crematory
1350 Simms St.
Lakewood, CO 80401
303-232-0985
Funeral home affiliated
Available: 24 hours

Cost of cremation only: $150
Body container requirements:
 rigid combustible
Cardboard casket: $35
Cost of mailing cremains:
 postage
Payment: negotiable

Montrose Valley Crematory
505 S. Second
P.O. Box 66
Montrose, CO 81401
303-249-3814
Montrose Funeral Home
Available: 24 hours

Cost of cremation only: $300
Body container requirements:
 no glue, pressboard or
 plywood; pine preferred
Cardboard casket: not carried
Cost of mailing cremains: $10
Payment: negotiable

Almont Crematory, Inc.
401 Broadway
Pueblo, CO 81004
303-542-4434
Funeral home affiliated
Available: 24 hours

Cost of cremation only: $173
Body container requirements:
 rigid combustible
Cardboard casket: $25
Cost of mailing cremains:
 postage
Payment: negotiable

Davis Memorial Crematory
128 Broadway
Pueblo, CO 81004
303-542-1984
Funeral home affiliated
Available: 24 hours

Cost of cremation only: $90
Body container requirements:
 rigid combustible
Cardboard casket: $40
Cost of mailing cremains: $10
Payment: negotiable

One other crematory in Denver declined to accept a body from other than a funeral director.

There may be additional crematories that are not on the lists I used for this research.

▸ **Body Donation**

University of Colorado
Anatomical Board
4200 E. 9th St.
Denver, CO 80262
303-394-8554
   399-1211 after hours

Cost to family: transportation
   beyond 100 mile radius;
   return of cremains - $110
Prior enrollment: required
Over-enrollment: not yet
   occurred
Disposition: cremation; return
   of cremains on request
Body rejection: standard*,
   emaciation, obesity, other
   dangerous diseases.

*autopsy, decomposition, mutilation, severe burn victim,
meningitis, hepatitis, AIDS

▸ **State Funeral Board**

Colorado no longer has a state funeral board since it was
eliminated by sunset laws in 1981-2. As a result, there is no
state license required to operate as a funeral director or
embalmer in Colorado.

The Colorado Funeral Directors and Embalmers Association, a
voluntary professional organization, has established the
Mortuary Science Commission. This commission "certifies"
those applying for recognition who have successfully completed training and apprenticeship. The Commission has five
members. Three are funeral directors, one represents the
clergy and one is a consumer representative.

(This section was reviewed by the Secretary for the Mortuary
Science Commission and the Colorado State Registrar's
Office.)

In Connecticut

Please refer to Chapter 9 as you use this section.

Persons in Connecticut may be limited in caring for their
own dead. The statutes in Connecticut are vague and

conflicting.

Sec. 45-253 **Custody of remains of deceased persons.** (a) The custody and control of the remains of deceased residents of this state shall belong to the surviving spouse . . . or if there is no spouse . . . then such custody and control shall belong to the next of kin. . .

Sec. 7-64 **Disposal of Bodies.** The body of each person who dies in this state shall be buried, removed or cremated within a reasonable time after death. The person to whom the custody and control of the remains of any deceased person are granted by law shall see that the certificate of death required by law has been completed and filed in accordance with section 7-62b prior to final disposition. . . (1979)

Sec. 7-62b **Death Certificates.** The licensed funeral director . . . in charge of the burial of the deceased person shall complete the death certificate . . . and shall file it. . . . Only a licensed embalmer may assume charge of the burial of a deceased person who died from a communicable disease, as designated in the public health code. . . (1983)

Sec. 7-69 **Removal of body from one town to another.** . . . and no burial or removal permit shall be issued unless the death certificate has been signed by a licensed embalmer or funeral director. . . (1985)

It is interesting to note that the Public Assembly in 1967 took a sentence out of 7-62 requiring the death certificate to be signed by the funeral director before it was amended as cited above. While this statute now says that when a funeral director is in charge he must sign the death certificate, it does not seem to require that a funeral director always be in charge unless the death was due to a communicable disease. Indeed, Sec. 45-253 appears to grant a family the fundamental right to control disposition. Section 7-69 requires the signature of a funeral director in most instances, but does not address the issue of who is in charge.

In the statutes regulating the business of funeral directing is found:

Sec. 20-212 **Embalming, care and disposal of bodies restricted.** . . . and no person, firm or corporation shall enter, engage in, carry on or manage for another the business of caring for, preserving or disposing of dead human bodies until each person, firm or corporation so engaged has obtained from the department of health services and holds a license as provided in this chapter; nor shall any person be employed to remove a dead human body, except a licensed embalmer, a registered student embalmer, a licensed funeral director, or a person authorized in each instance by the chief medical examiner, deputy chief medical examiner or assistant medical examiner . . . except that once a dead human body has been prepared in accordance with the public health code . . . an embalmer or funeral director licensed in this state may authorize a non-licensed employee to remove such body. . .

This statute was cited to me by a representative of the Connecticut State Funeral Board who flatly stated that it was illegal for a family to transport a body or make its own arrangements in Connecticut. However, this statute does not appear in the public health portion of the laws. The intent of this statute would seem to apply only to those in the funeral industry or those who are employed in a business transaction.

Except for the case of death from a contagious disease, or while a body might be under the jurisdiction of a medical examiner, and when no embalming is desired, I found no other restrictions to limit a family from managing arrangements provided all other procedures as listed below are followed. (Unfortunately, a church group might be considered to be doing business for "another" if it assisted a family in handling death arrangements.)

▸ **Death Certificate**

The death certificate must be signed by a physician within 24 hours of death and filed, prior to final disposition, in the town where death occurred. In view of the Connecticut statutes, it would be wise to seek the signature of a funeral director in all cases. A charge for "professional services" should be expected for this request. In the four other states where a funeral director must sign the death certificate or obtain the burial-transit permit before a family takes over, charges range from "No charge. . . we would do it as a courtesy" to "Well, our charge for professional services is $465." $45 or $50 was a more common response.

▶ **Fetal Death**

A fetal death report is required after 20 weeks of gestation. All other procedures apply if disposition is handled by the family.

▶ **Transporting and Disposition Permit**

The local registrar will issue a burial permit or a removal permit when disposition is planned outside the town or state. According to a Funeral Board member, a funeral director may serve as a sub-registrar. If cremation is planned, obtain the cremation certificate from the medical examiner before applying to the registrar for a cremation permit.

▶ **Burial**

Home burial is not permitted in Connecticut. A burial permit must be obtained from the registrar of the town in which burial will occur. Burial must be 350 feet from a dwelling place, and the top of the casket must be two and one-half feet from the surface of the earth. The sexton will return the burial permit to the registrar in a monthly report.

▶ **Cremation**

There is no fee for a cremation certificate if the death is under the jurisdiction of a medical examiner. In all other cases a cremation certificate from the medical examiner must be obtained. The usual fee for this is $50. Once the cremation certificate has been obtained, a registrar will issue a cremation permit. The charge for this is $1.00. Sub-registrars may not issue a cremation permit.

There is a 48-hour wait before cremation. A crematory may charge for storage or refrigeration if the body is delivered much before that time. Most crematories insist that a pacemaker be removed, and authorization from next-of-kin usually is required.

▶ **Other Requirements**

Connecticut has no other requirements controlling the time schedule for the disposition of unembalmed bodies. Weather and reasonable planning should be considered.

Persons dying of a contagious disease must be either embalmed or washed and wrapped with five layers of cloth saturated with a disinfecting solution. Disposition may be controlled by the local director of health.

A body to be transported by common carrier must be embalmed.

▶ **Crematories**

(These crematories are willing to accept a body from a family if it is legal for them to do so.)

Mt. Grove Cemetery
2675 North Avenue
Bridgeport, CT 06604
203-336-3579
Independent
Available: 7:30-4 M-F, or
  by appointment

Cost of cremation only: $155
Body container requirements:
  rigid combustible
Cardboard casket: not carried
Cost of mailing cremains: $10
Payment: negotiable

Fountain Hill Cemetery and
  Crematory
6 River Street
Deep River, CT 06417
203-526-2498
Independent
Available: 8-4 M-F, other
  times by appointment

Cost of cremation only: $135
Body container requirements:
  rigid combustible
Cardboard casket: not carried
Cost of mailing cremains:
included
Payment: at time of delivery

Cedar Hill Cemetery
453 Fairfield Avenue
Hartford, CT 06114
203-522-3311
Independent
Available: 8-4:30 M-F,
  Sat. by arrangement

Cost of cremation only: $165
Body container requirements:
  rigid combustible
Cardboard casket: available
Cost of mailing cremains:
  included
Payment: at time of delivery

Evergreen Cemetery
92 Winthrop Avenue
New Haven, CT 06511
203-624-5505
Independent
Available: 7:30-4 M-F,
  8-12 Sat. or by arrangement

Cost of cremation only: $150
Body container requirements:
  rigid combustible
Cardboard casket: available
Cost of mailing cremains:
  none within state; postage
  out of state
Payment: negotiable

Pine Grove Cemetery Assn.
850 Meriden Road
Waterbury, CT   06705
203-753-0776
Independent
Available: 8-4 M-F

Cost of cremation only: $145
Body container requirements:
  rigid combustible
Cardboard casket: not carried
Cost of mailing cremains:
  included
Payment: at time of delivery

The crematory in Norwich would consider accepting a body from a family if it were legal but asked not to be listed in the book.

There may be additional crematories that are not on the lists I used for this research.

▶ **Body Donation**

University of Connecticut
School of Medicine
Farmington, CT 06032
203-679-2117
203-223-4340

Cost to family: transportation
  if death occurs outside of
  the state
Prior enrollment: not required
Over-enrollment: has not
  occurred
Disposition: cremation; return
of cremains by request
Body rejection: standard*,
  under 18, obesity, TB,
  emaciation, widespread
  cancer, Alzheimer's, and
  other infectious diseases.

Yale University
School of Medicine
New Haven, CT 06520

Repeated requests for
information have not been
returned by this school.

*autopsy, decomposition, mutilation, severe burn victim, meningitis, hepatitis, AIDS

▶ **State Funeral Board**

The Connecticut State Funeral Board has five members. There are two consumer representatives.

(After much previous correspondence and contact, this section was sent for review to the Connecticut Department of Health and the Chairman of the Connecticut Funeral Board. No response was received from the Department of Health. I finally reached a representative of the Connecticut

Funeral Board. He disagrees with my interpretation of the statutes. However, it has been my experience that authorities will go along with your plans if you are well-informed and follow all procedures accurately.)

In Delaware

Please refer to Chapter 9 as you use this section.

Persons in Delaware may care for their own dead. The legal authority to do so is found in:

> Title 16, section 3125 . . .(c) The person in charge of interment shall file with the local registrar . . .a certificate of death. . .

There are no other statutes or regulations which might require you to use a funeral director when no embalming is desired.

▶ **Death Certificate**

The family doctor or a local medical examiner will supply and sign the death certificate stating the cause of death within 72 hours. The remaining information must be supplied, typewritten or with ball point pen in black ink. (There are three carbons which must be clear.) The death certificate, copies one and two, must be filed with the local registrar of the county in which death occurred within three days and before final disposition. (Copy four may be retained by the hospital or physician.)

▶ **Fetal Death**

A fetal death report is required after 20 weeks of gestation. If there is no family physician involved, the local medical examiner must sign the fetal death certificate. All other procedures apply if disposition is handled by the family.

▶ **Transporting and Disposition Permit**

A body may be moved with medical permission. Copy three of

the death certificate may be retained to serve as a burial-transit permit if needed.

▸ **Burial**

Home burial is permissible outside town limits. Check with the local registrar or health officer. The top of the casket must be 18 inches below the natural surface of the earth.

▸ **Cremation**

A permit for cremation may be obtained from the Office of Vital Records in Dover or from a funeral director. This permit must then be signed by the medical examiner (or deputy examiner), and subsequently signed by the attorney general (or a deputy), in that order. There is no fee for this authorization. (These signatures could be difficult to obtain over a weekend. However, both parties involved - as officers of the state in this regard - can be expected to serve at any time. The telephone numbers to contact may be obtainable through a funeral director or local law enforcement personnel.) The family member serving as the "funeral director" must also sign this permit on the line indicated. Most crematories insist that a pacemaker be removed, and authorization by next-of-kin usually is required. Delaware state statute allows a family to view cremation.

▸ **Other Requirements**

Body disposition must be accomplished within five days. If disposition does not occur within 24 hours, the body must be embalmed or refrigerated.

Embalming is required if a person has died of smallpox, plague, anthrax or "other disease which the State Board of Health may specify." Check with the physician involved.

▸ **Crematories**

Hockessin Crematory
Lancaster Pike
P.O. Box 480
Hockessin, DE 19707
302-478-7100
Chandler Funeral Home
Available: 24 hours

Cost of cremation only: $105
Body container requirements: rigid combustible
Cardboard casket: available
Cost of mailing cremains: $25
Payment: negotiable

Two other crematories declined to accept a body from other

than a funeral director: one in Lewes and one in Wilmington. One had concerns about other funeral business. The other felt a family "can't get the proper signatures."

There may be additional crematories that are not on the lists I used for this research.

▸ **Body Donation**

There are no medical schools in Delaware. Those considering body donation should check the nearest neighboring state.

▸ **State Funeral Board**

The Delaware Board of Funeral Service Practitioners has seven members. Two are not connected with funeral service.

(This section was reviewed by the Director of the Office of Vital Statistics for the state of Delaware.)

In the District of Columbia

Please refer to Chapter 9 as you use this section.

Persons in the District of Columbia may care for their own dead. The legal authority to do so is found in:

Title 6-211: "The funeral director or person acting as such . . . "

There are no other statutes or regulations which might require you to use a funeral director when no embalming is desired.

▸ **Death Certificate**

The family doctor or a local medical examiner will supply and sign the death certificate within 48 hours stating the cause of death. The remaining information must be supplied, typewritten or in black ink. The death certificate must be filed with the local registrar within five days and before final disposition.

▶ **Fetal Death**

A fetal death report is required after 20 weeks of gestation or when the weight is 500 grams or more. If there is no family physician involved, the local medical examiner must sign the fetal death certificate. All other procedures apply if disposition is handled by the family.

▶ **Transporting and Disposition Permit**

A body may be moved with the consent of the physician or medical examiner certifying death. The next-of-kin must authorize final disposition and file it with the mayor within one month.

▶ **Burial**

Because of the metropolitan nature of the District of Columbia, home burial is not feasible here.

▶ **Cremation**

A permit for cremation must be obtained from the medical examiner. There may be a fee for this. Most crematories insist that a pacemaker be removed, and authorization by next-of-kin usually is required.

▶ **Other Requirements**

The District of Columbia has no other requirements controlling the time schedule for the disposition of unembalmed bodies. Weather and reasonable planning should be considered.

If the person died of a contagious or communicable disease, the doctor in attendance should be consulted.

▶ **Crematories**

Cedar Hill Cemetery
4000 Suitland Road S.E.
Washington, D.C. 20023
202-568-5400
Independent
Available: 8-4:30 M-F,
  9-4 S-S

Cost of cremation only: $110
Body container requirements:
  rigid combustible
Cardboard casket: not carried
Cost of mailing cremains: $10
Payment: at time of delivery

The other crematory contacted in the District declined to accept a body from other than a funeral director.

There may be additional crematories that are not on the lists I used for this research.

▶ **Body Donation**

George Washington University
Department of Anatomy
2300 "I" St. N.W.
Washington, D. C. 20037
202-676-3511
202-676-3125

Cost to family: transportation beyond a 50-mile radius
Prior enrollment: not required
Over-enrollment: has not occurred
Disposition: cremation, return upon request
Body rejection: under 18, autopsy, missing thoracic organs, burn victim, decomposition, AIDS

Georgetown University
School of Medicine &
   Dentistry
Department of Anatomy
3900 Reservoir Rd. N.W.
Washington, D. C. 20007
202-625-2271
   8:30-5 M-F

Cost to family: transportation beyond 25-mile radius
Prior enrollment: not required
Over-enrollment: has not occurred
Disposition: cremation, no return
Body rejection: standard*, under 20, previously embalmed, widespread cancer

Howard University
College of Medicine
Department of Anatomy
Washington, D. C. 20059
202-636-6655
   -6555
   -6556

Cost to family: transportation beyond 50 miles
Prior enrollment: preferred but not required
Over-enrollment: shared
Disposition: cremation
Body rejection: standard*

*autopsy, decomposition, mutilation, severe burn victim, meningitis, hepatitis, AIDS

▶ **State Funeral Board**

The District of Columbia Funeral Board has four members. There are no consumer representatives.

(This section was sent to the District of Columbia Department of Human Services for review, but no response was received by the time of publication.)

In Florida

Please refer to Chapter 9 as you use this section.

Persons in Florida may care for their own dead. The authority to do so is found in:

FS 382.061. **Burial-transit permit** - (1) The funeral director or person acting as such who first assumes custody of a dead body or fetus shall obtain a burial-transit permit prior to final disposition. . .

FS 382.14 . . . the undertaker or person acting as such, when burying a body in a cemetery or burial grounds having no person in charge, shall sign the burial or removal permit, giving the date of burial and shall write across the face of the permit the words "No person in charge,. . . "

There are no other statutes or regulations which might require you to use a funeral director when no embalming is desired. This has been verified in 1987 correspondence with state officials.

In making calls to this state, I found no one had ever heard of a religious group or family members desiring to handle their own arrangements. (In other states, many funeral directors or crematories have experienced this once or twice a year.) A lot of the funeral directors in Florida had been convinced such a thing was illegal and seemed sure that no health department would issue a burial-transit permit to a family. If, as a person who is handling a death personally, you meet with reluctance on the part of any registrar, you might suggest that the registrar call Mr. R.C. Blanton, Jr., Executive Director, State Funeral Board, Department of Professional Regulations in Jacksonville, 904-359-6321, or an attorney for the state Department of Health in Tallahassee, 904-488-2381. On weekends and after hours, most funeral directors act as deputy registrar. Since they are acting as state officials, they should not charge for the permit.

▶ **Death Certificate**

The family doctor or a local medical examiner will supply and sign the death certificate within 48 hours stating the cause of death. The remaining information must be supplied, typewritten or in black ink. The death certificate must be filed with the local registrar within three days and before final disposition.

▶ **Fetal Death**

A fetal death report is required after 20 weeks of gestation. If there is no family physician involved, the local medical examiner must sign the fetal death certificate. All other procedures apply if disposition is handled by the family.

▶ **Transporting and Disposition Permit**

The local registrar in the health department or a deputy (usually a funeral director) will issue the burial-transit permit. This permit must be obtained within 72 hours of death and prior to final disposition of the body.

▶ **Burial**

Check with the county registrar for local zoning laws regarding home burial. There are no state burial statutes or regulations with regard to depth.

When burial is arranged, the family member acting as the funeral director must sign the burial-transit permit and deliver it to the local registrar within 10 days. If there is no person in charge, the words "no person in charge" must be written across the face of the permit.

▶ **Cremation**

A medical examiner's permit is required for cremation. The usual charge for this varies from one county to the next. There is a 48-hour wait before cremation. After the first 24 hours, refrigeration is required. Most large hospitals have refrigeration facilities, but if the storage becomes crowded removal may be requested. All but a few crematories have refrigerated storage for which a fee is charged. Fees ranged from $30 to $135 a day at the time of my calls, but they may be negotiable. Most crematories insist that a pacemaker be removed, and authorization by next-of-kin usually is required. The crematory will sign the disposition permit which must be filed with the local registrar within 10 days.

▶ **Other Requirements**

Refrigeration or embalming is required after 24 hours.

If the person died of a contagious or communicable disease, the doctor in attendance should be consulted.

▶ **Crematories**

Highlands Crematory
111 E. Circle
Avon Park, FL 33825
813-453-3101
Stephenson-Nelson-Smith
Funeral Home
Available: 24 hours
Refrigeration available

Cost of cremation only: $100
Body container requirements:
   rigid combustible
Cardboard casket: $25
Cost of mailing cremains:
   postage
Payment: negotiable

Lake Forest Crematory
507 U.S. 27 N
Avon Park, FL 33852
813-453-3134
Fountain Funeral Home
Available: 24 hours
Refrigeration available

Cost of cremation only: $100
Body container requirements:
   rigid combustible
Cardboard casket: $25
Cost of mailing cremains: $10
Payment: at time of delivery,
   negotiable

Palm Beach Memorial Park
3691 Seacrest Blvd.
Boynton Beach, FL 33435
305-585-6444
Funeral home affiliated
Available: 8:30-4:30 M-F,
   24-hour phone
Refrigeration available

Cost of cremation only: $125
Body container requirements:
   rigid combustible
Cardboard casket: $25
Cost of mailing cremains:
   postage
Payment: at time of delivery

Tampa Bay Crematory
401 W. Brandon Blvd.
Brandon, FL 33511
813-689-9156
Stowers Funeral Home
Available: 24 hours
Refrigeration available

Cost of cremation only: $100
Body container requirements:
   rigid combustible
Cardboard casket: $15
Cost of mailing cremains: $25
Payment: at time of delivery

National Cremation Society
2451 E. Bay Drive
Clearwater, FL 33546
813-536-0494
SCI affiliated
Available: 24 hours
Refrigeration available

Cost of cremation only: $125
Body container requirements:
cardboard
Cardboard casket: $30
Cost of mailing cremains: $45
Payment: at time of delivery,
negotiable

Delray Crematory
320 N. 5th
Delray Beach, FL 33444
305-276-7474
Scobee-Ireland-Potter Funeral
Home
Available: 24 hours
Refrigeration available

Cost of cremation only: $300
Body container requirements:
rigid combustible
Cardboard casket: $75
Cost of mailing cremains: $70
Payment: negotiable

Stephen R. Baldauff Funeral
Home
1600 Saxon Road
P.O. Box 128
Deltona, FL 32728-0128
904-775-2101
Available: 24 hours
Refrigeration available

Cost of cremation only: $150
Body container requirements:
rigid combustible
Cardboard casket: $25
Cost of mailing cremains: $35
Payment: at time of delivery,
negotiable

Roberts Funeral Home
E. Penn Ave.
P.O. Box 88
Dunellon, FL 32630
904-489-2429
Available: 24 hours
Refrigeration available

Cost of cremation only: $120
Body container requirements:
rigid combustible
Cardboard casket: $89
Cost of mailing cremains: $25
Payment: at time of delivery

Broward Crematory
4343 N. Federal Hwy.
Ft. Lauderdale, FL 33308
305-492-4000
Baird-Case Funeral Home
Available: 24 hours
Refrigeration available

Cost of cremation only: $150
Body container requirements:
rigid combustible
Cardboard casket: $25
Cost of mailing cremains: $30
Payment: negotiable

Fairchild Funeral Home &
  Crematory
3501 W. Broward Blvd.
Ft. Lauderdale, FL 33312
305-581-6100
Available: 24 hours
Refrigeration available

Cost of cremation only: $125
Body container requirements:
  rigid combustible
Cardboard casket: $20
Cost of mailing cremains: $25
Payment: negotiable

All State Cremation Service
6061 N.E. 14th Ave.
Ft. Lauderdale, FL 33334
305-523-6700
Forest Lawn Star of David
Available: 9-5 daily,
  24-hour phone
Refrigeration available

Cost of cremation only: $150
Body container requirements:
  rigid combustible
Cardboard casket: $35
Cost of mailing cremains: $20
Payment: at time of delivery

Harvey Crematory
1600 Colonial Blvd.
Ft. Myers, FL 33907
813-936-2177
Funeral home affiliated
Available: 24 hours
Refrigeration available

Cost of cremation only: $150
Body container requirements:
  rigid combustible
Cardboard casket: $25
Cost of mailing cremains: $25
Payment: negotiable

Ft. Pierce Crematory
1101 S. U.S. #1
Ft. Pierce, FL 33450
305-461-7000
Yates Funeral Home
Available: 24 hours
Refrigeration available

Cost of cremation only: $150
Body container requirements:
  rigid combustible
Cardboard casket: available
Cost of mailing cremains:
  postage
Payment: negotiable

Haisley-Hobbs Crematory
3015 Okeechobee Rd.
Ft. Pierce, FL 33450
305-461-5211
Available: 24 hours
Refrigeration available

Cost of cremation only: $150
Body container requirements:
  rigid combustible
Cardboard casket: $25
Cost of mailing cremains: $35
Payment: at time of delivery

Johnson-Hayes Funeral Home
311 S. Main Street
Gainesville, FL 32601
904-376-5361
Available: 24 hours
Refrigeration available

Cost of cremation only: $175
Body container requirements:
  rigid combustible
Cardboard casket: $55
Cost of mailing cremains: $25
Payment: at time of delivery,
  negotiable

Casto Funeral Home, Inc.
2772 Santa Barbara Blvd.
Golden Gate, FL 33999
813-455-2221
Available: 24 hours
Refrigeration available

Cost of cremation only: $175
Body container requirements:
  rigid combustible
Cardboard casket: $55
Cost of mailing cremains: $25
Payment: at time of delivery,
  negotiable

Fred Hunter Funeral Home
  and Crematory
6301 Taft Street
Hollywood, FL 33024
305-989-1550
800-835-7070
Available: 24 hours
Refrigeration available

Cost of cremation only: $150
Body container requirements:
  rigid combustible
Cardboard casket: $25
Cost of mailing cremains: $35
Payment: at time of delivery,
  negotiable

Directors Crematory, Inc.
U.S. Hwy. 41 S.
P.O. Box 1373
Inverness, FL 32651
904-726-8323
Davis Funeral Home
Available: 24 hours
Refrigeration available

Cost of cremation only: $125
Body container requirements:
  rigid combustible
Cardboard casket: $25
Cost of mailing cremains: $35
Payment: at time of delivery,
  negotiable

The Evergreen Cemetery
4535 Main St.
Jacksonville, FL 32206
904-353-3649
Independent
Available: 9-4 M-F, Sat. by
  arrangement
Refrigeration not available

Cost of cremation only: $105
Body container requirements:
  rigid combustible
Cardboard casket: not carried
Cost of mailing cremains: $20
Payment: at time of delivery

Earl Smith Crematory
3772 S. Military Trail
Lake Worth, FL 33460
305-964-3772
Funeral home affiliated
Available: 24 hours
Refrigeration available

Cost of cremation only: $200
Body container requirements:
  rigid combustible
Cardboard casket: $60
Cost of mailing cremains: $45
Payment: negotiable

Lakeland Crematory
1833 S. Florida Ave.
P.O. Box 2159
Lakeland, FL 33806-2158
813-682-3155
Thornton & Holcom Memorial
  Home
Available: 24 hours
Refrigeration available

Cost of cremation only: $80
Body container requirements:
  rigid combustible
Cardboard casket: $20
Cost of mailing cremains: $25
Payment: at time of delivery,
  negotiable

Lee Memorial Park
Highway 82
P.O. Box 568
Lehigh, FL 33970
813-334-4880
Funeral home affiliated
Available: 24 hours
Refrigeration available

Cost of cremation only: $110
Body container requirements:
  rigid combustible
Cardboard casket: $45
Cost of mailing cremains:
  postage
Payment: at time of delivery

Lithgow Funeral Centers, Inc.
7200 N.W. 2nd
Miami, FL 33150
305-757-5544
Funeral home affiliated
Available: 24 hours
Refrigeration available

Cost of cremation only: $150
Body container requirements:
  rigid combustible
Cardboard casket: available
Cost of mailing cremains: $40
Payment: at time of delivery

So. Florida Crematory, Inc.
1495 N.W. 17th Ave.
Miami, FL 33125
305-325-1174
800-327-7385
Florida Mortuary Service
Available: 24 hours
Refrigeration available

Cost of cremation only: $100
Body container requirements:
  rigid combustible
Cardboard casket: $10
Cost of mailing cremains: $25
Payment: at time of delivery

Woodlawn Park Cemetery
3260 S.W. 8th Street
Miami, FL 33135
305-445-5425
Independent
Available: 24 hours
Refrigeration planned but not
  available at present

Cost of cremation only: $150
Body container requirements:
  rigid combustible
Cardboard casket: included
Cost of mailing cremains:
  postage
Payment: at time of delivery

Cremations, Inc.
6107 Miramar Blvd.
Miramar, FL 33023
305-925-7577
Wintter Funeral Chapel
305-925-7575
Available: 24 hours
Refrigeration available

Cost of cremation only: $175
Body container requirements:
  rigid combustible
Cardboard casket: not carried
Cost of mailing cremains: $25
Payment: at time of delivery

David K. Johnson Crema-
  torium
4424 E. Tamiami Trail
Naples, FL 33940
813-774-3444
Funeral home affiliated
Available: 24 hours
Refrigeration available

Cost of cremation only: $185
Body container requirements:
  rigid combustible
Cardboard casket: $75
Cost of mailing cremains:
  postage
Payment: negotiable

Earl G. Hodges Funeral
  Chapel
3520 Tamiami Trail N.
Naples, FL 33940
813-261-1237
Available: 24 hours
Refrigeration available

Cost of cremation only: $175
Body container requirements:
  rigid combustible
Cardboard casket: $55
Cost of mailing cremains: $25
Payment: at time of delivery,
  negotiable

Rivermead Funeral Home and
  Crematory
950 Park Ave.
P.O. Box 1957
Orange Park, FL 32067-1957
904-264-2481
Available: 24 hours
Refrigeration available

Cost of cremation only: $115
Body container requirements:
  rigid combustible
Cardboard casket: $25
Payment: at time of delivery

Orange Co. Crematory
600 Wilkinson
Orlando, FL 32803
305-898-7882
Garden Chapel Home
Available: 9-9 daily,
  24-hour phone
Refrigeration available

Cost of cremation only: $150
Body container requirements:
  rigid combustible
Cardboard casket: $25
Cost of mailing cremains: $20
Payment: at time of delivery,
  negotiable, 30 days

Fountainhead Memorial Park
& Crematory
2929 S. Babcock St.
P.O. Box 368
Palm Bay, FL 32906
305-724-2861 or 727-3993
Funeral home affiliated
Available: 24 hours
Refrigeration available

Cost of cremation only: $200
Body container requirements:
 rigid combustible
Cardboard casket: $75
Cost of mailing cremains: $25
Payment: negotiable

Curlew Hills Memory Gardens
1750 Curlew Rd.
Palm Harbor, FL 33563
813-785-4428
Funeral home planned '88
Available: 24 hours
Refrigeration available

Cost of cremation only: $150
Body container requirements:
 rigid combustible
Cardboard casket: $15
Cost of mailing cremains: $50
Payment: at time of delivery,
 negotiable

Robertson Crematory
2151 Tamiami Trail
P.O. Box 2966
Port Charlotte, FL 33949
813-629-3141
Funeral home affiliated
Available: 24 hours
Refrigeration available

Cost of cremation only: $195
Body container requirements:
 rigid combustible
Cardboard casket: $30
Cost of mailing cremains: $45
Payment: at time of delivery

Adams-Sasser Funeral Home
 and Crematory
22 S. Madison St.
Quincy, FL 32351
904-627-7535
Available: 24-hour phone
Refrigeration not available

Cost of cremation only: $100
Body container requirements:
 rigid combustible
Cardboard casket: $25
Cost of mailing cremains:
 included
Payment: at time of delivery

Lew Funeral Home
5750 Swift Rd.
Sarasota, FL 33581
813-922-3551
Available: 24 hours
Refrigeration not available

Cost of cremation only: $190
Body container requirements:
 rigid combustible
Cardboard casket: available
Cost of mailing cremains: $50
Payment: negotiable

Manasota Memorial Park, Inc.
P.O. Box 3109
Sarasota, FL 33578
813-755-2688
Independent
Available: 8-4:30 M-F,
  9-1:30 Sat., 24-hr. phone
Refrigeration available

Cost of cremation only: $200
Body container requirements:
  rigid combustible
Cardboard casket: included
Cost of mailing cremains: $25
Payment: at time of delivery

Sara-mana Crematory
135 N. Lime Ave.
Sarasota, FL 33597
813-365-1767
Hawkins Funeral Home
Available: 24 hours
Refrigeration available

Cost of cremation only: $225
Body container requirements:
  rigid combustible
Cardboard casket: available
Cost of mailing cremains:
  postage
Payment: at time of delivery,
  negotiable

Tri-County Crematory
505 S. Federal
Stuart, FL 30497
305-287-1717
Aycock Funeral Home
Available: 9-5 M-F,
  24-hour phone
Refrigeration available

Cost of cremation only: $175
Body container requirements:
  rigid combustible
Cardboard casket: $140
Cost of mailing cremains: $30
Payment: at time of delivery

Crematory of Venice
265 S. Nokomis Ave.
Venice, FL 33595
813-488-2291
Farley Funeral Home
Available: 24 hours
Refrigeration available

Cost of cremation only: $175
Body container requirements:
  rigid combustible
Cardboard casket: $75
Cost of mailing cremains: $50
Payment: at time of delivery

One crematory in Daytona agreed to accept a body from a family on a case-by-case basis but preferred not to be listed in this book. Seven other crematories declined to accept a body from other than a funeral director, one each in Clearwater, Lake Worth, Lakeland, Orlando, Pompano Beach, St. Petersburg and Stuart. Their concerns were, "My funeral directors would flip out. . . the competition here is wild". . . " We deal only with funeral directors wholesale" (even though he admitted that it might be only one body at a time). . . "If we can't get a reasonable fee, we wouldn't be interested. . . We have overhead and taxes to pay" . . . "Time is money - I don't have time to talk about cremation and all that crap". . . . "We don't give interviews over the phone". . . "Absolutely not! . . . beyond sensibility . . . a guilt trip . . . just to challenge the law."

There may be additional crematories that are not on the lists I used for this research.

▶ Body Donation

There is one agency for body donation in Florida.

Florida State Anatomical Board
1 Hillis Miller Health Center
Box J-235
Gainesville, FL 32610
904-392-3588
(This appears to be the only state where the family of a deceased must pay for transportation and embalming before body donation. Funeral directors report that the need is frequently met and that schools are "picky" about accepting bodies.)

Cost to family: embalming, transportation to Gainesville
Prior enrollment: not required
Over-enrollment: shared within state only
Disposition: cremation; return of cremains by request
Body rejection: autopsy, decomposition, AIDS, meningitis, hepatitis, or other contagious disease

▶ State Funeral Board

The Florida State Board of Funeral Directors and Embalmers has seven members. There are two consumer representatives.

(This section was reviewed by the General Counsel, Florida Department of Health and Rehabilitative Services and the Executive Director of the Florida State Funeral Board.)

In Georgia

Please refer to Chapter 9 as you use this section.

Persons in Georgia may care for their own dead. The legal authority to do so is found in:

Title 31-10-15 (b) The funeral director or person acting as such who first assumes custody of the dead body. . .

Title 31-10-20 (e) When there is no person in charge of the place for final disposition, the funeral director or other person shall endorse the authorization and retain such in the director's or other person's files.

There are no other statutes or regulations which might require you to use a funeral director when no embalming is desired.

▸ **Death Certificate**

The family doctor or a local medical examiner will supply and sign the death certificate within 48 hours stating the cause of death. The remaining information must be supplied, typewritten or in black ink. The death certificate must be filed with the local registrar within 72 hours and before final disposition.

▸ **Fetal Death**

A fetal death report is required for each fetal death. If there is no family physician involved, the local medical investigator must sign the fetal death certificate. All other procedures apply if disposition is handled by the family.

▸ **Transporting and Disposition Permit**

A body may be moved with the consent of a physician or county coroner. After receiving the death certificate, the local registrar will issue a final disposition permit if cremation or out-of-state disposition is planned. No burial-transit permit is required by statute for in-state burial, although a local ordinance may require one.

▸ **Burial**

Check with the county registrar for local zoning laws regarding home burial. If a local ordinance requires a disposition permit for burial, the family member acting as the funeral director must sign the authorization for disposition and retain it on file. There are no state burial statutes or regulations with regard to depth.

▶ **Cremation**

The registrar's permit for disposition is required before cremation. There is no fee for this. Most crematories insist that a pacemaker be removed, and authorization by next-of-kin usually is usually required.

▶ **Other Requirements**

Georgia has no other requirements controlling the time schedule for the disposition of unembalmed bodies. Weather and reasonable planning should be considered.

If the person died of a contagious or communicable disease, the doctor in attendance or the local health officer should be consulted.

▶ **Crematories**

Kimbrell-Stern, Inc.
1503 Dawson Rd.
P.O. Box 92
Albany, GA 31702
912-883-4152
Funeral home affiliated
Available: 24 hours

Cost of cremation only: $150
Body container requirements:
  rigid combustible
Cardboard casket: $55
Cost of mailing cremains: $15
Payment: 30 days

Atlanta Crematory
Stone Mountain
P.O. Box 605
Atlanta, GA 30086
404-469-5577
Wages Funeral Home
Available: 24 hours,
  call first

Cost of cremation only: $210
Body container requirements:
  "none"
Cardboard casket: available
Cost of mailing cremains: $15
Payment: negotiable

Hart's Crematory
765 Cherry St.
Macon, GA 31201
912-746-4321
Hart's Mortuary
Available: 24 hours,
  call first

Costs: not for publication
Body container requirements:
  "none"
Cost of mailing cremains: $10
Payment: negotiable

Two crematories declined to accept a body from other than a funeral director, one in Athens and one in Atlanta. Concerns expressed were, "That's not our practice.". . . "We don't want to compete with funeral directors."

There may be additional crematories that are not on the lists
I used for this research.

▶ **Body Donation**

Emory University
School of Medicine
Atlanta, GA 30322
404-727-6242

Cost to family: transportation
beyond 50-mile radius
Prior enrollment: required
Over-enrollment: shared
Disposition: cremation; return
of cremains by request
Body rejection: standard*,
under 16, prefer no
previous embalming

Morehouse School of
Medicine
720 Westview Dr., S.W.
Atlanta, Ga. 30310
404-752-1560 9-5, M-F
404-752-1500 other times

Cost to family: transportation
beyond 50 miles
Prior enrollment: not required
Over-enrollment: has not
occurred
Disposition: cremation; return
of cremains by request
Body rejection: standard*,
under 10

Medical College of Georgia
Augusta, GA 30912

Repeated requests for
information have not been
returned from this school.

Mercer University
School of Medicine
1550 College St.
Macon, GA 31207
912-744-2555
912-474-2308

Cost to family: transportation
to funeral home where
embalming will occur
(check with school)
Prior enrollment: not required
Over-enrollment: shared
Disposition: cremation; return
of cremains by request
Body rejection: autopsy,
AIDS, decomposition,
demyelinating diseases.

*autopsy, decomposition, mutilation, severe burn victim,
meningitis, hepatitis, AIDS

▶ **State Funeral Board**

The Georgia State Board of Funeral Service has six members
appointed by the Governor; no consumer representatives.

(The Georgia section was reviewed by the Georgia Department of Health, Vital Records.)

In Hawaii

Please refer to Chapter 9 as you use this section.

Persons in Hawaii may care for their own dead. The legal authority to do so is found in:

Title 338-1 (5) "Person in charge of disposition of the body" means any person who . . . disposes thereof.

There are no other statutes or regulations which might require you to use a funeral director when no embalming is desired.

▶ **Death Certificate**

The family doctor or a local medical examiner will supply and sign the death certificate within 24 hours stating the cause of death. The remaining information must be supplied, typewritten or in black ink. The death certificate must be filed with the local registrar or health agent within three days and before final disposition.

▶ **Fetal Death**

A fetal death report is required after 24 weeks of gestation. If there is no family physician involved, the local health officer must be notified. All other procedures apply if disposition is handled by the family.

▶ **Transporting and Disposition Permit**

A burial-transit permit must be obtained within 72 hours of death from the local registrar or deputy and prior to final disposition of the body. The permit fee is $5.

The family member, acting as funeral director, must sign the permit and within 10 days file it with the registrar of the district where disposition took place.

▸ **Burial**

Check with the county registrar for local zoning laws regarding home burial. Burial must be on land approved as a cemetery by the county council. A written certificate of dedication exclusively to cemetery purposes must be filed with the registrar along with a map. Burial depth must be sufficient to avoid a public health nuisance and to make it impossible for animals to disturb the grave.

▸ **Cremation**

The burial-transit permit is sufficient for cremation and no additional permit is needed. Most crematories insist that a pacemaker be removed, and authorization by next-of-kin usually is required.

▸ **Other Requirements**

A body shall be embalmed, cremated, or buried within 30 hours after death or release by the medical examiner or placed in refrigerated storage in a State-approved hospital.

If the person died of a contagious or communicable disease, the doctor in attendance should be consulted.

► **Crematories**

Borthwick Mortuary
1330 Maunakea St.
Honolulu, HI 96817
808-531-3566
Available: 24 hours

Cost of cremation only: $150
Body container requirements:
  rigid combustible
Cardboard casket: included
Cost of mailing cremains:
  postage
Payment: at time of delivery,
  negotiable

Diamond Head Mortuary
529 18th St.
Honolulu, HI 96816
808-735-2872
Available: 24 hours

Cost of cremation only: $220
Body container requirements:
  rigid combustible
Cardboard casket: available
Payment: at time of delivery

Windward Crematory
45-425 Hamehameha Hwy.
P.O. Box 4417
Kaneoke, HI 96744
808-247-0437
Funeral home affiliated
Available 24 hours

Cost of cremation only: $180
Body container requirements:
  rigid combustible
Cardboard casket: $36
Cost of mailing cremains: $37
Payment: at time of delivery,
  negotiable

There may be additional crematories that are not on the lists
I used for this research.

► **Body Donation**

University of Hawaii
Department of Anatomy
1960 East-West Rd., T311
Honolulu, HI 96822
808-948-7132 or call
Island Wide Mortuary Service
941-4734

Cost to family: transportation
  outside Oahu
Prior enrollment: not required
Over-enrollment: not shared
Disposition: cremation; return
  of cremains by request
Body rejection: standard*,
  over-enrollment, cancer,
  possibly if outside Oahu

*autopsy, decomposition, mutilation, severe burn victim,
meningitis, hepatitis, AIDS or other infectious disease

► **State Funeral Board**

There is no Hawaii State Funeral Board. Funeral directors are
governed by the Professional & Vocational Licensing Division
of the Department of Commerce and Consumer Affairs.

(The Hawaii section was sent to the Hawaii Department of Health for review, but no response was received by the time of publication.)

In Idaho

Please refer to Chapter 9 as you use this section.

Persons and religious groups in Idaho may care for their own dead. The legal authority to do so is found in:

Title 39-260: (re death registration). . . The person in charge of interment or of removal of the body from the district shall be responsible for obtaining and filing the certificate.

Title 54-1104 Exemptions from provisions of act (re licensing of morticians). . . C. Any duly authorized representative of any church, fraternal order or other association or organization honoring the dead who performs a funeral or other religious service. . .

There are no other statutes or regulations which might require you to use a funeral director when no embalming is desired.

▶ **Death Certificate**

The family doctor or a local medical examiner will supply and sign the death certificate within 72 hours stating the cause of death. The remaining information must be supplied, typewritten or in black ink. Since there are three carbons, use a ball-point pen. The completed death certificate must be filed with the local registrar within five days.

▶ **Fetal Death**

A fetal death report is required after 20 weeks of gestation or when weight is 350 grams or more. If there is no family physician involved, the local medical examiner must sign the fetal death certificate. All other procedures apply if disposition is handled by the family.

▶ Transporting and Disposition Permit

A body may be moved with medical permission. The death must be recorded with the local registrar within 24 hours, in person or by mail. Use the fourth (pink) page of the four-copy death certificate for this purpose. Even if some items on the death certificate are not yet complete, be sure that the name of the deceased, the date of death, the name of the doctor and the person acting as the funeral director have been filled in. The third (yellow) page serves as the burial-transit permit. It is necessary to have a physician's or coroner's authorization before removal from the state.

▶ Burial

Home burial is permissible in Idaho. There are no state burial statutes or regulations with regard to depth. Check with the county registrar for local zoning laws.

▶ Cremation

A permit for cremation must be obtained from the county coroner. There is no fee for this. Most crematories insist that a pacemaker be removed, and authorization by next-of-kin usually is required.

▶ Other Requirements

If disposition will not take place within 24 hours of death, the body must be embalmed or refrigerated.

If the person died of a contagious or communicable disease, the doctor in attendance should be consulted.

Bodies transported by commercial carrier must be embalmed.

▶ Crematories

Alden-Waggoner Funeral
  Chapel and Crematory
5400 Fairview Avenue
Boise, ID 83706
208-376-5400
Available: 24 hours

Cost of cremation only: $200
Body container requirements:
  rigid combustible
Cardboard casket: $45
Cost of mailing cremains: $10
Payment: at time of delivery,
  negotiable

Mt. View Crematory
8400 Fairview
Boise, ID 83707
208-322-3999
Funeral home affiliated
Available: 9-5:30 M-Sat.

Cost of cremation only: $150
Body container requirements:
  rigid combustible
Cardboard casket: not carried
Cost of mailing cremains: $25
Payment: negotiable

English Funeral Chapel
1133 N. 4th
Coeur d'Alene, ID 83814
208-664-3143
Available: 8:30-5:30 M-Sat.,
  24-hour phone

Cost of cremation only: $150
Body container requirements:
  rigid combustible
Cardboard casket: $25
Cost of mailing cremains:
  postage
Payment: at time of delivery,
  negotiable

Yates Funeral Home and
  Crematory
744 N. 4th St.
Coeur d'Alene, ID 83814
208-664-3151
Available: 24 hours

Cost of cremation only: $150
Body container requirements:
  rigid combustible, no nails
Cardboard casket: $65
Cost of mailing cremains:
  postage
Payment: negotiable

Coeur d'Alene Memorial
  Chapel
7315 N. Government Way
Coeur d'Alene, ID 83814
208-772-4015
Funeral home affiliated
Available: 24 hours

Cost of cremation only: $100
Body container requirements:
  rigid combustible
Cardboard casket: $15
Cost of mailing cremains:
  included
Payment: negotiable

Lewis Clark Memorial Garden
7th and Cedar
Lewiston, ID 83501
208-743-9464
Mt. View Funeral Home
Available: 24 hours, call first

Cost of cremation only: $150
Body container requirements:
  rigid combustible
Cardboard casket: available
Cost of mailing cremains:
  postage
Payment: negotiable

White Mortuary
136 4th Ave. E.
Twin Falls, ID
208-733-6600
Available: 8-5 M-Sat.,
  3-8 Sun., 24 hr. phone

Cost of cremation only: $150
Body container requirements:
  rigid combustible
Cardboard casket: $25
Cost of mailing cremains:
  included
Payment: negotiable

There may be additional crematories that are not on the lists I used for this research.

▶ **Body Donation**

There are no medical schools in Idaho. Persons considering body donation should check the nearest neighboring state.

▶ **State Funeral Board**

The Idaho Board of Morticians has three members. There are no consumer representatives.

(This section was reviewed by telephone with the Idaho Department of Vital Statistics.)

In Illinois

Please refer to Chapter 9 as you use this section.

In Illinois, the signature of a funeral director is required on the death certificate, Title 73-18 (1) (c). The phrase, "or person acting as such," was deleted from this statute in 1985.

The health department regulations also define "funeral director or person acting as such" to be a licensed funeral director or employee (re the statute for obtaining the permit for disposition).

Title 31-10.7 (re coroners) reads:
    Public policy release of body to next of kin -
    . . . That as soon as may be consistent with the performance of his duties under this act the coroner shall release the body of the decedent to the decedent's next of kin, personal representative, friends, . . . or to the funeral director. . .

Once the death certificate is filed and the permit for disposition is obtained, there are no other statutes or regulations which might require the further use of a funeral director when embalming is not desired. Therefore, a family may manage a death personally in Illinois but should be prepared to pay for the signature of a funeral director on the death certificate and the time required to obtain the permit for disposition.

▶ **Death Certificate**

The attending physician, local medical examiner, or coroner will supply and sign the death certificate within 24 hours stating the cause of death. The remaining information must be supplied, typewritten or in black ink. The death certificate must be filed with the local registrar within five days and prior to cremation or removal from the state. The filing of the death certificate is the responsibility of a licensed funeral director.

▶ **Fetal Death**

A fetal death report is required after 20 weeks of gestation. If no family physician is involved, the local medical examiner or coroner must sign the fetal death certificate. All other procedures apply if disposition is handled by the family.

▶ **Transporting and Disposition Permits**

A licensed funeral director must report the death to the local registrar of the district where death occurred, within 24 hours, on a form which will serve as authorization to transport or bury within the state. While this can be obtained before the death certificate is filed, persons handling a death on their own will find it easier when a death certificate is on hand and a final authorization for disposition can be granted by the registrar. If cremation is planned, it is necessary to have a coroner's authorization before applying for the final disposition permit. The "Permit for Disposition" must be signed by the person in charge of the cemetery or crematory where disposition is made and presented to the registrar of that district within three days.

▶ **Burial**

Home burial may be permissible in Illinois and an additional permit may be required. Check with the county registrar for local zoning laws and burial procedures. The top of the coffin must be covered by 18 inches of earth.

▶ **Cremation**

A permit for cremation must be obtained from the county

coroner. This must be obtained before the permit for disposition. The usual fee for this is about $15 in Cook County. There seems to be no charge in other counties. Most crematories insist that a pacemaker be removed, and authorization by next-of-kin usually is required.

▶ **Other Requirements**

Illinois has no other requirements controlling the time schedule for the disposition of unembalmed bodies. Weather and reasonable planning should be considered.

When death occurs due to a contagious or communicable disease embalming is required. In deaths due to smallpox, cholera or plague the local health officer must sign the "Permit for Disposition."

▶ **Crematories**

River Hills Memorial Park
E. River Rd., P.O. Box 22
Batavia, IL 60510
312-879-7400
Independent
Available: 8-4:30 M-F,
  9-1 Sat.

Cost of cremation only: $270
Body container requirements:
  rigid combustible
Cardboard casket: $15
Cost of mailing cremains:
  included
Payment: at time of delivery

Acacia Park Cemetery
7800 W. Irving Park
Chicago, IL 60634
312-625-7800
Independent
Available: 9-4:30 M-Sat.

Cost of cremation only: $135
Body container requirements:
  rigid combustible
Cardboard casket: not carried
Cost of mailing cremains:
  included
Payment: at time of delivery

Graceland Cemetery Co.
4001 N. Clark
Chicago, IL 60613
312-525-1105
Independent
Available: 8:30-4:30 M-Sat.

Cost of cremation only: $130
Body container requirements:
  rigid combustible
Cardboard casket: not carried
Cost of mailing cremains:
  postage
Payment: at time of delivery,
  negotiable

The Oakwoods Cemetery
1035 E. 67th St.
Chicago, IL 60637
312-288-3800
Independent
Available: 8:30-4:15 M-F,
  weekends by arrangement

Cost of cremation only: $130
Body container requirements:
  rigid combustible
Cardboard casket: not carried
Cost of mailing cremains: $10
Payment: at time of delivery

Graceland-Fairlawn Cemetery
2101 N. Oakland Avenue
Decatur, IL 62525
217-429-5439
Larry Karlovsky, Funeral
  Director
Available: 24 hours

Cost of cremation only: $75
Body container requirements:
  rigid combustible
Cardboard casket: $75
Cost of mailing cremains: $14
Payment: at time of delivery,
  negotiable

York Crematory
435 North York
Elmhurst, IL 60126
312-834-1133
Pedersen-Ryberg Mortuary
Available: 24 hours

Charge for signing death
  certificate: $275
Cost of cremation only: $125
Body container requirements:
  rigid combustible
Cardboard casket: $50
Cost of mailing cremains:
  postage
Payment: negotiable

Woodlawn Memorial Cemetery
23060 W. Jefferson
Joliet, IL 60435
815-725-1152
Independent
Available: 9-5 M-Sat.,
  weekends by arrangement

Cost of cremation only: $165
Body container requirements:
  rigid combustible
Cardboard casket: not carried
Cost of mailing cremains:
  postage
Payment: at time of delivery

Lain-Sullivan Funeral Home
  and Crematory
50 Westwood Drive
Park Forest, IL 60466
312-747-3700
Available: 24 hours

Charge for signing death
  certificate: $50
Cost of cremation only: $175
Body container requirements:
  rigid combustible
Cardboard casket: $90
Cost of mailing cremains: $25
Payment: at time of delivery

Three crematories declined to accept a body from other than
a funeral director, one each in Elmhurst, Pekin, and
Rosemont. Their concerns were, "I don't deal with the public
at all" (situated in an industrial building serving funeral
directors only). . . "not legal". . . "health hazard."

There may be additional crematories that are not on the lists I used for this research.

▶ **Body Donation**

All body donations in Illinois are handled through one agency.

Demonstrators Association of Illinois
2240 W. Fillmore
Chicago, IL 60612
312-733-5283

Cost to family: transportation
Prior enrollment: not required
Over-enrollment: shared
Disposition: cremation
Body rejection: under 18, previous embalming, autopsy, decomposition, meningitis, hepatitis, AIDS, sepsis, septicemia.

▶ **State Funeral Board**

The Illinois State Funeral Board has five members. There are no consumer representatives.

(This section was reviewed by the Illinois Department of Health, Vital Records.)

In Indiana

Please refer to Chapter 9 as you use this section.

Persons in Indiana must use a funeral director to sign the death certificate and obtain the permits. The legal authority restricting a family's right to do so is found in the Embalmers and Funeral Directors Act (which otherwise deals with the licensing and regulation of funeral directors):

> Title 25-15-8-25 Sec. 25. A local health officer may issue a permit under IC 16-1-17-7 only to a funeral director acting as an agent of a funeral home licensee or another individual acting under the direct supervision of a funeral director who is an agent of a funeral home licensee.

However, there are no other statutes or regulations which might require the use of a funeral director when no embalming is desired. Indeed, under the public health statutes there are no similar restrictions:

Title 16-1-17-1. The person in charge of interment shall file a certificate of death. . .

Title 16-1-17-7. Upon receipt of a properly executed certificate of death or of a stillbirth or of a provisional certificate of death . . . a local health officer in the county in which the death occurred shall issue a permit for the disposal of the body.

Once the permit for disposition has been acquired by a funeral director, a family in Indiana may care for its own dead. The funeral directors with whom I spoke indicated that the charge for obtaining the authorization for disposition and signing the death certificate will probably cost several hundred dollars in this state. In the four other states where a funeral director must sign the death certificate or obtain the burial-transit permit before a family takes over, charges ranged from "No charge. . . we would do it as a courtesy" to "Well, our charge for professional services is $465." However, $45 or $50 was a more common response in those states.

▶ **Death Certificate**

The family doctor or a local health officer will sign a death certificate stating the cause of death. The remaining information must be supplied, typewritten or in black ink. The death certificate must be filed with the local health officer prior to final disposition.

▶ **Fetal Death**

A death certificate is required in a case of stillbirth after 20 weeks of gestation. All other procedures apply if disposition is handled by the family.

▶ **Transporting and Disposition Permit**

The local health officer will issue the authorization for disposition to a funeral director only. A burial-transit permit must be obtained if the body is to be moved across county lines. If a body is brought into Indiana from another state, the burial-transit permit must be recorded with the local health officer having jurisdiction.

▸ **Burial**

Burial in Indiana must occur in an "established cemetery," and have "a cover of not less than two feet of earth. . . "

▸ **Cremation**

There is a 48 hour wait before cremation unless waived by the city or county health officer, or by the coroner if the death is under a coroner's jurisdiction. If a family were to seek such a waiver, the "holding fee" many crematories or funeral homes charge may be eliminated. Most crematories insist that a pacemaker be removed, and authorization by next-of-kin usually is required.

Cremains may be disposed in any manner if reduced to particle size of one-eighth inch or less. Disposal may be on uninhabited public land, on a waterway, or on property of a consenting owner. When disposition occurs on property of a consenting owner, a record must be filed with the county recorder within 10 days stating the date and manner of disposal and a brief legal description of the property.

▸ **Other Requirements**

Disposition must occur within a "reasonable time" after death. Indiana has no other requirements controlling the time schedule for the disposition of unembalmed bodies.

If the person died of a contagious or communicable disease, the doctor in attendance should be consulted. The body of a person dying of cholera, plague, typhus, leprosy, yellow fever and smallpox must be placed in a sealed casket if a public funeral is held.

▸ **Crematories**

Northwest Indiana Cremation
 Service
10101 Broadway
Crown Point, IN 46307
219-662-0661
Funeral home affiliated
Available: 24 hours

Cost of cremation only: $120
Body container requirements:
 rigid combustible, no
 plastic
Cardboard casket: $100
Cost of mailing cremains:
 included
Payment: at time of delivery,
 negotiable

The Lindenwood Cemetery
2324 W. Main
Fort Wayne, IN 46808
219-432-4542
Independent
Available: 9-5 M-F, 9-4 Sat.

Cost of cremation only: $145
Body container requirements:
  rigid combustible
Cardboard casket: not carried
Cost of mailing cremains: $15
Payment: at time of delivery,
  negotiable

The Crown Hill Cemetery
700 W. 38th
Indianapolis, IN 46208
317-925-8231
Independent
Available: 8:30-5 M-F,
  8:30-4 Sat.

Cost of cremation only: $165
Body container requirements:
  rigid combustible
Cardboard casket: not carried
Cost of mailing cremains: $17
Payment: at time of delivery,
  negotiable

Leppert & Copeland Crema-
  tory
740 E. 86th
Indianapolis, IN 46240
317-844-3966
Funeral home affiliated
Available: 24 hours

Cost of cremation only: $145
Body container requirements:
  rigid combustible
Cardboard casket: $60
Cost of mailing cremains: $18
Payment: negotiable

M. L. Meeks & Sons
415 E. Washington
Muncie, IN 47305
317-288-6669
Funeral home affiliated
Available: 24 hours

Cost of cremation only: $120
Body container requirements:
  rigid combustible
Pressboard casket: $75
Cost of mailing cremains: $12
Payment: negotiable

Michiana Crematory
52803 U. S. 33 N
Mail: 521 N. William
South Bend, IN 46616
219-232-4857
Welsheimer Funeral Home
Available: 24 hours

Cost of cremation only: $120
Body container requirements:
  rigid combustible
Cardboard casket: $25
Cost of mailing cremains: $ -
Payment: at time of delivery,
  negotiable

Riverview Cemetery
2300 Portage
South Bend, IN 46616
219-233-2420
Independent
Available 8-5 M-F,
  8-12 Sat, 24 hr. phone

Cost of cremation only: $125
Body container requirements:
  rigid combustible
Cardboard casket: $30
Cost of mailing cremains:
  postage
Payment: at time of delivery

Terre Haute Crematory
3000 Lafayette
Terre Haute, IN 47805
812-466-5204
Mattox Wood Funeral Home
Available: 24 hours

Cost of cremation only: $125
Body container requirements:
  rigid combustible
Cardboard casket: $40
Cost of mailing cremains: $15
Payment: negotiable

One crematory in Portage declined to accept a body from other than a funeral director. They had "never been asked."

There may be additional crematories that are not on the lists I used for this research.

Body Donation

All body donations in Indiana are handled through one agency.

Indiana State Anatomical
  Board
Medical Science Building
Room 258
635 Barnhill Drive
Indianapolis, IN 46223
317-274-7450
317-892-4242

Cost to family: embalming
  and transportation minus
  $200 paid by the Board to
  an Indiana funeral director
Prior enrollment: not required
Over-enrollment: has not
  occurred
Disposition: cremation, return
  of cremains by request
Body rejection: under 16,
  standard*, over 200 lbs.,
  over 6 feet tall, Alz-
  heimer's, pre-senile
  dementia, amyotrophic
  lateral sclerosis

*autopsy, decomposition, mutilation, severe burn victim, meningitis, hepatitis, AIDS

▸ **State Funeral Board**

The Indiana State Board of Embalmers and Funeral Directors

has six members. Five are practicing embalmers and funeral directors. There is one consumer representative.

(The Indiana section was reviewed by the Office of Legal Affairs, Indiana State Board of Health.)

In Iowa

Please refer to Chapter 9 as you use this section.

Persons in Iowa may care for their own dead. The legal authority to do so is found in:

Title 144.27 (re filing a death certificate). . . When a person other than a funeral director assumes custody of a dead body, the person shall be responsible for carrying out the provisions of this section.

Title 156.2 Persons excluded (from the Practice of Funeral Directing and Mortuary Science regulations) (5) Persons burying their own dead under burial permit from the registrar of vital statistics.

There are no other statutes or regulations which might require you to use a funeral director when embalming is not desired.

▶ **Death Certificate**

The family doctor or a local medical examiner will supply and sign the death certificate within 24 hours stating the cause of death. The remaining information must be supplied, typewritten or in black ink. The death certificate must be filed with the local registrar within three days and before final disposition.

▶ **Fetal Death**

A fetal death report is required after 20 weeks of gestation. If there is no family physician involved, the local medical examiner must sign the fetal death certificate. All other procedures apply if disposition is handled by the family.

▶ **Transporting and Disposition Permit**

The local registrar will issue the burial-transit permit. This authorization must be obtained within 72 hours of death and prior to final disposition of the body.

▶ **Burial**

Check with the county registrar for local zoning laws regarding home burial. There are no state burial statutes or regulations with regard to depth.

When burial is arranged, the family member acting as the funeral director must sign the burial-transit permit and return it within 10 days to the issuing registrar.

▶ **Cremation**

The burial-transit permit serves as a permit for cremation. Most crematories insist that a pacemaker be removed, and authorization by next-of-kin usually is required. The crematory will return the disposition authorization to the issuing registrar.

▶ **Other Requirements**

Iowa has no other requirements controlling the time schedule for the disposition of unembalmed bodies. Weather and reasonable planning should be considered.

If the person died of a contagious or communicable disease, the doctor in attendance should be consulted.

▶ **Crematories**

Cedar Memorial Park
  Cemetery
4200 1st N.E.
Cedar Rapids, IA 52406
319-393-8000
Funeral home affiliated
Available: 24 hours

Cost of cremation only: $160
Body container requirements:
  rigid combustible
Cardboard casket: $40
Cost of mailing cremains:
  postage
Payment: at time of delivery,
  negotiable

Larkin Funeral Home
604 W. Adams St.
Creston, IA 50801
515-782-8428
Available: 24 hours

Cost of cremation only: $150
Body container requirements:
  rigid combustible
Cardboard casket: $100
Cost of mailing cremains:
  included
  Payment: at time of
  delivery, negotiable

Fairmont Cemetery Assoc.
3902 Rockingham Rd.
Davenport, IA 52802
319-322-8663
Independent
Available: 9-4 M-F,
  24-hour phone

Cost of cremation only: $150
Body container requirements:
  rigid combustible
Cardboard casket: no charge
Cost of mailing
cremains:$9.50
Payment: at time of delivery

Quad Cities Crematory
  Service
838 E. Kimberly Rd.
Davenport, IA 52807
319-391-6202
Runge Mortuary
Available: 24 hours

Cost of cremation only: $150
Body container requirements:
  rigid combustible
Cardboard casket: $30
Cost of mailing cremains: $20
Payment: at time of delivery,
  negotiable

Dunn's Funeral Home
2121 Grand
Des Moines, IA 50312
515-244-2121
Available: 24 hours

Cost of cremation only: $160
Body container requirements:
  rigid combustible
Cardboard casket: $75
Cost of mailing cremains: $46
Payment: 30 days

Heisman Funeral Home and
  Crematory
606 Main St.
La Porte, IA 50651
319-342-3131
Available: 24 hours

Cost of cremation only: $150
Body container requirements:
  rigid combustible
Cardboard casket: $40
Cost of mailing cremains: $10
Payment: at time of delivery,
  negotiable

Two crematories declined to accept a body from other than a funeral director: one in Marion and one in Sioux City. A concern of one was "liability."

There may be additional crematories that are not on the lists I used for this research.

▶ **Body Donation**

Palmer College of Chiro-
    practic
Department of Anatomy
1000 Brady Street
Davenport, IA 52803
319-326-9692 8-5 M-F
319-355-4433

Cost to family: transportation
beyond 250 miles; over $200;
disposition other than
cremation
Prior enrollment: not required
Over-enrollment: has not
    occurred
Disposition: return of remains
    or cremation, w. return of
    cremains by request
Body rejection: standard*,
    under 18, by-pass surgery,
    missing body parts

University of Osteopathic
    Medicine and Health Sci.
3200 Grand Ave.
Des Moines, IA 50312
515-271-1481 8-4:30
515-271-1400

Cost to family: transportation
    over $150 inside Polk Co.,
    $250 outside Polk Co.
Prior enrollment: required
Over-enrollment: not shared
Disposition: Cremation; return
    of cremains by request
Body rejection: standard*,
    under 18, missing limbs

University of Iowa
Department of Anatomy, BSB
Iowa City, IA 52242
319-353-5905
319-356-1616 after hours

Cost to family: transportation;
    embalming if not delivered
    within 10 hrs.
Prior enrollment: required
    unless need exists
Over-enrollment: shared by
    request
Disposition: cremation; return
    of cremains by request
Body rejection: standard*

*autopsy, decomposition, mutilation, severe burn victim,
meningitis, hepatitis, AIDS

▶ **State Funeral Board**

The Iowa State Funeral Board has five members. There are
two consumer representatives.

(This section was sent to the Iowa Department of Health for
review, but no response was received by the time of publication.)

In Kansas

Please refer to Chapter 9 as you use this section.

Persons in Kansas may care for their own dead. The legal authority to do so is found in:

Title 65-1713b. Every funeral service or interment, or part thereof, hereafter conducted in this state must be in the actual charge and under the supervision of a Kansas licensed funeral director, or of the duly licensed assistant funeral director: Provided, however, that this shall not prevent a family from burying its own dead where death did not result from a contagious, infectious or communicable disease, nor shall it prevent a religious group or sect whose religious beliefs require the burial of its own dead from conducting such services where death did not result from a contagious, infectious or communicable disease.

There are no other statutes or regulations which might require you to use a funeral director when embalming is not desired.

A pamphlet entitled "Provisions for the Final Disposition of the Deceased" written for a family or persons handling their own arrangements may be obtained from:

The Kansas Department of Health and Environment
Office of Vital Statistics, Registration Section
Building 740, Forbes Field
Topeka, Kansas 66620

▶ Death Certificate

The family doctor (or a coroner) will sign within 24 hours the death certificate stating the cause of death. The remaining information must be supplied, typewritten or in black ink. The death certificate must be filed with the registrar within three days and before final disposition.

► **Fetal Death**

A fetal death report is required when the weight is 350 grams or more. If there is no family physician involved, the local coroner must sign the fetal death certificate. All other procedures apply if disposition is handled by the family.

► **Transporting and Disposition Permit**

A body may be moved with medical permission. If out-of-state disposition is planned, the local registrar will issue a transit permit.

► **Burial**

Home burial is permissible in Kansas. Check with the county or local registrar for zoning laws regarding home burial. There are no statutes or regulations with regard to depth.

► **Cremation**

A permit for cremation must be obtained from the local coroner. There is no fee for this. Most crematories insist that a pacemaker be removed, and authorization by next-of-kin usually is required.

► **Other Requirements**

If disposition will not take place within 24 hours, embalming is required. A reasonable extension of this may be permitted if no health hazard or nuisance will result.

When death has occurred resulting from a contagious or infectious disease, the body must be embalmed. When death has occurred from any unusual and highly communicable disease, the body shall be handled . . . only by a licensed embalmer and immediately placed in a casket or coffin which shall be permanently closed.

► **Crematories**

Ryan Mortuary
137 N. 8th St.
Salina, Kansas 67401
913-825-4242
Available: 24 hours

Cost of cremation only: $180
Body container requirements:
 rigid combustible
Cardboard casket: $40
Cost of mailing cremains: $10
Payment: at time of delivery,
 negotiable

Amos Family, Inc.
10901 Johnson Drive
Shawnee, Kansas 66203
913-631-5566
Funeral home
Available: 24 hours

Cost of cremation only: $150
Body container requirements:
    rigid combustible
Cardboard casket: available
Cost of mailing cremains:
    included
Payment: at time of delivery,
    negotiable

Mount Hope Cemetery
4700 W. 17th
Topeka, Kansas 66604
913-272-1122
Independent
Available: 8-5 M-F,
    weekends by arrangement

Cost of cremation only: $200
Body container requirements:
    rigid combustible
Cardboard casket: not carried
Cost of mailing cremains:
    included
Payment: at time of delivery,
    negotiable

Shawnee Co. Crematory
1321 W. 10th
P.O. Box 2729
Topeka, Kansas 66601
913-354-8558
Penwell-Gabel Inc.
Available: 24 hours

Cost of cremation only: $200
Body container requirements:
    rigid combustible
Cardboard casket: $75
Cost of mailing cremains:
    postage
Payment: negotiable

Downing & Lahey Crematory
6555 E. Central
Wichita, Kansas 67206
316-682-4553
Funeral home affiliated
Available: 24 hours

Cost of cremation only: $170
Body container requirements:
    rigid combustible
Cardboard casket: $45
Cost of mailing cremains: $10
Payment: 30 days

There may be additional crematories that are not on the lists
I used for this research.

▶ **Body Donation**

University of Kansas
Department of Anatomy
Medical Center
39th & Rainbow
Kansas City, Kansas 66103
913-588-7000 8-5 M-F
913-588-5000

Cost to family: transportation
  beyond Kansas City area
Prior enrollment: not required
Over-enrollment: shared
Disposition: cremation; return
  of cremains by request
Body rejection: autopsy,
  decomposition, mutilation,
  severe burn victim, missing
  body parts, meningitis,
  hepatitis, AIDS, other
  infectious diseases

▶ **State Funeral Board**

The Kansas State Board of Mortuary Arts has five members.
There are two consumer representatives.

(This section was reviewed by the Director of Vital Statistics, Kansas Department of Health and Environment, and the Executive Secretary for the State Board of Mortuary Arts.)

In Kentucky

Please refer to Chapter 9 as you use this section.

Persons in Kentucky may care for their own dead. The legal authority to do so is found in:

Title 213.080 **Certificate of Death** . . . The statement of facts relating to the disposition of the body shall be signed by the undertaker or person acting as such.

There are no other statutes or regulations which might require you to use a funeral director when embalming is not desired. Letters from the attorney for the Cabinet for Human Resources and the Executive Secretary for the State Board of Embalmers and Funeral Directors confirm this information.

► **Death Certificate**

If the deceased was not attended by a physician during the last 36 hours of life, the death must be reported to the coroner, regardless of the cause of the death. The death certificate, obtainable from the health department or a funeral director, must be presented to the medical person certifying death within five days. The non-medical information must be supplied, typewritten or in unfading ink. The physician will file the completed death certificate with the county health department within fifteen days.

A provisional death certificate will be needed to obtain the burial-transit permit. This may be procured from the county health department or a funeral director.

► **Fetal Death**

A fetal death must be reported when gestation is 20 weeks or more or when the weight is 350 grams. If no physician is in attendance, the registrar must be notified, who in turn will notify the local health officer or coroner. All other procedures apply if disposition is handled by the family.

► **Transporting and Disposition Permit**

The local registrar will issue the burial-transit permit. This authorization must be obtained prior to final disposition of the body.

► **Burial**

Check with the county registrar for local zoning laws regarding home burial. There must be three feet of earth over a box unless the casket is impervious, in which case the container must be covered by two feet of earth.

When burial is arranged by the family, the family member acting as the funeral director must sign the authorization for disposition and return it to the registrar of that locale within 10 days.

► **Cremation**

A coroner's signature on the burial-transit permit is required for cremation. Most crematories insist that a pacemaker be removed, and authorization by next-of-kin usually is required. The crematory may offer to file the burial-transit permit.

▶ **Other Requirements**

Kentucky has no other requirements controlling the time schedule for the disposition of unembalmed bodies. Weather and reasonable planning should be considered.

If the person died of a contagious or communicable disease, the physician or local health officer should be consulted.

▶ **Crematories**

Louisville Crematory
641 Baxter
Louisville, KY 40204
502-584-7566
Independent
Available: 8-4:30 M-F,
   8-12 Sat., 24-hour phone

Cost of cremation only: $150
Body container requirements:
   rigid combustible
Cardboard casket: $40
Cost of mailing cremains: $16
Payment: at time of delivery

Resthaven Memorial Park
4400 Bardstown
Louisville, KY 40218
502-491-5950
Independent
Available 9-4:30 M-F

Cost of cremation only: $175
Body container requirements:
   rigid combustible
Cardboard casket: not carried
Cost of mailing cremains:
   postage
Payment: at time of delivery

Three other crematories declined to accept a body from other than a funeral director, one each in Lexington, Louisville, and Owensboro. Their concerns were "not legal," "repeat business from funeral directors. . . not interested in dealing with the public," and "don't want to assume responsibility."

There may be additional crematories that are not on the lists I used for this research.

▶ **Body Donation**

University of Kentucky
Department of Anatomy
University Medical Center
Lexington, Kentucky 40536
606-233-5276
after hours: 233-5811

Cost to family: none inside
   Kentucky
Prior enrollment: not required
Over-enrollment: not shared
Disposition: cremation; return
   of cremains by request
Body rejection: standard*,
   under 16, (body delivery
   within 6 hours unless
   embalmed)

University of Louisville
Health Science Center
Department of Anatomy
Louisville, Kentucky 40292
502-588-5744
after hours: 368-3396

Cost to family: transportation over $50 local or $1.25 per mile within 50-mile radius
Prior enrollment: not required
Over-enrollment: used, not shared
Disposition: cremation and burial in University plot; return of remains or cremains at family expense
Body rejection: autopsy, decomposition, burn victim, mutilation

*autopsy, decomposition, mutilation, severe burn victim, meningitis, hepatitis, AIDS

▶ **State Funeral Board**

The Kentucky Board of Embalmers and Funeral Directors has five members. There is one consumer representative.

(This section was reviewed by the Registrar of Vital Statistics, Kentucky Department of Health.)

In Louisiana

Please refer to Chapter 9 as you use this section.

Persons in Louisiana are limited in caring for their own dead. Existing public health statutes refer to "the funeral director or person acting as such," but in 1986 the following statute was passed:

LSA-R.S. 40:32 **Definitions** - (17) "Funeral director or person acting as such" is a licensed funeral director or embalmer. . .

Therefore, the use of a licensed funeral director is now

mandatory in order to file the death certificate. Even a medical examiner or medical school personnel may not file a death certificate.

Furthermore, in the statutes covering Professions and Occupations dealing primarily with the licensing of funeral directors (and which were most likely drafted by funeral directors) this restrictive statute was added in 1983:

> LSA-R.S. 37:848 **Unlawful practice** - D. (5) Every dead human body shall be disposed of and prepared through a funeral establishment and under the supervision of a licensed funeral home or embalmer.

No similar restriction is in the Public Health Statutes and nothing in those statutes appears to prohibit a family member from transporting a body.

▸ **Death Certificate**

The family doctor will sign the death certificate within 24 hours, stating the cause of death. If the death is a coroner's case the coroner may take 48 hours. The remaining information must be supplied, typewritten or in black ink. The death certificate must be filed by a licensed funeral director, with any parish registrar, within five days and before final disposition.

▸ **Fetal Death**

A fetal death report is required after 20 weeks of gestation or when the weight is 350 grams or more. If there is no family physician involved, the local coroner must sign the fetal death certificate. All other procedures apply if disposition is handled by the family.

▸ **Transporting and Disposition Permit**

Once the death certificate has been filed, the local registrar will issue a burial-transit permit which is a separate document, not attached to the death certificate. This permit must be obtained prior to final disposition of the body. The fee for this is $2.00. The permit may be obtained and filed by a family member in the district of disposition, but the permit must be signed by the licensed funeral director supervising burial or cremation.

▶ **Burial**

Burial must be in a duly authorized cemetery. Home burial would probably be permissible if the property were dedicated as such with local authorities and registered with the Louisiana Cemetery Board. Check with the parish registrar for local zoning laws. The casket must have a covering of two feet of soil unless a burial vault or lawn crypt is used.

When burial occurs, the burial-transit permit must be filed with the registrar of the parish where disposition takes place within 10 days.

▶ **Cremation**

A permit to cremate must be obtained from the coroner in the parish where death occurred. The charge for this varies and may be nothing in one parish, $5 in the next, $25 in another. Most crematories insist that a pacemaker be removed, and authorization by next-of-kin usually is required. The crematory will sign the burial-transit permit. This permit must be filed with the parish registrar within 10 days.

▶ **Other Requirements**

If disposition is not arranged within 30 hours of death, the body must be embalmed or refrigerated below 45 degrees.

If the person died of a contagious or communicable disease, the doctor in attendance should be consulted.

▶ **Crematories**

Memorial Crematory
2156 Airline Dr.
Bossier City, LA 71111
318-742-5361
Boone Funeral Home
Available: 24 hours

Filing of certificate: $45
Cost of cremation only: $195
Body container requirements:
   rigid combustible
Cardboard casket: $30
Cost of mailing cremains:
   included
Payment: at time of delivery,
   negotiable

Tharp-Southeimer Crematory
4117 S. Claibourne Ave.
P.O. Box 750140
New Orleans, LA 70175
504-821-8411
Funeral home affiliated
Available: 24 hours

Filing of certificate: $45
Cost of cremation only: $140
Body container requirements:
  rigid combustible
Cardboard casket: $60
Cost of mailing cremains: $20
Payment: at time of delivery,
  negotiable

Metairie Cemetery
5100 Pontchartrain
P.O. Drawer 19925
New Orleans, LA 70179
504-486-6331
Lake Lawn Metairie Funeral
  Home
Available: 24 hours

Filing of certificate: $2
Cost of cremation only: $145
Body container requirements:
  rigid combustible
Cardboard casket: $48
Cost of mailing cremains: $20
Payment: negotiable

Two crematories, one in Lafayette and one in New Orleans, declined to accept a body from other than a funeral director. One "does not do any outside business." The other said, "I made up my mind years ago."

There may be additional crematories that are not on the lists I used for this research.

▶ **Body Donation**

One agency handles body donation in Louisiana.

Department of Health and
  Human Resources
Anatomical Services
1901 Perdido St.
New Orleans, LA 70112-1393

New Orleans area:
  Anatomy Department - LSU
  504-568-4012 days
Anatomy Department - Tulane
  504-588-5255 days
  other times:
  J.T. Willie Funeral Home
  504-861-0383 or 522-1441
Shreveport area:
  Anatomy Department - LSU
  318-226-3312 days
  other times:
  LSU Security Office
  318-226-3369

Cost to family: none if
  previously registered and
  death is in state or within
  100-mile radius
Prior enrollment: not
  required, but priority given
  to registered donors
Over-enrollment: shared
  within state
Disposition: cremation; return
  of cremains on request
Body rejection: autopsy, burn
  victim, decomposition,
  embalming if trocar is used

▸ **State Funeral Board**

The Louisiana State Board of Embalmers and Funeral
Directors has seven members: three embalmers and four
funeral directors. There are no consumer representatives.

(This section was reviewed by the Office of General Counsel
for the Louisiana Department of Health and Human Services,
the Registrar of Vital Records and the Secretary for the
Louisiana Board of Embalmers and Funeral Directors.)

In Maine

Please refer to Chapter 9 as you use this section.

Persons in Maine may care for their own dead. The legal
authority to do so is found in:

Title 22, Sec. 2846 - Authorized Person. For the purposes
of this chapter, the "authorized person" responsible for
obtaining or filing a permit or certificate shall mean a

member of the immediate family of the deceased, a person authorized in writing by a member of the immediate family. . . or a person authorized in writing by the deceased.

There are no other statutes or regulations which might require you to use a funeral director when no embalming is desired.

▶ **Death Certificate**

The family doctor or a local medical examiner will supply and sign the death certificate within 24 hours, stating the cause of death. The remaining information must be supplied, typewritten or in black ink. Do not use a felt-tip pen; there are three carbons. The death certificate must be filed with the local town or city clerk within three days.

▶ **Fetal Death**

A fetal death report is required after 20 weeks of gestation. If there is no family physician involved, the local medical examiner must sign the fetal death certificate. All other procedures apply if disposition is handled by the family.

▶ **Transporting and Disposition**

The local town clerk will issue a burial-transit permit. The fee for this is $2.00. The death certificate must be obtained first, as well as a medical examiner's release if cremation, burial-at-sea or out-of-state disposition is planned. If death occurs after usual business hours, a funeral director may be asked to supply the permit. The burial transit permit must be filed within seven days, with the clerk of the town where burial or cremation takes place. If this is in another district, an additional $2.00 may be charged to file the permit.

▶ **Burial**

Check with the town clerk for local zoning laws regarding home burial. Family burial grounds of not more than a quarter of an acre are protected as a "burial place forever." This plot must be recorded in the registry of deeds in the county or town where burial takes place and enclosed by a fence to be "exempt from attachment and execution." There are no state burial statutes or regulations regarding depth.

▸ **Cremation or Burial at Sea**

A permit for cremation or burial at sea must be signed by a local medical examiner. The usual fee for this is $15. There is a 48-hour wait unless the deceased person is diseased. A rigid combustible container must be used, without a canvas or plastic bag. Most crematories insist that a pacemaker be removed before cremation, and authorization by next-of-kin usually is required.

▸ **Other Requirements**

There are no other requirements affecting the time schedule of disposition of an unembalmed body. Weather and reasonable planning should prevail.

Death from a "disease" may involve a medical examiner. Check with the family physician to be sure.

▸ **Crematories**

Gracelawn Memorial Park
980 Turner
Auburn, ME 04210
207-782-3741
Independent
Available: 24 hours

Cost of cremation only: $125
Body container requirements:
  rigid combustible
Cardboard casket: available
Cost of mailing cremains:
  included
Payment: at time of delivery

Mt. Hope Cemetery Group
1038 State
Bangor, ME 04401
207-945-6589
Independent
Available: 8-4:30 M-F

Cost of cremation only: $200
Body container requirements:
  rigid combustible
Cardboard casket: available
Cost of mailing cremains:
  postage
Payment: at time of delivery

Laurel Hill Cemetery
293 Beach
Saco, ME 04072
207-282-9351
Independent
Available: 7:30-4:30 M-F
  or call

Cost of cremation only: $145
Body container requirements:
  rigid combustible
Cardboard casket: available
Cost of mailing cremains:
  included
Payment: at time of delivery

One other crematory, in Portland, declined to accept a body from other than a funeral director. The reason given: "We work with funeral directors."

There may be additional crematories that are not on the lists I used for this research.

▶ **Body Donation**

Univ. of N.E. College of
  Osteopathic Medicine
11 Hills Beach Rd.
Biddeford, ME 04005
207-283-0171 ext. 202/206
  or 284-8870

Cost to family: none; the school will provide transportation outside "several hundred miles"
Prior enrollment: not required
Over-enrollment: has not occurred
Disposition: cremation/Univ. plot; return of cremains by request
Body rejection: autopsy, burn victim, decomposition, AIDS, previous embalming

▶ **State Funeral Board**

The Maine Board of Funeral Service has seven members. There is one consumer representative.

(This section was reviewed by the chairman of the Maine Board of Funeral Service.)

In Maryland

Please refer to Chapter 9 as you use this section.

Persons in Maryland may care for their own dead. Correspondence with Charles R. Buck, Jr., Secretary of Health and Mental Hygiene, states:

> Under English Common Law, which is carried over in our State law, the immediate families may dispose of their dead either by burial or cremation. They must, however, conform to the laws . . .

There are no statutes or regulations which might require you to use a funeral director when embalming is not desired.

▸ **Death Certificate**

The family doctor or a local medical examiner will sign the death certificate within 24 hours, stating the cause of death. The remaining information must be supplied, typewritten or with ball-point pen. There are three carbons. The first two pages of the death certificate must be filed with the Department of Health and Mental Hygiene, Division of Vital Records, within 72 hours. The hospital or physician will retain the fourth copy.

▸ **Fetal Death**

A fetal death report is required after 20 weeks of gestation. If there is no family physician involved, the local medical examiner must sign the fetal death certificate. All other procedures apply if disposition is handled by the family.

▸ **Transporting and Disposition Permit**

Page three of the death certificate serves as the burial-transit permit. The physician's or medical examiner's signature is required.

▸ **Burial**

Contact the county Health Department and Zoning Board for local ordinances or regulations that may apply to home burial. There are no state burial statutes or regulations with regard to depth.

When burial is arranged, the family member acting as the funeral director must sign the burial-transit permit and return it to the Department of Health and Mental Hygiene, Division of Vital Records, within 10 days.

▸ **Cremation**

The burial-transit permit serves as the permit for cremation. A cot and pouch or a receptacle is required when a body is transported to a crematory. The body must be identified and cremation approved by the next-of-kin or other person who is authorized to arrange for final disposition. There is a 12-hour waiting period before cremation. Most crematories insist that a pacemaker be removed. The crematory may offer to file the burial-transit permit.

▶ **Other Requirements**

Maryland has no other requirements controlling the time schedule for the disposition of unembalmed bodies. Weather and reasonable planning should be considered.

If the person died of a contagious or communicable disease, the doctor in attendance should be consulted.

▶ **Crematories**

The Green Mount Cemetery
Greenmont & Oliver
Baltimore, MD 21202
301-539-0641
Independent
Available: 7:30-4 M-F,
  7:30-12 Sat.

Cost of cremation only: $100
Body container requirements:
  rigid combustible
Cost of mailing cremains:
  included
Payment: at time of delivery

Cremation Society of
  Maryland
299 Frederick Rd.
Catonsville, MD 21228
301-788-1800
Funeral home affiliated
Available: 24 hours

Cost of cremation only: to be
  arranged
Body container requirements:
  none
Cardboard casket: available
Payment: at time of delivery

Lee Crematory
6633 Old Alexander Ferry Rd.
Clinton, MD 20735
301-868-0900
Funeral home affiliated
Available: 24 hours

Cost of cremation only: to be
  arranged
Body container requirements:
  none
Cardboard casket: available
Cost of mailing cremains: $25
Payment: at time of delivery,
  negotiable

Resthaven Memorial Gardens
9501 Rt. 15 N
P.O. Box 150
Frederick, MD 21701
301-898-7177
Independent
Available: 9-5 M-F,
  9-12 Sat., 24-hour phone

Cost of cremation only: $125
Body container requirements:
  rigid combustible
Cardboard casket: $40
Cost of mailing cremains:
  postage
Payment: at time of delivery,
  negotiable

Carroll Cremation Service
934 S. Main St.
P.O. Box 617
Hempstead, MD 21074
301-239-8163
Eline Funeral Home
Available: 24 hours

Cost of cremation only: $125
Body container requirements:
  rigid combustible
Cardboard casket: $25
Cost of mailing cremains: $15
Payment: at time of delivery

Chambers Funeral Home &
  Crematory
8653 Georgia Ave.
Silver Spring, MD 20910
301-565-3200
Available: 24 hours

Cost of cremation only: $110
Body container requirements:
  none
Cardboard casket: $85
Cost of mailing cremains: $35
Payment: at time of delivery,
  negotiable

Smithsburg Crematory
Pennsylvania Ave.
Smithsburg, MD 21783
301-791-1230
Funeral home affiliated
Available: 24 hours

Cost of cremation only: $125
Body container requirements:
  rigid combustible
Cardboard casket: not carried
Cost of mailing cremains:
  included
Payment: at time of delivery

A London Park Cemetery crematory in Baltimore declined to accept a body from other than a funeral director although it would be considered on an individual basis.

There may be additional crematories that are not on the lists I used for this research.

▶ **Body Donation**

The State Anatomy Board
Department of Health and
  Mental Hygiene
655 W. Baltimore St.
Bressler Research Building,
  Room B-026
Baltimore, MD 21201
301-547-1222

Cost to family: none if death
  occurs within state
Prior enrollment: preferred
  but not required
Over-enrollment: shared
  within state
Disposition: cremation; return
  of cremains on request
Body rejection: none if pre-
  enrolled; otherwise autopsy
  or diseased

▶ **State Funeral Board**

The Maryland State Board of Embalmers and Funeral Directors has 12 members. There are two consumer representatives.

(This section was reviewed by the Director of the Maryland State Anatomy Board. He is also a member of the State Board of Morticians.)

In Massachusetts

Please refer to Chapter 9 as you use this section.

Persons in Massachusetts probably may not care for their own dead. There are no public health or other limiting statutes, yet there are restrictions issued by the Board of Registration in Embalming and Funeral Directing in regulations which carry the weight of law:

239 CMR, 3.11: **Issuance of Burial and Transportation Permits.** (1) In order to preserve public health and to insure enforcement of the rules and regulations provided therefore, no burial or transportation permit shall be issued to anyone other than a funeral director registered and licensed under the laws of Massachusetts.

3.12: **Custody of Bodies.** (1) In order to preserve the public health and in order to enforce the rules and regulations provided therefore, no dead human body shall be handled, moved or transported, except as follows:
(a) Under the supervision and with the personal attendance in the vehicle of a person registered by this Board;
(b) Under the personal supervision or order of a duly authorized medical examiner
(c) By a duly authorized physician, or medical school for purposes of autopsy or dissection;
(d) Transportation on or through a public street or highway shall be in a closed hearse or other vehicle used exclusively for the purpose of transporting dead human bodies or funeral equipment, with the personal attendance in the vehicle of a person registered by this Board.

There is an interesting legal case, however, <u>Wyeth v. Thomas</u> (1909) 200 Mass. 474, which is noted in the statutes under

Title 114, section 45. "The rule adopted by the board of registration in embalming. . . which provided that no permits for burial shall be issued to any person who is not a registered embalmer, could not be sustained on the theory that the regulation promoted the public health, especially since. . . (statutes). . . recognized ways of ascertaining whether death was from a contagious disease without employing an embalmer for that purpose."

The statutes in the Public Health section would seem permissive:

Title 46, sec. 9. **Death certificates.** A physician. . . shall immediately furnish for registration a standard certificate of death. . . to an undertaker or other authorized person or a member of the family of the deceased. . .

It is my experience that authorities will go along with your plans if the plans are well-formed and meet public health concerns. One family, in another state that appeared to be blatantly restrictive was allowed to carry out personal wishes by following all procedures carefully.

▶ **Death Certificate**

The family doctor or a medical examiner will "immediately" supply the death certificate stating the cause of death. The remaining information must be supplied, typewritten or in black ink. The death certificate must be filed with the local town clerk or Board of Health within five days.

▶ **Fetal Death**

A fetal death report is required after 20 weeks of gestation or when the weight is 350 grams or more. If there is no family physician involved, the local medical examiner must sign the fetal death certificate. All other procedures apply if disposition is handled by the family.

▶ **Transporting and Disposition Permit**

The local board of health or town clerk will issue the burial-transit permit. This authorization must be obtained prior to final disposition of the body.

▶ **Burial**

The Board of Health in each town regulates burial grounds.

There are no state burial statutes or regulations with regard to depth or home burial.

When burial is arranged, the sexton of the cemetery or the funeral director signs the coupon on the burial-transit permit and must return it to the issuing registrar.

▸ **Cremation**

A permit for cremation must be obtained from the medical examiner. There may be a charge for this. There is a 48 hour waiting period before cremation unless the death was due to a contagious or infectious disease. Most crematories insist that a pacemaker be removed, and authorization by next-of-kin usually is required.

▸ **Other Requirements**

Massachusetts has no other requirements controlling the time schedule for the disposition of unembalmed bodies. Weather and reasonable planning should be considered.

If the person died of a contagious or communicable disease, the doctor in attendance should be consulted.

▸ **Crematories**

Because of the restrictive regulations, I did not contact the crematories in this state.

▶ **Body Donation**

Boston Univ. School of Med.
80 E. Concord St.
Boston, MA 02118
617-638-4245
after hours 638-4144

Harvard Medical School
25 Shattuck St.
Boston, MA 02115
617-732-1735
after hours 732-1111

Tufts Univ. School of Med.
136 Harrison Ave.
Boston, MA 02111
617-956-6685
after hours 956-6610

Univ. of Mass. Med. School
55 Lake Ave. North
Worcester, MA 01605-2397
617-856-2460 24 hrs.

Coordinated donor program:

Cost to family: none; transportation supplied within
Commonwealth
Prior enrollment: not required
Over-enrollment: shared
among Massachusetts medical
schools
Disposition: cremation for
donors at University of
Massachusetts and burial of
cremains in state plot if no
return of cremains requested; for other three, burial
in state plot; or return of
remains at request and
expense of family
Body rejection: autopsy,
decomposition, mutilation,
severe burn victim,
meningitis, hepatitis, AIDS,
missing body parts,
previous embalming

State Funeral Board

The Massachusetts State Board of Embalmers and Funeral
Directors has five members, including one consumer representative.

(This section was reviewed by the Massachusetts Department
of Health.)

In Michigan

Please refer to Chapter 9 as you use this section.

Persons in Michigan probably may not care for their own
dead. One restrictive statute found in the Public Health Code

is:

> Title 333.2843 **Funeral Director or Agent; report of death;
> medical certification; filing death record**
> (1) A funeral director or his or her authorized agent who
> first assumes custody of a dead body shall report the
> death. . .

Furthermore, the Occupational Code governing Mortuary
Science states:

> Article 18, Sec. 1801 (d) "Practice of funeral directing"
> means engaging in . . . the supervising of the burial and
> disposal of a dead human body;. . .

> Article 18, Sec. 1810 A person shall be subject to the
> penalties of article 6 if the person commits. . . (d) aiding
> and abetting an unlicensed person to engage in the
> practice of funeral directing. . . "

Correspondence in 1986, with both George Van Amburg, State
Registrar, Michigan State Department of Public Health, and
Suzanne Jolicoeur, Administrative Secretary, Michigan State
Department of Licensing and Regulation, verifies the restric-
tions against family management of death in Michigan.

▶ **Death Certificate**

The family doctor or a local medical examiner will sign the
death certificate within 48 hours, stating the cause of death.
The remaining information must be supplied, typewritten or
in black ink. The death certificate must be filed with the
local registrar within 72 hours by a licensed funeral director
and before final disposition.

▶ **Fetal Death**

A fetal death report is required for each fetal death. All
other procedures apply if disposition is handled by the
family.

▶ **Transporting and Disposition Permit**

A body may be moved from the place of death to be
prepared for final disposition with the consent of the
physician or medical examiner who certifies the cause of
death. The local registrar will issue the authorization for
disposition in the form of a burial-transit permit. This

authorization must be obtained within 72 hours of death and prior to final disposition of the body. Funeral directors can also issue permits after hours.

▶ **Burial**

Family graveyards under one acre outside city or village limits are permissible. Such land is exempt from taxation and must be recorded with the county clerk. Permission from the local health department is required to establish a private cemetery. There are no state burial statutes or regulations with regard to depth.

The presence of a funeral director or mortuary science licensee is required to supervise the burial or disposition of dead human bodies. (Op. Atty. Gen. 1973, No. 4770, p. 60)

▶ **Cremation**

A signature of the medical examiner in the county where death occurred is required on the burial-transit permit for cremation. Most crematories insist that a pacemaker be removed, and authorization by next-of-kin usually is required.

▶ **Other Requirements**

A body of one who has died of diphtheria, meningococcic infections, plague, poliomyelitis, scarlet fever, or small pox must be embalmed. The attending physician may determine the appropriate precautions to be taken in the case of AIDS.

A body which will not reach its destination within 48 hours must be embalmed.

▶ **Crematories**

Because of the restrictive statutes, I did not contact the crematories in this state.

▸ **Body Donation**

University of Michigan
  Medical School
Department of Anatomy and
  Cell Biology
Medical Science II Building
Ann Arbor, MI 48109
313-764-4359 8-5 M-F
313-764-1817, ask for person
  on call

Cost to family: transportation
  to medical school
Prior enrollment: not required
Over-enrollment: shared
Disposition: cremation and
  burial in University plot;
  return of cremains by
  request. $25 fee unless
  picked up
Body rejection: obesity,
  decomposition, burn victim,
  mutilation, contagious
  diseases, i.e., Jacob-
  Kreutzfeld, AIDS, meningitis, hepatitis

Wayne State University
  Medical School
Department of Anatomy
540 E. Canfield
Detroit, MI 48201
313-577-1188
nights: 577-1198

Cost to family: transportation
  outside SE lower Michigan
Prior enrollment: not required
Over-enrollment: shared
Disposition: cremation with
  burial at University; return
  of remains by request
Body rejection: standard*,
  recent major surgery,
  metastatic cancer, previous
  embalming

Michigan State University
College of Human Medicine
East Lansing, MI 48823

Repeated requests for
information have not been
returned by this school.

*autopsy, decomposition, mutilation, severe burn victim,
meningitis, hepatitis, AIDS

▸ **State Funeral Board**

The Michigan Board of Mortuary Science has nine members.
There are three public representatives.

(This section was reviewed by the State Registrar, Michigan
Department of Public Health.)

In Minnesota

Please refer to Chapter 9 as you use this section.

Religious groups in Minnesota may care for their own dead. The legal authority to do so is found in:

Department of Health Regulations, Chapter 4610, Sec.0800 regarding **Transportation of the Dead** (requiring the use of a funeral director). . . This part does not apply to nor shall it in any way interfere with the duties of. . . or to the customs or rites of any recognized religion in the burial of their dead.

There are no other statutes or regulations which might require you to use a funeral director when embalming is not desired.

▶ **Death Certificate**

The family doctor or a local medical examiner will sign the death certificate stating the cause of death. The remaining information must be supplied, typewritten or in black ink. The death certificate must be filed with the local registrar within five days and before final disposition.

▶ **Fetal Death**

A fetal death report must be made when gestation is 20 weeks or more. All other procedures apply if disposition is handled by the family.

▶ **Transporting and Disposition Permit**

The local registrar, health officer, clerk of district court, or city administrator will issue the burial-removal-transit permit. Morticians serve as subregistrars. This authorization must be obtained within five days and prior to final disposition of the body. The vehicle used to move the body must be enclosed.

▶ **Burial**

Any private person and any religious corporation may establish a cemetery on his or its own land. The land must be surveyed and a plat recorded with the county recorder. Family graveyards so dedicated are exempt from taxation. Check with the local health officer for zoning laws regarding home burial. There are no state burial statutes or regulations with regard to depth.

The original copy of the burial-transit permit is to be filed with the place of disposition. In the case of home burial, the original should be retained with your deed unless the clerk of the court requires it to be recorded with official land records. The second copy of the burial-transit permit must be filed with the Department of Health.

▶ **Cremation**

A permit for cremation must be obtained from the local coroner or medical examiner. There is no fee for this. Most crematories insist that a pacemaker be removed, and authorization by next-of-kin usually is required.

▶ **Other Requirements**

Disposition must be within a "reasonable time." If the destination cannot be reached within 18 hours embalming is required. Refrigeration may be substituted up to 72 hours.

Communicable diseased must be embalmed within 18 hours of death.

Embalming is required if public transportation is to be used.

▶ **Crematories**

Park Hill Cemetery Assn.
2500 Vermillion Rd.
Duluth, MN 55803
218-724-7149
Funeral home affiliated
Available: 8:30-4:30 M-F

Cost of cremation only: $185
Body container requirements:
  rigid combustible
Cardboard casket: not carried
Cost of mailing cremains:
  included
Payment: at time of delivery

Woodland Hills Inc.
1605 Woodland Ave.
P.O. Box 121
Mankato, MN 56001
507-387-5504
Funeral home affiliated
Available: 24 hours

Cost of cremation only: $165
Body container requirements:
  rigid combustible
Cardboard casket: $50
Cost of mailing cremains: $10
Payment: 30 days

Cremation Society of Minn.
4343 Nicollet Ave.
Minneapolis, MN 55409
612-825-2435
Waterston Funeral Home
Available: 24 hours

Cost of cremation only: $95
Body container requirements:
 none
Cardboard casket: $25
Cost of mailing cremains: $25
Payment: at time of delivery

Hillside Memorium
2600 19th Ave. N.E.
Minneapolis, MN 55418
612-781-3391
Funeral home affiliated
Available: 8-9 daily,
 24-hour phone

Cost of cremation only: $115
Body container requirements:
 rigid combustible
Cardboard casket: $25
Cost of mailing cremains: $10
Payment: at time of delivery,
 negotiable

Lakewood Cemetery Assoc.
3600 Hennepin Ave.
Minneapolis, MN 55408
612-822-2172
Independent
Available: 8-5 M-F,
 8-12 Sat.

Cost of cremation only: $145
Body container requirements:
 rigid combustible
Cardboard casket: not carried
Cost of mailing cremains:
 included
Payment: at time of delivery

Sunset Memorial Park
St. Anthony Blvd. and 22nd
N.E., P.O. Box 984
Minneapolis, MN 55418
612-789-3596
Funeral home affiliated
Available: 24-hour phone

Cost of cremation only: $100
Body container requirements:
 rigid combustible
Cardboard casket: $35
Cost of mailing cremains:
 postage
Payment: at time of delivery,
 negotiable

Fairview Crematory
RFD #1, Box 157
Mound, MN 55364
612-472-3925
Funeral home affiliated
Available: 9-5 M-Sat.

Cost of cremation only: $125
Body container requirements:
 rigid combustible
Cardboard casket: $50
Cost of mailing cremains:
 included
Payment: negotiable

Southern Minn. Crematory
1705 Elton Dr.
Rochester, MN 55901
507-289-3600
Ranfranz Funeral Home
Available: 24-hour phone
 M-F, weekends by arrange-
 ment

Cost of cremation only: $150
Body container requirements:
 rigid combustible
Cardboard casket: $35
Cost of mailing cremains: $15
Payment: 30 days

Benson Crematory
1111 25th Ave. S.
St. Cloud, MN 56301
612-252-3132
Funeral home affiliated
Available: 8-5 M-F,
  24-hour phone

Cost of cremation only: $125
Body container requirements:
  rigid combustible
Cardboard casket: $20
Cost of mailing cremains:
  included
Payment: negotiable

Forest Park Memorial Park
  Association
1800 Edgerton St.
St. Paul, MN 55117
612-776-6420
Independent
Available: 8-4:30 M-F,
  8-12 Sat.

Cost of cremation only: $125
Body container requirements:
  rigid combustible
Cardboard casket: not carried
Cost of mailing cremains:
  included
Payment: at time of delivery

Northern Minnesota Crema-
  tion Service
516 1st St. S.
Virginia, MN 55792
218-741-9593
Funeral home affiliated
Available: 24 hours

Cost of cremation only: $165
Body container requirements:
  rigid combustible
Cardboard casket: $25
Cost of mailing cremains:
  included
Payment: at time of delivery,
  negotiable, 30 days

One crematory in Rochester declined to accept a body from
other than a funeral director. It provides "a service to
funeral directors only."

There may be additional crematories that are not on the lists
I used for this research.

► **Body Donation**

University of Minnesota
Bequest Program
4-135 Jackson Hall
321 Church St.
Minneapolis, MN 55455
612-625-1111

Cost to family: transportation
  outside the metropolitan
  area; disposition if return
  of remains is requested
Prior enrollment: required
Over-enrollment: not shared
Disposition: cremation; return
  of remains by request
Body rejection: standard*,
  other diseases

Mayo Clinic Foundation
Rochester, MN 55901
507-284-2511

Cost to family: transportation
  beyond 200 miles or over
  $.75 per mile
Prior enrollment: not required
Over-enrollment: not shared
Disposition: cremation/
  retained in Clinic vault;
  return of cremains by
  request; return of remains
  by request and at expense
  of family
Body rejection: standard*,
  over-enrollment

Northwestern College of
  Chiropractic
2501 W. 84th
Bloomington, MN

Repeated requests for
information have not been
returned from this school.

*autopsy, decomposition, mutilation, severe burn victim,
meningitis, hepatitis, AIDS

▸ **State Funeral Board**

The Minnesota Advisory Council in Mortuary Science has five
members. There is one consumer representative.

(This section was reviewed by the Minnesota Department of
Health, Mortuary Science Unit.)

In Mississippi

Please refer to Chapter 9 as you use this section.

Persons in Mississippi may care for their own dead. The legal
authority to do so is found in:

Health Department Rule 38: When death occurs at a place
other than an institution and the death does not affect
the public interest, the funeral director or person acting
as such who first assumes custody of the body shall
initiate preparation of the certificate. . .

There are no other statutes or regulations which might require you to use a funeral director when embalming is not desired.

▶ **Death Certificate**

The attending physician or local medical examiner will sign the death certificate within 72 hours, stating the cause of death. The remaining information must be supplied, and the use of a typewriter is preferred. There are three carbons. The original (white copy) must be filed with the Office of Vital Records within five days and before final disposition. The third page may be retained by a hospital or nursing home, and physician's copy is the fourth page.

The medical examiner will certify the cause of death in violent or unexpected circumstances and when a physician was not in attendance within 36 hours, except in cases where terminal illness has been diagnosed.

▶ **Fetal Death**

A fetal death report is required after 20 weeks of gestation or when weight is 350 grams or more. If there is no family physician involved and the death is not subject to the jurisdiction of the coroner or medical examiner, the person attending or the parents may file the fetal death report with the State Registrar within five days. A fetal death report may be obtained from a physician, hospital or the county health department.

▶ **Transporting and Disposition Permit**

A body may be moved with the consent of a physician, coroner, or medical examiner. If the body is moved out of state, it must be accompanied by a burial-transit permit. This is the yellow page of the four-copy death certificate obtained from the person certifying the cause of death.

▶ **Burial**

Check with the county Board of Supervisors for local zoning laws if home burial is planned. The top of the coffin must be 24 inches below the natural surface of the earth.

When burial is arranged, the family member acting as the funeral director must sign the death certificate and file it with the Office of Vital Records within five days.

▶ **Cremation**

The death certificate must be filed with the Office of Vital Records before cremation. Most crematories insist that a pacemaker be removed, and authorization by next-of-kin usually is required.

▶ **Other Requirements**

When death is from a contagious disease which may constitute a public hazard the matter must be referred to a medical examiner.

When the destination cannot be reached within 24 hours, or disposition does not take place within 48 hours, a body must be embalmed or refrigerated.

▶ **Crematories**

Mississippi Gulf Coast
  Crematory
314 E. Howard Ave.
Biloxi, MS 39530
601-374-5650
Bradford-O'Keefe Funeral
  Home
Available: 24 hours

Cost of cremation only: $170
Body container requirements:
  rigid combustible
Cardboard casket: $110
Cost of mailing cremains: $25
Payment: at time of delivery,
  negotiable

Cremation Services, Inc.
505 Storm Ave.
Brookhaven, MS 39601
601-833-6680
Independent
Available: 24 hours

Cost of cremation only: $175
Body container requirements:
  rigid combustible
Cardboard casket: available
Cost of mailing cremains:
  included
Payment: at time of delivery,
  negotiable

There may be additional crematories that are not on the lists I used for this research.

▸ **Body Donation**

University of Mississippi
Medical Center
Jackson, MS 39216
601-984-1000

Cost to family: transportation
  beyond 300 miles
Prior enrollment: not required
Over-enrollment: shared
Disposition: cremation/ burial
  at University; return of
  cremains by request; return
  of remains by request and
  at expense of the family
Body rejection: autopsy,
  decomposition, burn victim,
  severe trauma, under 18,
  previous embalming unless
  under the direction of the
  University

▸ **State Funeral Board**

The Mississippi State Board of Funeral Service has nine
members. There are two consumer representatives.

(This state section was reviewed by the Mississippi Department of Health.)

In Missouri

Please refer to Chapter 9 as you use this section.

Persons in Missouri may care for their own dead. The legal
authority to do so is found in:

  Title 193.145: . . . 4. The funeral director or person
  acting as such in charge of final disposition of the dead
  body shall file the certificate of death.

There are no other statutes or regulations which might
require you to use a funeral director when embalming is not
desired.

▶ **Death Certificate**

The family doctor or a local medical examiner will sign the death certificate within 72 hours, stating the cause of death. The remaining information must be supplied, typewritten or in black ink. The death certificate must be filed with the local registrar within five days. A "notification of death" must be filed with or mailed to the local registrar prior to final disposition if the death certificate has not been completed. This form can be obtained from the registrar or a funeral director.

▶ **Fetal Death**

A fetal death report is required after 20 weeks of gestation or when weight is 350 grams or more. If there is no family physician involved, the local medical examiner must sign the fetal death certificate. The fetal death certificate must be filed within seven days. All other procedures apply if disposition is handled by the family.

▶ **Transporting and Disposition Permit**

A body may be moved with the consent of a physician, medical examiner or coroner. An out-of-state disposition permit can be obtained from a funeral director or the Bureau of Vital Records.

▶ **Burial**

Home burial is permissible in Missouri. Land, not to exceed one acre, must be deeded in trust and the deed filed with the county court within 60 days. There are no state burial statutes or regulations with regard to depth. The state does not require a permit for disposition. Check with the local registrar for zoning laws regarding home burial.

▶ **Cremation**

While there is no state-required permit for cremation, a crematory will expect verbal or written permission from the physician certifying the cause of death. If the death certificate has been completed, this may serve. Most crematories insist that a pacemaker be removed, and authorization by next-of-kin usually is required.

▶ **Other Requirements**

If the destination cannot be reached within 24 hours, a body must be embalmed or encased in an airtight metal or metal-lined burial case that is closed and hermetically sealed.

Shipping by common carrier also requires embalming or a hermetically sealed coffin.

Embalming or the use of a hermetically sealed coffin is required if death is due to Asiatic cholera, typhus, typhoid or ship fever, yellow fever, bubonic plague, diphtheria, scarlet fever, glanders, anthrax, leprosy, TB, puerperal fever, erysipelas, measles or "other dangerous or communicable diseases."

▶ **Crematories**

Parker Crematory
10th & Walnut
Columbia, MO 65201
314-449-4153
Independent
Available: 24 hours

Cost of cremation only: $135
Body container requirements:
  rigid combustible
Cardboard casket: $80
Cost of mailing cremains:
  postage
Payment: at time of delivery,
  negotiable

D.W. Newcomer's Sons
1331 Brush Creek Blvd.
Kansas City, MO 64110
816-561-0024
Funeral home affiliated
Available: 24 hours

Cost of cremation only: $160
Body container requirements:
  rigid combustible
Cardboard casket: $50
Cost of mailing cremains: $12
Payment: at time of delivery,
  negotiable

Parklawn Crematory
8251 Hillcrest Rd.
Kansas City, MO 64138
816-523-1233
Parklawn Funeral Home
Available: 24 hours

Cost of cremation only: $70
Body container requirements:
  rigid combustible
Cardboard casket: not carried
Cost of mailing cremains: $15
Payment: at time of delivery,
  negotiable

Memorial Park Cemetery
Hwy. 70 at Lucas & Hunt Rd.
St. Louis, MO 63121
314-389-3500
nights: 993-5258
Independent
Available: 9-4:30 daily

Cost of cremation only: $140
Body container requirements:
 rigid combustible
Cardboard casket: not carried
Cost of mailing cremains:
 postage
Payment: at time of delivery

Valhalla Chapel of Memories
7600 St. Charles Rock Rd.
St. Louis, MO 63133
314-721-4900
Independent
Available: 10-4 M-Sat.,
 24-hour phone

Cost of cremation only: $145
Body container requirements:
 rigid combustible
Cardboard casket: $24
Cost of mailing cremains: $15
Payment: at time of delivery,
 negotiable

Greenlawn Funeral Home &
 Crematory
3506 N. National Blvd.
Springfield, MO 65803
417-833-1111
Available: 24 hours

Cost of cremation only: $345
Body container requirements:
 rigid combustible
Cardboard casket: not carried
Cost of mailing cremains:
 included
Payment: negotiable

Four other crematories declined to accept a body from other
than a funeral director: two in Kansas City, and one each in
St. Louis and Springfield. Their concerns were, "we will lose
all of our business,". . . "it's not legal,". . . "not proper. . .
don't want more trouble than it's worth,". . ."we deal directly
with the funeral director."

There may be additional crematories that are not on the lists
I used for this research.

▶ **Body Donation**

Logan College of Chiropractic
1851 Schoettler Rd.
P.O. Box 100
Chesterfield, MO 63017
314-227-2100, ext. 135
314-962-0271

Cost to family: transportation
 over $75
Prior enrollment: not required
Over-enrollment: not shared
Disposition: cremation/burial
 of cremains on school
 grounds
Body rejection: AIDS, autopsy
(rare exceptions)

University of Missouri -
Columbia
Department of Anatomy
School of Medicine
Columbia, MO 65212
314-882-2288

Cost to family: transportation
Prior enrollment: required
Over-enrollment: shared
Disposition: cremation/burial
of cremains in local
cemetery
Body rejection: standard*,
under 18, other dangerous
infection

Cleveland Chiropractic
College
6401 Rockhill Rd.
Kansas City, MO 64131

Because it does not have
facilities for embalming
Cleveland Chiropractic
College obtains it bodies
through other schools in the
state.

University of Missouri -
Kansas City
Department of Anatomy
2411 Holmes St.
Kansas City, MO 64108
816-276-1984
474-8831

Cost to family: transportation
beyond 50 miles
Prior enrollment: not required
Over-enrollment: shared
Disposition: cremation; return
of cremains by request
Body rejection: standard*
All prior donations accepted.

Kirksville College of
Osteopathic Medicine
800 W. Jefferson
Kirksville, MO 63501
816-626-2468

Cost to family: embalming,
transportation
Prior enrollment: preferred
but not required
Over-enrollment: shared
Disposition: cremation; return
of cremains by request
Body rejection: standard*,
under 12

St. Louis University
School of Medicine
Department of Anatomy
1402 South Grand Blvd.
St. Louis, MO 63104
314-577-8271
nights: 577-8078

Cost to family: transportation
Prior enrollment: required
Over-enrollment: shared
Disposition: cremation/burial
of cremains by school
Body rejection: previous
embalming unless with
school permission, autopsy

Washington University
Department of Anatomy
4566 Scott Ave.
St. Louis, MO 63110
314-362-3597

Cost to family: transportation
Prior enrollment: required
Over-enrollment: shared
Disposition: cremains are
    scattered on University
    hillside; no return of
    cremains
Body rejection: autopsy, burn
    victim, decomposition,
    mutilation, previous
    embalming

*autopsy, decomposition, mutilation, severe burn victim,
meningitis, hepatitis, AIDS

▸ **State Funeral Board**

The Missouri State Board of Embalmers and Funeral Directors
has six members. There is one consumer representative.

(This section was reviewed by the Missouri Department of
Health, Bureau of Vital Records.)

In Montana

Please refer to Chapter 9 as you use this section.

Persons in Montana may care for their own dead. The legal
authority to do so is found in:

Title 35-21-301: Right to control disposition of remains-

The right to control the disposition of the remains of a
deceased person, unless other directions have been given
by the deceased, vests in. . .
   a) the surviving spouse
   b) the surviving children of the decedent
   c) the surviving parents of the decedent

There are no other statutes or regulations which might
require you to use a funeral director when embalming is not
desired.

▶ **Death Certificate**

The family doctor or a local medical examiner will sign the death certificate stating the cause of death. The remaining information must be supplied, typewritten or in black ink. The death certificate must be filed with the local registrar within three days and before final disposition.

▶ **Fetal Death**

A fetal death report is required for each fetal death. All other procedures apply if disposition is handled by the family.

▶ **Transporting and Disposition Permit**

A permit for removal or disposition will be issued by the local registrar. This must be filed with the registrar in the district of disposition within ten days.

▶ **Burial**

Check with the county registrar for local zoning laws regarding home burial. There are no state burial statutes or regulations with regard to depth.

When burial is arranged, the family member acting as the funeral director must sign the authorization for disposition and file it with the local registrar within 10 days.

▶ **Cremation**

The permit for disposition is sufficient for cremation. Most crematories insist that a pacemaker be removed, and authorization by next-of-kin usually is required. The crematory may offer to file the disposition authorization with the registrar.

▶ **Other Requirements**

A "proper covering" is required when a body is transported by private carrier.

A body which will not reach its destination within 48 hours must be embalmed or refrigerated.

The local health officer must be notified (and embalming is required for most) if death is due to anthrax, diphtheria, emphysema, meningococcic meningitis, typhoid and typhus fever, small pox, cholera, pneumonic plague, lassa fever, ebola fever, Marburg virus disease, TB, and any other undiagnosable febrile disease occurring shortly after returning from international travel.

▶ **Crematories**

Terrace Gardens
304 34th St. W.
Billings, MT 59102
406-245-6427
Funeral home affiliated
Available: 24 hours

Cost of cremation only: $165
Body container requirements:
  rigid combustible
Cardboard casket: $50
Cost of mailing cremains: $10
Payment: negotiable

Dahl Funeral Home
P.O. Box 1063
Bozeman, MT 59715
406-586-5298
Available: 24 hours

Cost of cremation only: $195
Body container requirements:
  rigid combustible
Cardboard casket: $60
Cost of mailing cremains:
  included
Payment: negotiable, 30 days

Hillcrest Lawn Memorial
  Association
1410 13th St. South
Great Falls, MT 59403
406-453-3847
Independent
Available: 9-5 M-Sat.

Cost of cremation only: $150
Body container requirements:
  rigid combustible
Cardboard casket: not carried
Cost of mailing cremains: $15
Payment: negotiable

O'Connor Crematory
2425 8th Ave. North
P.O. Box 2374
Great Falls, MT 59403
406-453-7257
Livingston-Malletta Funeral
  Home, 406-549-2857
Available: 24 hours

Cost of cremation only: $150
Body container requirements:
  rigid combustible
Cardboard casket: $35
Cost of mailing cremains: $10
Payment: negotiable

Sunset Memorial Garden
7100 N. Montana
Helena, MT 59601
406-458-5732
Independent
Available: 8-4, on call 24
  hours

Cost of cremation only: $150
Body container requirements:
  rigid combustible
Cardboard casket: not carried
Cost of mailing cremains:
  included
Payment: at time of delivery,
  negotiable

194 **Montana**

Weatherford Crematory
1890 Highway 93 N
Kalispell, MT 59901
406-755-3432
Funeral home affiliated
Available 9-5 M-Sat.

Cost of cremation only: $265
Body container requirements:
rigid combustible
Cardboard casket: $45
Cost of mailing cremains: $10
Payment: negotiable, 30 days

Sunset Memorial Cemetery
7405 Mullan Rd.
Missoula, MT 59802
406-549-2857
Livingston-Malletta Funeral
Home
Available: 9-5 M-F,
24-hour phone

Cost of cremation only: $195
Body container requirements:
rigid combustible
Cardboard casket: available
Cost of mailing cremains: $14
Payment: at time of delivery

One funeral home, in Billings, declined to accept a body from other than a funeral director. "Too much bother outside business hours." This company dealt in vaults as well and personnel were not always available.

There may be additional crematories that are not on the lists I used for this research.

▶ **Body Donation**

There are no medical schools in Montana. Persons considering body donation should check the nearest neighboring state.

▶ **State Funeral Board**

The Montana Board of Morticians has five members. There is one consumer representative.

(This section was reviewed by the Department of Health and Environmental Sciences, Bureau of Records and Statistics.)

In Nebraska

Please refer to Chapter 9 as you use this section.

Persons in Nebraska may not care for their own dead. The terms "funeral director" and "licensed funeral director" are pervasive in all statutes regarding death, including those found in the Public Health and Welfare title.

▸ **Death Certificate**

The family doctor or a local medical examiner will sign the death certificate within 24 hours, stating the cause of death. The remaining information must be supplied, typewritten or in permanent ink. The death certificate must be filed with the Bureau of Vital Statistics within five business days.

▸ **Fetal Death**

A fetal death report is required after 20 weeks of gestation. If there is no family physician involved, the county attorney must be notified. All other procedures apply if disposition is handled by the family.

▸ **Transporting and Disposition Permit**

A transit permit is required for every body shipped out of state. A funeral director will issue this permit.

▸ **Burial**

Check with the county registrar for local zoning laws regarding home burial. Family graveyards are exempt from taxation and must be registered with the county clerk. When burial is arranged, even on private land, it must be under the "direct supervision" of a licensed funeral director. There are no state burial statutes or regulations with regard to depth.

▸ **Cremation**

A permit for cremation must be obtained from the county

attorney. There is no fee for this. Most crematories insist that a pacemaker be removed, and authorization by next-of-kin usually is required.

▶ **Other Requirements**

Nebraska has no other requirements controlling the time schedule for the disposition of unembalmed bodies. Weather and reasonable planning should be considered.

If the person died of a contagious or communicable disease, the doctor in attendance should be consulted.

▶ **Crematories**

Because of the restrictive statutes in Nebraska, I did not contact the crematories in this state.

▶ **Body Donation**

Anatomical Board, State of
  Nebraska
Creighton University and
University of Nebraska
Schools of Medicine
42nd & Dewey Ave.
Omaha, NE 68105
402-280-2914 (Creighton)
402-559-4030 (University of
  Nebraska)
  or: 559-6249
  or: 331-2839

Cost to family: transportation exceeding 200 miles or $184
Prior enrollment: required
Over-enrollment: shared in Nebraska
Disposition: cremation/ burial of cremains in Catholic cemetery; return of cremains by request; return of remains by request and at expense of family
Body rejection: autopsy, decomposition, TB, obesity, emaciation, mutilation, over age 76

▶ **State Funeral Board**

The Nebraska State Board of Embalmers and Funeral Directors has four members. There is one consumer representative.

(The Nebraska section was reviewed by a staff attorney for the Nebraska Department of Health.)

In Nevada

Please refer to Chapter 9 as you use this section.

Persons in Nevada may probably care for their own dead. The
Office of Vital Statistics (Department of Human Resources,
Health Division) accepts a liberal interpretation of the
statutes. According to 1986 correspondence, "The funeral
industry has hotly contested this viewpoint. . . " The
relevant statutes are:

NRS 440.370: **Signature of statements as to disposition of
body.** The statement of facts relating to the disposition
of the body must be signed by the funeral director or
person acting as such.

NRS 642.550: **Applicability of chapter (re funeral directors and embalmers).** Nothing in this chapter shall be
construed to apply: 1. To persons engaged as layers-out
or to those who shroud the dead.

However, NAC 451.100 (1) provides that:

The bodies of persons who have died from any cause
must not be received for transportation by a common
carrier or transported by agencies or other persons
authorized to carry human bodies unless the body has
been embalmed and prepared by an embalmer licensed
under the laws of Nevada.

And NAC 451.120 states:

Nothing in NAC 451.100 to 451.140, inclusive, prohibits or
limits in any respect the transportation of dead human
bodies within Nevada by licensed funeral directors or
embalmers in properly licensed motor vehicles or aircraft
owned, operated, chartered or leased by licensed funeral
directors or mortuaries, nor prohibits the transportation
of embalmed bodies within Nevada by relatives or other
authorized persons.

In 451.100 "persons authorized to carry human bodies" is

stated in the plural and can be reasonably construed as applying to those in business. While NAC 451.120 allows family members to transport an embalmed body, the transportation of an unembalmed body by relatives is apparently not dealt with in the statutes.

To interpret that a body must be embalmed before a family could care for its own dead would make Nevada the only state requiring embalming in a "routine" death. This would be in contradiction of the spirit of the Federal Trade Commission rule, 1-1-86 edition. (See Appendix.)

It is my experience that authorities will go along with your plans if the plans are well-formed and meet public health concerns. One family, in another state that appeared to be restrictive, was allowed to carry out personal wishes by following all regulations carefully. The majority of crematories in this state appeared eager to meet families' needs.

▶ **Death Certificate**

The family doctor, local health officer or coroner will sign the death certificate stating the cause of death. The remaining information must be supplied, typewritten or in black ink. The death certificate must be filed with the local registrar within 72 hours and before final disposition.

▶ **Fetal Death**

A fetal death report is required for each fetal death. If there is no family physician involved, the local health officer or coroner must sign the fetal death certificate. All other procedures apply if disposition is handled by the family.

▶ **Transporting and Disposition Permit**

A body may be moved with the permission of the person certifying death. The local registrar (health officer) will issue the final burial or removal permit. This must be obtained within 72 hours of death.

▶ **Burial**

Check with the county registrar for local zoning laws regarding home burial. There are no state burial statutes or regulations with regard to depth.

When burial is arranged, the family member acting as the

funeral director must sign the burial permit and file it with the local health officer within 10 days.

▶ Cremation

No additional permit is required for cremation. Most crematories insist that a pacemaker be removed, and authorization by next-of-kin usually is required.

▶ Other Requirements

If disposition has not taken place within 18 hours, embalming or refrigeration must be arranged.

If the person died of a contagious or communicable disease, the doctor in attendance should be consulted for state health guidelines. Embalming may be required.

▶ Crematories

Memory Gardens Cemetery &
  Crematory
7251 Lone Mountain Rd.
Las Vegas, NV 89108
702-645-1174
Bunker's Mortuary
702-385-1441
Available: 8-4:30 M-F,
  24-hour phone

Cost of cremation only: $125
Body container requirements:
  rigid combustible
Cardboard casket: $40
Cost of mailing cremains: $35
Payment: at time of delivery

Palm Mausoleum and
Memorial Park
1325 N. Main St.
Las Vegas, NV 89101
702-382-1340
Funeral home affiliated
Available: 24 hours

Cost of cremation only: $132
Body container requirements:
  rigid combustible
Cardboard casket: available
Cost of mailing cremains: $40
Payment: at time of delivery,
  negotiable

Paradise Valley Chapel
6200 S. Eastern Ave.
Las Vegas, NV 89119
702-736-6200
Davis Funeral Home
Available: 24 hours

Cost of cremation only: $160
Body container requirements:
  rigid combustible
Cardboard casket: not carried
Cost of mailing cremains: $35
Payment: at time of delivery

One crematory in Reno declined to answer any questions. Because the gentleman said he was busy I eagerly volunteered to call back at his convenience, but he replied, "I don't have any time."

There may be additional crematories that are not on the lists I used for this research.

▶ **Body Donation**

University of Nevada
Department of Anatomy
School of Medicine
Reno, NV 89557
702-784-6113
    784-6169

(This school has temporarily restricted new bequests because of the large number of currently enrolled donors on file.)

Cost to family: transportation costs above $75
Prior enrollment: required, except in rare cases
Over-enrollment: only a few shared
Disposition: cremation
Body rejection: autopsy, decomposition, missing limbs, suicide, meningitis, hepatitis, AIDS, other infectious diseases

▶ **State Funeral Board**

The Nevada State Board of Embalmers and Funeral Directors has three members. There is one consumer representative.

(This section was sent to the Nevada Department of Health for review, but no response was received by the publication date.)

In New Hampshire

Please refer to Chapter 9 as you use this section.

Persons in New Hampshire probably may not care for their own dead. The legal restrictions are found in:

Title 290:3 **Burial Permits, Obtaining.** It shall be the duty of the funeral director to add to the death certificate the date and place of burial, and having signed the same, to forward it to the clerk of the town, and obtain a permit for burial.

Title 290:11 **Transfer of Body.** No body of a human being may be released or transferred from any residence, hospital, or other facility to any person other than a funeral director or his designee, who shall be responsible for the completion of forms as required. . .

▸ **Death Certificate**

The family doctor or a local medical examiner will sign the death certificate stating the cause of death. The remaining information must be supplied, typewritten or in black ink. The death certificate must be filed with the local town clerk by a licensed funeral director.

▸ **Fetal Death**

A fetal death report is required for each fetal death. All other procedures apply if disposition is handled by the family.

▸ **Transporting and Disposition Permit**

The town clerk will issue a burial permit to a funeral director only.

▸ **Burial**

Check with the town clerk for local zoning laws regarding home burial. No cemetery shall be laid out within 100 feet of any dwelling house, schoolhouse or school lot, store or other place of business without the consent of the owner of the same and may not be laid out within 50 feet of the right-of-way of all classifications of highways. There are no state burial statutes or regulations with regard to depth.

▸ **Cremation**

A permit for cremation must be obtained from the medical examiner. The usual fee for this is $15. There is a 48-hour wait before cremation unless death was due to a contagious or infectious disease. Most crematories insist that a pacemaker be removed, and authorization by next-of-kin usually is required.

▸ **Other Requirements**

New Hampshire has no other requirements controlling the

time schedule for the disposition of unembalmed bodies. Weather and reasonable planning should be considered.

If the person died of a contagious or communicable disease, the doctor in attendance should be consulted.

▶ **Crematories**

Because of the restrictive statutes in New Hampshire I did not contact any crematories in this state.

▶ **Body Donation**

Dartmouth Medical School
Department of Anatomy
Hanover, NH 03756
8-4: 603-646-7636
after hours: 646-5000
 (Hitchcock Medical Center)

Cost to family: none
Prior enrollment: required
Over-enrollment: not shared
Disposition: cremation/burial
 of cremains in college plot;
 return of cremains to
 family by request
Body rejection: standard*,
 over-enrollment, previous
 embalming, under 21

*autopsy, decomposition, mutilation, severe burn victim, meningitis, hepatitis, AIDS

▶ **State Funeral Board**

The New Hampshire State Board of Embalmers and Funeral Directors has four members. There is one consumer representative.

(This section was reviewed by the New Hampshire Department of Health, Bureau of Vital Records.)

In New Jersey

Please refer to Chapter 9 as you use this section.

Persons in New Jersey probably may not care for their own dead. The restrictive statutes are found in:

Title 26:6-6 **Death certificate and Burial or Removal Permit** - The funeral director in charge of the funeral or disposition of the body of any person dying in this State shall be responsible for the proper execution of a death certificate.

Title 26:6-31 **Delivery of burial or removal papers** - The undertaker shall deliver the burial or removal permit . . . to the person in charge of the place of burial or of final disposition before interring or otherwise disposing of the body.

It is my experience that authorities will go along with your plans if the plans are well-formed and meet public health concerns. One family, in another state that appeared to be blatantly restrictive was allowed to carry out personal wishes by following all regulations carefully.

▸ **Death Certificate**

The family doctor or medical examiner (or registered nurse in the case of an expected death as in a nursing home or hospice setting) will sign the death certificate stating the cause of death. The remaining information must be supplied, typewritten or in durable blue or black ink. The death certificate must be filed with the registrar of the district where death occurred or where disposition will take place.

▸ **Fetal Death**

A fetal death report is required after 20 weeks of gestation. If there is no family physician involved, the local medical examiner must sign the fetal death certificate. All other procedures apply if disposition is handled by the family.

▸ **Transporting and Disposition Permit**

The registrar will issue the burial, removal, or transit permit. The fee is $1.00. If no registrar is available, a judge or magistrate may issue an emergency permit. No additional permit is required when disposition occurs in a district away from the district where death occurred.

▸ **Burial**

Check with the local registrar for zoning laws regarding home burial. The top of the coffin shall be at least four feet below the natural surface of the ground.

The person in charge of burial must file the permit with the local registrar within 10 days. If there is no person in charge, the funeral director must write across the face of the permit, "No person in charge," and file accordingly.

▶ **Cremation**

There is a 24-hour wait before cremation. Most crematories insist that a pacemaker be removed, and authorization by next-of-kin usually is required.

▶ **Other Requirements**

New Jersey has no other requirements controlling the time schedule for the disposition of unembalmed bodies. Weather and reasonable planning should be considered.

If the person died of a contagious or communicable disease, the doctor in attendance should be consulted for the guidelines issued by the state.

▶ **Crematories**

Because of the restrictive statutes in this state, I did not contact any crematories in New Jersey.

▶ **Body Donation**

Fairleigh Dickinson
University
College of Dental Medicine
140 University Plaza Drive
Hackensack, NJ 07601
201-692-2577/2571 9-5
201-748-0240

Cost to family: transportation beyond 100 mile radius; disposition if burial is preferred
Prior enrollment: not required
Over-enrollment: shared
Disposition: cremation; return of cremains or remains by request
Body rejection: standard*, missing major body parts, extensive surgery on dental area

UMDNJ
Robert Wood Johnson Medical
  School
Rutgers Pathology and
  Anatomy Association
P.O. Box 101
Piscataway, NJ 08854
201-463-4580
  other times: 463-4586

Cost to family: transportation
  outside New Jersey
Prior enrollment: not required
Over-enrollment: shared
Disposition: cremation/ burial
  of cremains in college plot;
  return of cremains by
  request ($15)
Body rejection: standard*,
  TB, previous embalming

*autopsy, decomposition, mutilation, severe burn victim,
meningitis, hepatitis, AIDS

▶ **State Funeral Board**

The New Jersey Board of Mortuary Science has five members.
There are no consumer representatives.

(This section was reviewed by telephone with the New Jersey
Department of Health.)

In New Mexico

Please refer to Chapter 9 as you use this section.

Persons in New Mexico may care for their own dead. The
legal authority to do so is found in these and ensuing
statutes:

Title 24-14-20: **Death registration.** The funeral science
practitioner or person acting as a funeral science
practitioner who first assumes custody of the dead body
shall file the death certificate.

Title 24-14-23: **Permits; authorization for final
disposition.** . . B. A burial-transit permit shall be issued
by the state registrar or a local registrar for those
bodies which are to be transported out of the state for
final disposition or when final disposition is being made
by a person other than a funeral service practitioner or
direct disposer.

There are no other statutes or regulations which might require you to use a funeral director when embalming is not desired.

The Medical Investigator's Office is eager to assist with information and guidance regarding disposition arrangements. The central office is in Albuquerque, 505-277-3053.

▶ **Death Certificate**

The family doctor or a medical investigator will sign the death certificate within 48 hours, stating the cause of death. The remaining information must be supplied, typewritten or in black ink. Do not use a felt-tip pen; there are five copies. The death certificate must be filed with any registrar within five days and before final disposition.

▶ **Fetal Death**

A fetal death report is required when the weight is 500 grams or more. If there is no family physician involved, the state medical investigator must sign the fetal death certificate. The fetal death certificate must be filed with state registrar within ten days. All other procedures apply if disposition is handled by the family.

▶ **Transporting and Disposition Permit**

A body may be moved with medical permission. No burial-transit permit is required if disposition is under the direction of a funeral service practitioner or direct disposer and if disposition occurs within the state. In other cases, the local registrar must sign the burial-transit permit (page four of the death certificate) before final disposition.

▶ **Burial**

Check with the county registrar for local zoning laws regarding home burial. Prior arrangements must be made with the county clerk's office to record a map designating the burial site. There are no state burial statutes or regulations with regard to depth. Unless the registrar in the district of disposition requests the burial-transit permit, persons acting as the sexton should retain it for their records.

▶ **Cremation**

A permit for cremation must be obtained from the state

medical investigator. There is no charge for this when a family is handling arrangements. Most crematories insist that a pacemaker be removed, and authorization by next-of-kin usually is required.

▶ **Other Requirements**

New Mexico has no other requirements controlling the time schedule for the disposition of unembalmed bodies. Weather and reasonable planning should be considered.

If the person died of a contagious or communicable disease, the Office of the Medical Investigator should be consulted. Embalming or a sealed casket may be required.

The County Finance Office can assist family members whenever they cannot afford burial expenses.

▶ **Crematories**

Fairview Memorial Park
700 Yale Blvd.
Albuquerque, NM 87106
505-262-1454
Independent
Available: 8-4:30 M-F,
    8-12 Sat.

Cost of cremation only: $125
Body container requirements:
    rigid combustible, plywood
    bottom
Cardboard casket: not carried
Cost of mailing cremains: $15
Payment: at time of delivery

Sunrise at Vista Verde
Sara Rd. at Meadowlark Ln.
Albuquerque, NM 87124
505-892-9920
Independent
Available: 24-hour phone

Cost of cremation only: $125
Body container requirements:
    rigid combustible
Cardboard casket: $35
Cost of mailing cremains: $20
Payment: at time of delivery,
    negotiable

Sunset Memorial Park
924 Menaul N.E. , P.O. Box 94
Albuquerque, NM 87125
505-345-3536
French Mortuary
505-843-6333
Available: 8-5 M-F, 8-12 Sat.,
  24-hour phone

Cost of cremation only: $150
Body container requirements:
  rigid combustible
Cardboard casket: $35
Cost of mailing cremains: $15
Payment: at time of delivery,
  negotiable

McGee Memorial Chapel
1320 Luisa St.
Santa Fe, NM 87501
505-983-9151
Funeral home affiliated
Available: 24 hours

Cost of cremation only: $145
Body container requirements:
  rigid combustible
Cardboard casket: $75
Cost of mailing cremains: $15
Payment: at time of delivery

Two crematories declined to accept a body from other than a funeral director, one in Deming and one in Dona Ana County. One was a cremation service with an answering machine and never returned my calls. The other said a "family couldn't get the permits."

There may be additional crematories that are not on the lists I used for this research.

▶ **Body Donation**

University of New Mexico
Department of Anatomy
Albuquerque, NM 87131
505-277-5555 or
medical investigator:
505-277-3053

Cost to family: transportation
  outside of New Mexico
Prior enrollment: preferred
  but not required
Over-enrollment: not shared
Disposition: burial or
  cremation by request of
  family
Body rejection: autopsy,
  missing extremities,
  infectious diseases,
  embalming if not under
  direction of school

▶ **State Funeral Board**

The New Mexico Board of Thanatopractice has five members. Three are funeral directors, one is a representative of the medical providers, and one is a consumer representative.

(The New Mexico section was reviewed by the Office of the Medical Investigator, and the Registrar of Vital Records, Health Department, State of New Mexico.)

In New York

Please refer to Chapter 9 as you use this section.

Persons in New York may care for their own dead in a very limited way. The restrictive statutes are found in:

> Title 4 sec. 4140. **Deaths; registration** 2. . . . no permit for the removal or other disposition of the body shall be issued by the registrar, except to a funeral director or undertaker licensed. . .

In addition, under the Sanitary Code, section 77.7 "Funeral Directing" subsection (b-1) states:

> In no case shall a dead human body be released from any hospital, institution or other place where the death occurred or from the place where the body is held by legal authority to any person not a duly licensed and registered funeral director or undertaker.

And subsection (a-4) requires:

> A licensed funeral director or undertaker shall be present and personally supervise the interment or cremation or the pick-up from or the delivery to a common carrier of a dead human body.

However, subsection (f) of the same article reads:

> Nothing contained in this section shall be deemed to require that a mere transporter, to whom or to which a dead human body has been duly released for the sole purpose of transportation or transfer, shall be a duly licensed and registered funeral director or undertaker.

That is, a family in New York, after hiring the services of a funeral director to obtain the burial-transit permit for disposition and to gain the release of the body if death occurred in a hospital, may transport the body privately. However, if disposition is within the state, there must be a funeral director present at the time of delivery to a crematory or even for burial on private land. In the five other states where a funeral director must sign the death certificate or obtain the burial-transit permit before a family takes over, charges ranged from "No charge. . . we would do it as a courtesy" to "Well, our charge for professional services is $465." A more common response was $45 or $50. I did not survey the per-hour cost of a funeral director's presence at a burial or crematory in New York.

▸ **Death Certificate**

The family doctor, coroner or local medical examiner will sign the death certificate stating the cause of death. The remaining information must be supplied, typewritten or in black ink. The death certificate must be filed with the local registrar within 72 hours and before final disposition.

▸ **Fetal Death**

A fetal death report is required for each fetal death. If there is no family physician involved, the local medical examiner must sign the fetal death certificate. All other procedures apply if disposition is handled by the family.

▸ **Transporting and Disposition Permit**

The local registrar will issue the burial and removal permit to a licensed funeral director only. This authorization must be obtained within 72 hours of death and prior to final disposition of the body. During transportation the body shall be obscured from public view.

▸ **Burial**

Any person may dedicate land to be used as a family cemetery provided that it is less than three acres and not closer than 100 rods to a dwelling house. Such land must be registered with the county clerk. Check with the county clerk for local zoning laws regarding home burial. There are no state burial statutes or regulations with regard to depth.

When a body is buried in a cemetery or burial place where no person is in charge, the funeral director shall sign the permit and write across the face of the permit the words "No person in charge." The permit must be filed within three days with the registrar of the district in which burial took place.

▶ **Cremation**

No additional permit is needed for cremation. Most crematories insist that a pacemaker be removed, and authorization by next-of-kin usually is required. The crematory will file the disposition permit with the local registrar. If there is no licensed funeral director on the crematory staff, the family must arrange for a funeral director to be present at the time of delivery.

▶ **Other Requirements**

New York has no other requirements controlling the time schedule for the disposition of unembalmed bodies. Weather and reasonable planning should be considered.

If the person died of a contagious or communicable disease, the doctor in attendance should be consulted for state guidelines.

▶ **Crematories with at least one staff member who is a licensed funeral director and which will accept a body directly from a family:**

Cayuga Crematorium, Inc.
55 W. Main St.
Dryden, NY 13053
607-844-8161
Available: 8-5 M-F,
   weekends by arrangement

Cost of cremation only: $125
Body container requirements:
   rigid combustible
Cardboard casket: $75
Cost of mailing cremains:
   included
Payment: at time of delivery

Whispering Maples Memorial
   Gardens
P.O. Box 163
Ellenburg Depot, NY 12935
518-594-7500
Available: 24 hours

Cost of cremation only: $125
Body container requirements:
   rigid combustible
Chipboard casket: $50
Cost of mailing cremains: $10
Payment: at time of delivery

Southern Tier Memorial
  Crematory
46 E. Falconer St.
Falconer, NY
716-665-4455
or 484-2241
Available: 8-5 M-Sat.
  and by arrangement

Cost of cremation only: $115
Body container requirements:
  rigid combustible
Cardboard casket: $65
Cost of mailing cremains:
  included
Payment: at time of delivery

Albany Rural Chapel and
  Crematory
Cemetery Ave.
Menands, NY 12204
518-463-7017
Available: 24 hours

Cost of cremation only: $125
Body container requirements:
  rigid combustible
Cardboard casket: $20
Cost of mailing cremains: $10
Payment: at time of delivery

Parkview Crematory
Fehr Ave.
Schenectady, NY 12309
518-377-3657
Griswolds Funeral Home
518-374-6188
Available 8-5 M-Sat.,
  24-hour phone

Cost of cremation only: $125
Body container requirements:
  rigid combustible
Cardboard casket: not carried
Cost of mailing cremains:
  $7.50
Payment: at time of delivery

Two such crematories, in Endicott and West Babylon, declined
to accept a body from other than another funeral director.

▸ **Crematories which have no funeral director on staff:**

The Woodlawn Cemetery
20 W. 233rd & Webster Ave.
Bronx, NY 10470
212-920-0500
Independent
Available: 9-4:30 M-Sat.

Cost of cremation only: $140
Body container requirements:
  rigid combustible
Cardboard casket: not carried
Cost of mailing cremains:
  included
Payment: at time of delivery

The Green-Wood Cemetery
17 Battery Place
Brooklyn, NY 10004
718-768-7300
Available: 8:30-3:30 M-Sat.

Cost of cremation only: $197
Body container requirements:
  rigid combustible
Cardboard casket: not carried
Cost of mailing cremains:
  included
Payment: at time of delivery

Buffalo Cremation Co. Ltd.
901 W. Delavan Avenue
Buffalo, NY 14209
716-885-3079
Independent
Available: 8-4:15 M-Sat.,
  9-1:30 Sun.

Cost of cremation only: $85
Body container requirements:
  rigid combustible
Cardboard casket: not carried
Cost of mailing cremains:
  $3-$6
Payment: at time of delivery,
  negotiable

Forest Lawn Cemetery
1411 Delaware Avenue
Buffalo, NY 14209
716-885-1600
Independent
Available: 8:30-4:30 M-Sat.,
  10-4 Sun.

Cost of cremation only: $110
Body container requirements:
  rigid combustible
Cardboard casket: not carried
Cost of mailing cremains:
  included
Payment: negotiable

Washington Memorial Park
Canal Road
Coram, NY 11727
516-473-0437
Available: 9-4 M-Sat.,
  Sun. by arrangement

Cost of cremation only: $110
Body container requirements:
  rigid combustible
Cardboard casket: not carried
Cost of mailing cremains:
  included
Payment: at time of delivery

Ferncliff Cemetery Assn.
Secor Road
Hartsdale, NY 10530
914-693-4700
Independent
Available: 8-4:30 daily

Cost of cremation only: $123
Body container requirements:
  rigid combustible
Cardboard casket: not carried
Cost of mailing cremains: $21
Payment: at time of delivery

Elmlawn Cemetery and
  Crematory
3939 Delaware Avenue
Kenmore, NY 14217
716-876-8131
Available: 9-4:30 M-Sat.,
  Sun. by arrangement

Cost of cremation only: $100
Body container requirements:
  rigid combustible
Cardboard casket: not carried
Cost of mailing cremains:
  postage
Payment: at time of delivery

Niagara Falls Memorial Park
5871 Military Rd.
Lewiston, NY 14092
716-297-0811
Lanes Funeral Home affiliated
716-283-9660
Available: 9-4 M-F,
  or by arrangement

Cost of cremation only: $95
Body container requirements:
  rigid combustible
Cardboard casket: not carried
Cost of mailing cremains: $10
Payment: at time of delivery

Fresh Pond Crematory
61-40 Mt. Olivet Crescent
Middle Village, NY 11379
718-821-9700
Available: 9-4 M-Sat.

Cost of cremation only: $135
Body container requirements:
  rigid combustible
Cardboard casket: not carried
Cost of mailing cremains: $10
Payment: at time of delivery

Trinity Church Cemetery and
  Crematory
770 Riverside Dr.
New York, NY 10032
212-602-0787
Available: 8-8 daily

Cost of cremation only: $120
Body container requirements:
  rigid combustible
Cardboard casket: not carried
Cost of mailing cremains: $10
Payment: at time of delivery

Cedar Hill Cemetery Assn.
706-720 Rt. 9W North
Newburgh, NY 12550
914-562-0505
Available: 8-4:30 M-Sat.,
  24-hour phone

Cost of cremation only: $100
Body container requirements:
  rigid combustible
Cardboard casket: not carried
Cost of mailing cremains:
  included
Payment: at time of delivery

Oakwood Cemetery Assn.
763 Portage Road
Niagara Falls, NY 14301
716-284-5131
Available: 8-4:30 M-F,
  Sat. by arrangement

Cost of cremation only: $90
Body container requirements:
  rigid combustible
Cardboard casket: not carried
Cost of mailing cremains:
  postage
Payment: at time of delivery

South Port Crematory, Inc.
P.O. Box 136
Pine City, NY 14871
607-734-7373
Olthof Funeral Home
  affiliated
Available: 24 hours

Cost of cremation only: $125
Body container requirements:
  rigid combustible
Cardboard casket: $15
Cost of mailing cremains:
  included
Payment: at time of delivery

White Haven Memorial Park
210 Marsh Road
Pittsford, NY 14534
716-586-5250
Available: 8-4:30 M-F
  8-12 Sat.

Cost of cremation only: $110
Body container requirements:
  rigid combustible
Cardboard casket: not carried
Cost of mailing cremains:
  postage
Payment: at time of delivery

Poughkeepsie Rural Cemetery
342 South Rd.
P.O. Box 977
Poughkeepsie, NY 12602
914-454-6020
Available: 8-4:30 M-F,
  8-12 Sat.

Cost of cremation only: $125
Body container requirements:
  rigid combustible
Cardboard casket: available
Cost of mailing cremains: $10
Payment: at time of delivery

Mt. Hope Cemetery and
  Crematory
1133 Mt. Hope Ave.
Rochester, NY 14620
716-473-2755
Available: 7:30-3:30 M-Sat.

Cost of cremation only: $125
Body container requirements:
  rigid combustible
Cardboard casket: not carried
Cost of mailing cremains:
  postage
Payment: at time of delivery

Oakwood-Morningside Cem.
1001 Comstock Ave., P.O.
  Box 9, Colvin Station
Syracuse, NY 13205
315-475-2194
Available: 8-5 M-F,
  8-1 Sat.

Cost of cremation only: $135
Body container requirements:
  rigid combustible
Cardboard casket: not carried
Cost of mailing cremains:
  postage
Payment: negotiable

Gardner-Earle Memorial
  Chapel
Head of 101 St.
Troy, NY 12180
518-272-7520
Available: 9-4:30 M-F,
  9-12 Sat. or by
  arrangement,
  24-hour phone

Cost of cremation only: $125
Body container requirements:
  rigid combustible
Cardboard casket: not carried
Cost of mailing cremains:
  included
Payment: negotiable

Vestal Hills Memorial Park
3997 Vestal Road
Vestal, NY 13850
607-797-8407
Available: 24 hours

Cost of cremation only: $100
Body container requirements:
  rigid combustible
Cardboard casket: not carried
Cost of mailing cremains:
  included
Payment: negotiable

Waterville Cemetery Assn.
4883 Waterville Road
P.O. Box 2
Waterville, NY 13480
315-841-4883
Available: 24 hours

Cost of cremation only: $135
Body container requirements:
  rigid combustible
Cardboard casket: not carried
Cost of mailing cremains:
  included
Payment: at time of delivery

There may be additional crematories that are not on the lists I used for this research.

▶ **Body Donation**

Union University
Albany Medical College
Albany, NY 12208
518-445-5379 or 5375
after hours: 445-3125

Cost to family: transportation
  beyond 120 miles or $150
Prior enrollment: not required
Over-enrollment: shared
Disposition: cremation/burial
  of cremains in school plot;
  return of cremains by
  request
Body rejection: hepatitis,
decomposition, AIDS, TB

Yeshiva University
Albert Einstein College of
  Medicine
Bronx, NY 10461

Repeated requests for
information have not been
returned from this school.

S.U.N.Y.
Health Science Center at
  Brooklyn
450 Clarkson Ave.
Brooklyn, NY 11203
718-270-1014 or 2379
Any time:
718-227-1402 or 235-0505

Cost to family: transportation
  beyond 100 miles
Prior enrollment: not required
Over-enrollment: shared
Disposition: cremation/burial
  of cremains in school plot;
  return of remains or
  cremains by request at
  expense of family
Body rejection: autopsy,
  missing body parts, burn
  victim, decomposition,
  AIDS, under 10, previous
  embalming

S.U.N.Y.
Department of Anatomical
  Sciences
Buffalo, NY 14214
716-831-2912
other times:
834-8128

Cost to family: transportation
  beyond 100 miles
Prior enrollment: preferred
  but not always required
Over-enrollment: shared
Disposition: cremation/burial
  of cremains in University
  plot (Catholic or non-
  denominational)
Body rejection: standard*,
  under 18, previous
embalming

N.Y. Chiropractic College
P.O. Box 167
Glen Head, NY 11545

Repeated requests for
information have not been
returned from this school

City University of New York
Mt. Sinai School of Medicine
New York, NY 10029

Repeated requests for
information have not been
returned from this school

Columbia University
College of Physicians and
  Surgeons
630 West 168th St.
New York, NY 10032
212-305-3451

Cost to family: transportation
  beyond 100 miles
Prior enrollment: not required
Over-enrollment: shared
Disposition: cremation/burial
  of cremains in University
  plot; return of cremains by
  request and at cost of
  family
Body rejection: standard*,
  obesity, under 21, previous
  embalming

Cornell University
Medical College
Dept. of Cell Biology &
Anatomy
1300 York Ave.
New York, NY 10021
212-472-6400

Cost to family: transportation
beyond 60 miles
Prior enrollment: not required
Over-enrollment: has not
occurred
Disposition: city burial or
cremation; no return
Body rejection: under 18,
autopsy, AIDS, decompo-
sition

New York University
School of Medicine
New York, NY 10016
212-340-5360

Cost to family: transportation
outside Manhattan, case by
case
Prior enrollment: not required
Over-enrollment: has not
occurred
Disposition: burial or
cremation; return by
request
Body rejection: standard*,
previous embalming

New York Institute of
Technology
Old Westbury, NY 11568

Repeated requests for
information have not been
returned from this school.

University of Rochester
School of Medicine
Rochester, NY 14642

Repeated requests for
information have not been
returned from this school.

S.U.N.Y.
School of Medicine
Stony Brook, NY 11794
516-444-3111 or
599-0041

Cost to family: transportation
beyond 50 miles
Prior enrollment: not required
Over-enrollment: shared
Disposition: cremation
Body rejection: autopsy,
decomposition, AIDS, under
16, previous embalming

S.U.N.Y.
Health Science Center at
  Syracuse
Department of Anatomy and
Cell Biology
766 Irving Ave.
Syracuse, NY 13210
315-473-5120 or
473-5280

Cost to family: transportation
  beyond 200 miles at 23
  cents per mile
Prior enrollment: not required
Over-enrollment: shared
Disposition: cremation/burial
  of cremains in University
  plot; return of cremains by
  request
Body rejection: autopsy,
  decomposition, under 13

New York Medical College
Valhalla, NY 10595

Repeated requests for
information have not been
returned from this school

▸ **State Funeral Board**

Funeral directors in New York are regulated by the Department of Health. The New York State Board of Embalmers and Funeral Directors serves in an advisory capacity. It has ten members. There are four consumer representatives.

(This section was reviewed by the New York State Department of Health.)

In North Carolina

Please refer to Chapter 9 as you use this section.

Persons in North Carolina may care for their own dead. The legal authority to do so is found in this and ensuing statutes:

General Statute 130A-112 **Notification of Death.**
A. A funeral director or person acting as such who first assumes custody of a dead body or fetus of 20 completed weeks gestation or more shall submit a notification of death to the local registrar in the county where death . occurred within 24 hours of taking custody of the body or fetus. . .

There are no other statutes or regulations which might require you to use a funeral director when embalming is not desired.

▶ **Death Certificate**

A Notification of Death can be obtained from a registrar. This must be completed within 24 hours. The registrar will keep one copy; the other copy is for your records.

The family doctor or a local medical examiner will sign the death certificate within three days stating the cause of death. The remaining information must be supplied, type-written or in black ink. The death certificate must be filed with the local registrar within five days and before final disposition.

▶ **Fetal Death**

A fetal death report is required after 20 weeks of gestation. If there is no family physician involved, the local medical examiner must sign the fetal death certificate. All other procedures apply if disposition is handled by the family.

▶ **Transporting and Disposition Permit**

The physician or local medical examiner will authorize disposition. A burial-transit permit is required only if out-of-state disposition is planned or when the death is under the jurisdiction of the medical examiner. It is the third copy of the medical examiner's death certificate. In other cases, the burial-transit permit may be obtained from the local registrar at no cost.

▶ **Burial**

Check with the county registrar for local zoning laws regarding home burial. There are no state burial statutes or regulations with regard to depth.

▶ **Cremation**

A permit for cremation must be obtained from the local medical examiner. The usual fee for this is $10. Most crematories insist that a pacemaker be removed, and authorization by next-of-kin usually is required.

▶ **Other Requirements**

North Carolina has no other requirements controlling the time schedule for the disposition of unembalmed bodies. Weather and reasonable planning should be considered.

If the person died of a contagious or communicable disease, the doctor in attendance should be consulted.

▶ **Crematories**

Maple Springs Crematory
304 Merrimon Ave.
Ashville, NC 28804
704-252-1821
Morris Funeral Home
Available: 24 hours

Cost of cremation only: $175
Body container requirements:
  rigid combustible
Cardboard casket: $35
Cost of mailing cremains:
  postage
Payment: negotiable

Triangle Cremation Service
P.O. Box 2070
Chapel Hill, NC 27514
919-732-8605
Independent
Available: 24 hours

Cost of cremation only: $125
Body container requirements:
  none
Cardboard casket: included
Cost of mailing cremains: $20
Payment: negotiable

Vogler Crematory
Middlebrook Dr.
Clemmons, NC 27012
919-766-4714
Funeral home affiliated
Available: 24 hours

Cost of cremation only: $150
Body container requirements:
  wrapped
Cardboard casket: available
Cost of mailing cremains: $10
Payment: negotiable

Carolina Memorial Park
P.O. Box 3257
Concord, NC 28025
704-786-2161
Independent
Available: 8:30-5 M-F,
  8:30-1 Sat.

Cost of cremation only: $135
Body container requirements:
  rigid combustible
Cardboard casket: included
Cost of mailing cremains: $20
Payment: at time of delivery

Guilford Crematory
5926 W. Friendly Ave.
Greensboro, NC 27419
919-299-9171
Funeral home affiliated
Available: 24 hours

Cost of cremation only: $125
Body container requirements:
 wrapped
Cardboard casket: available
Cost of mailing cremains:
 postage
Payment: negotiable

Westminster Gardens, Inc.
3601 Whitehurst Rd.
P.O. Box 9159
Greensboro, NC 27408
919-288-7329
Funeral home affiliated
Available: 8-5 daily

Cost of cremation only: $140
Body container requirements:
 rigid combustible
Cardboard casket: $50
Cost of mailing cremains:
 postage
Payment: at time of delivery,
 negotiable

Sheppard Memorial Park, Inc.
P.O. Box 765
Hendersonville, NC 28739
704-693-3435 or
704-692-1463
Funeral home affiliated
Available: 24 hours

Cost of cremation only: $110
Body container requirements:
 rigid combustible
Cardboard casket: $15
Cost of mailing cremains:
 postage
Payment: negotiable

Brown-Wynne Funeral Home
716 W. North St.
P.O. Box 12195
Raleigh, NC 27605
919-828-4311
Available: 24 hours

Cost of cremation only: $205
Body container requirements:
 rigid combustible
Cardboard casket: $30
Cost of mailing cremains:
 postage
Payment: negotiable

McFarland's Crematory
Hwy. 108 N.
P.O. Box 280
Tryon, NC 28782
704-859-9341
Funeral home affiliated
Available: 24 hours

Cost of cremation only: $120
Body container requirements:
 rigid combustible
Cardboard casket: $15
Cost of mailing cremains:
 postage
Payment: negotiable

Bowman-Gray School of
Medicine Crematory
300 S. Hawthorne Rd.
Winston-Salem, NC 27103
919-748-2011
Independent
Available: 8:30-4:30 M-F

Cost of cremation only: $175
Body container requirements:
none
Payment: at time of delivery

Two crematories declined to accept a body from other than a funeral director, one in Charlotte and one in Whiteville. Both saw no circumstances under which their policies might change. Said one, "We would lose business."

There may be additional crematories that are not on the lists I used for this research.

▶ **Body Donation**

University of North Carolina
314 Berry Hill Hall 219-H
Chapel Hill, NC 27514
919-966-1134 8:30-4:30

Cost to family: transportation
Prior enrollment: not required
Over-enrollment: shared
Disposition: cremation/
scattering; return of
cremains by request
Body rejection: autopsy,
decomposition, meningitis,
hepatitis, AIDS, infant,
embalming if trocar used

Duke University
School of Medicine
Durham, NC 27710
919-684-4124
after hours: 684-8111

Cost to family: transportation
Prior enrollment: not required
Over-enrollment: shared with
permission
Disposition: cremation
Body rejection: standard*

E. Carolina University
School of Medicine
Department of Anatomy
Greenville, NC 27834
919-757-2849
757-2246

Cost to family: transportation
from outside of state
Prior enrollment: not required
Over-enrollment: shared
Disposition: cremation; return
of cremains by request
Body rejection: standard*,
herpes, Creutzfeldt-Jakob
and any other infectious
disease

Wake Forest University
Bowman-Gray School of
    Medicine
Winston-Salem, NC 27103

Repeated requests for
information have not been
returned from this school.

*autopsy, decomposition, mutilation, severe burn victim,
meningitis, hepatitis, AIDS

▸ **State Funeral Board**

The North Carolina State Board of Mortuary Science has
seven members. Six are funeral directors or embalmers. There
is one consumer representative.

(This section was reviewed by State Registrar of Vital
Records, North Carolina Division of Health Services.)

In North Dakota

Please refer to Chapter 9 as you use this section.

Persons in North Dakota may care for their own dead. The
legal authority to do so is found in:

Title 23-06-02. **Who is entitled to custody of body.** -
The person charged with the duty of burying the body of
a deceased person is entitled to the custody of such body
for the purpose of burying it. . .

Title 23-06-03. **Duty of burial.** The duty of burying the
body of a deceased person devolves upon the following
persons: 1. . .upon the surviving husband or wife. 2. If
the deceased was not married but left kindred, upon the
person or persons in the same degree, of adult age,
nearest of kin to the deceased living within the state...

There are no other statutes or regulations which might
require you to use a funeral director when embalming is not
desired.

▸ **Death Certificate**

The family doctor or county coroner will sign the death certificate stating the cause of death. The remaining information must be supplied, typewritten or in black ink. Do not use a felt-tip pen; the information must carry through to a third copy. The death certificate must be filed with the local registrar within 15 days. When a family is handling all arrangements, the death certificate should be completed and filed at the time of requesting the registrar's signature on the burial-transit permit.

▸ **Fetal Death**

A fetal death report is required after 20 weeks of gestation. If there is no family physician involved, the county coroner must sign the fetal death certificate. All other procedures apply if disposition is handled by the family.

▸ **Transporting and Disposition Permit**

The local registrar or sub-registrar in the district where death occurred must sign the burial-transit permit, which is on the third page attached to the death certificate.

▸ **Burial**

Check with the county registrar for local zoning laws regarding home burial. Burial must be in a "properly registered cemetery" authorized by the state Health Department. The land must be surveyed and the deed registered with the county registrar. The top of the casket must be three and one-half feet below the natural surface of the earth.

When burial is arranged, the family member acting as the funeral director must detach and sign the burial-transit permit and file it with the registrar of that district within 10 days.

▸ **Cremation**

No additional permit is needed for cremation. Most crematories insist that a pacemaker be removed, and authorization by next-of-kin usually is required. The crematory will sign the burial-transit permit which must be filed with the registrar in that district within 10 days.

▸ **Other Requirements**

Disposition must be made within eight days.

A body must be embalmed if the destination cannot be reached within 24 hours. Embalming is required if disposition is not accomplished within 48 hours.

If the person died of anthrax, cholera, meningococcus, TB, plague, meningitis, or smallpox, the body must be embalmed.

▸ **Crematories**

Riverside Cemetery Assn.
501 21st Ave.
Fargo, ND 58102
701-235-2671
Independent
Available: 8-5 M-F

Cost of cremation only: $195
Body container requirements:
   rigid combustible
Cardboard casket: not carried
Cost of mailing cremains:
   included
Payment: at time of delivery

This is the only crematory in North Dakota at the time of this publication.

▸ **Body Donation**

University of North Dakota
Department of Anatomy
Medical Science South
Grand Forks, ND 58202
701-777-2101 8-4:30 M-F
   or 772-7444
      775-5047
      772-0484

Cost to family: transportation
   and embalming (under
   school direction) over $275
Prior enrollment: not required
Over-enrollment: has not
   occurred
Disposition: cremation/burial
   of cremains; return of
   cremains by request
Body rejection: autopsy,
   decomposition, AIDS

▸ **State Funeral Board**

The North Dakota State Board of Embalmers has three members. The state medical officer serves as well. There are no consumer representatives.

(This section was reviewed by the North Dakota Department of Health, Division of Vital Records.)

In Ohio

Please refer to Chapter 9 as you use this section.

Members of a religious group in Ohio may care for their own dead. The legal authority to do so is found in:

RC 3705.26 - **Registration of death with local registrar;** certificate of death. Each death which occurs in Ohio shall be registered with the local registrar of vital statistics of the district in which the death occurred by the funeral director or other person in charge of interment or cremation of the remains.

RC 4717.10 - **Exceptions to provisions.** . . Sections 4717.01-4717.19 of the Revised Code do not prevent or interfere with the ceremonies, customs, religious rights, or religion of any people, denomination, or sect; . . . prevent or interfere with. . . preparing human bodies for burial; prevent or interfere with the use of any place, chapel or private home for the preparation of bodies for burial: . . . except in case of a contagious disease, where rules of the local board of health as to preparation for burial shall govern.

There are no other statutes or regulations which might require you to use a funeral director when embalming is not desired.

▶ **Death Certificate**

The family doctor or a coroner will sign the death certificate within 48 hours, stating the cause of death. The remaining information must be supplied, typewritten or in black ink. The death certificate must be filed with the local registrar within 48 hours and before final disposition.

▶ **Fetal Death**

A certificate of stillbirth is required for each fetal death. All other procedures apply when a family handles disposition.

▶ **Transporting and Disposition Permit**

The local registrar or sub-registrar will issue the burial-transit permit. The charge for this is 50 cents. This permit must be filed with the registrar in the district of disposition.

When a body is brought into the state a Certificate of Service must be filed with the local registrar after disposition.

▶ **Burial**

Check with the county registrar for local zoning laws regarding home burial. There are no state burial statutes or regulations with regard to depth.

When burial is arranged, the family member acting as the funeral director must sign the burial-transit permit and file it with the registrar where disposition takes place.

▶ **Cremation**

Most crematories insist that a pacemaker be removed, and authorization by next-of-kin usually is required. The crematory may offer to file the burial-transit permit.

▶ **Other Requirements**

Written permission from the local health commissioner is required before moving a body dead from a communicable disease. Disposition must be made within 24 hours, and handling of the body is restricted.

Ohio has no other requirements controlling the time schedule for the disposition of unembalmed bodies. Weather and reasonable planning should be considered.

▶ **Crematories**

Akron Crematory
2399 Gilchrist Rd.
Akron, OH 44305
216-784-5475
Independent
Available: 8-4:30 M-Sat.,
    24-hour phone

Cost of cremation only: $110
Body container requirements:
    rigid combustible
Cardboard casket: $20
Cost of mailing cremains:
    postage
Payment: at time of delivery

The Billow Co.
85 N. Miller Rd.
Akron, OH 44313
216-867-4141
Funeral home affiliated
Available: 24 hours

Cost of cremation only: $100
Body container requirements:
  rigid combustible
Cardboard casket: $50
Cost of mailing cremains:
  postage
Payment: at time of delivery,
  negotiable

Hillcrest Memorial Park
  Cemetery
26700 Aurora
Bedford Heights, OH 44146
216-232-0035
Independent
Available: 8-4:30 M-F,
  9-3:30 Sat., 11-3:30 Sun.

Cost of cremation only: $65
Body container requirements:
  rigid combustible
Cardboard casket: $25
Cost of mailing cremains: $10
Payment: at time of delivery

Spring Grove Memorial
Mausoleum
4521 Spring Grove
Cincinnati, OH 45232
513-541-0600
Independent
Available: 8-5 daily

Cost of cremation only: $145
Body container requirements:
  rigid combustible
Cardboard casket: available
Cost of mailing cremains:
  postage
Payment: negotiable

Cincinnati Crematory Co.
525 Dixmyth
Cincinnati, OH 45220
513-861-1021
Funeral home affiliated
Available: 9-4 M-Sat.,
  24-hour phone

Cost of cremation only: $150
Body container requirements:
  rigid combustible
Cardboard casket: $20
Cost of mailing cremains:
  postage
Payment: at time of delivery,
  negotiable

Ball Funeral Home and
  Crematory
1486-1490 Crawford Road
Cleveland, OH 44106
216-421-1455
Available: 24 hours

Cost of cremation only: $100
Body container requirements:
  rigid combustible
Cardboard casket: available
Cost of mailing cremains:
  postage
Payment: at time of delivery

Cook and Son
1631 Parsons
Columbus, OH 43207
614-444-7861
Funeral home affiliated
Available: 8-4:30 daily,
  24-hour phone

Cost of cremation only: $130
Body container requirements:
  rigid combustible
Cardboard casket: $25
Cost of mailing cremains:
  postage
Payment: negotiable

Green Lawn Cemetery Assn.
1000 Greenlawn Ave.
Columbus, OH 43223
614-444-1123
Independent
Available: 8:30-4:30 M-F,
  8:30-12 Sat.

Cost of cremation only: $125
Body container requirements:
  rigid combustible
Cardboard casket: not carried
Cost of mailing cremains:
  included
Payment: at time of delivery

Schoedinger Crematory
229 E. State St.
Columbus, OH 43215
614-224-6105
Funeral home affiliated
Available: 8 a.m.-9:30 p.m.
  daily, 24-hour phone

Cost of cremation only: $150
Body container requirements:
  rigid combustible
Cardboard casket: $50
Cost of mailing cremains:
  postage
Payment: at time of delivery

Spears Funeral Home
2693 W. Broad St.
Columbus, OH 43204
614-274-5092
Available: 24 hours

Cost of cremation only: $115
Body container requirements:
  rigid combustible
Cardboard casket: $100
Cost of mailing cremains:
  postage
Payment: at time of delivery

Cridersville Crematory
311 W. Main Street
Cridersville, OH 45806
419-645-4501
Funeral home affiliated
Available: 24 hours

Cost of cremation only: $150
Body container requirements:
  rigid combustible
Cardboard casket: $15
Cost of mailing cremains:
  included
Payment: negotiable

Woodland Cemetery Assn.
118 Woodland Avenue
Dayton, OH 45409
513-228-3221
Independent
Available: 8-4:30 M-F,
  8-12 Sat.

Cost of cremation only: $165
Body container requirements:
  rigid combustible
Cardboard casket: not carried
Cost of mailing cremains: $35
Payment: negotiable

S & S Crematory
209 N. Wilheim Street
Holgate, OH 43527
419-264-3401
Funeral home affiliated
Available: 24 hours

Cost of cremation only: $135
Body container requirements:
  rigid combustible
Cardboard casket: $60
Cost of mailing cremains: $15
Payment: negotiable

N.E. Ohio Crematory
7474 Mentor Ave.
Mentor, OH 44060
216-942-1702
Dicicco & Sons Funeral Home
Available 8:30-5 M-F,
  8:30-1 Sat.

Cost of cremation only: $117
Body container requirements:
  rigid combustible
Cardboard casket: available
Cost of mailing cremains:
  postage
Payment: negotiable

Sunset Memorial Park
6265 Columbia Rd.
P.O. Box 87
North Olmsted, OH 44070
216-777-0450
Dostal Funeral Service
Available: 9-5 M-F, 9-12 Sat.,
  24-hour phone

Cost of cremation only: $95
Body container requirements:
  rigid combustible
Cardboard casket: $20
Payment: at time of delivery

Sandusky Cremation Service
2001 Columbus Ave.
P.O. Box 362
Sandusky, OH 44870
419-625-4221
Andres-Tucker Funeral Home
Available: 24 hours

Cost of cremation only: $120
Body container requirements:
  rigid combustible
Cardboard casket: not carried
Cost of mailing cremains:
  included
Payment: at time of delivery

Bennett Funeral Home
3434 Secor Rd.
Toledo, OH 43606
419-535-7726
Available: 24 hours

Cost of cremation only: $400
Body container requirements:
  rigid combustible
Cardboard casket:
  included
Cost of mailing cremains:
  postage
Payment: negotiable

West Shore Crematory
2914 Dover Center Rd.
Westlake, OH 44145
216-871-0711
Jenkins Funeral Chapel
Available: 24 hours

Cost of cremation only: $110
Body container requirements:
  rigid combustible
Cardboard casket: $20
Cost of mailing cremains:
  postage
Payment: negotiable

Rutherford Crematory
517 High St.
Worthington, OH 43085
614-885-4006
Funeral home affiliated
Available: 9-5 M-F,
  24-hour phone

Cost of cremation only: $150
Body container requirements:
  rigid combustible
Cardboard casket: $75
Cost of mailing cremains: $20
Payment: at time of delivery

Lake Park Cemetery Assn.
1459 E. Midlothian Blvd.
Youngstown, OH 44502
216-782-4221
Independent
Available: 8-4:30 M-Sat.

Cost of cremation only: $140
Body container requirements:
  rigid combustible
Cardboard casket: not carried
Cost of mailing cremains: $7
Payment: negotiable

Seven crematories declined to accept a body from other than a funeral director: one each in Cincinnati, Chesterland, Cleveland, Miamisburg, Sylvania, and two in Toledo. Their concerns were: "I'm a wholesaler," "We're not in competition with our clientele," "Can't see it, burden of responsibility," "Not until it's a more accepted practice," "State law," "Maybe down the road."

There may be additional crematories that are not on the lists I used for this research.

► **Body Donation**

Ohio University
College of Osteopathic
Medicine
Athens, OH 45701
614-593-1800 8-5 M-F,
or 594-2416

Cost to family: transportation
beyond 150 miles
Prior enrollment: not required
Over-enrollment: has not
occurred
Disposition: cremation/burial
of cremains in University
plot; return of cremains by
request
Body rejection: standard*,
fetal death, MS, A-L
sclerosis, Creutzfeld-Jacob,
Parkinson's, Guillain-Barre,
Alzheimer's, neurofibroma-
tosis, scleroderma, ataxia
telangiectasis, demyeli-
nating enceph., embalmed
(except by direction of
school)

University of Cincinnati
College of Medicine
231 Bethesda Ave., ML 521
Cincinnati, OH 45267
513-872-5674 8:30-5 M-F
or Hamilton County Coroner's
Office, 513-872-5612

Cost to family: transportation
Prior enrollment: not required
Over-enrollment: shared
Disposition: burial or return
by request
Body rejection: autopsy
(check first), burn victim,
decomposition, meningitis,
AIDS, under 21, previous
embalming, (accepts almost
all prior enrollees)

Case Western Reserve
University
School of Medicine
Department of Anatomy
2119 Abington Rd.
Cleveland, OH 44106
216-368-3430
or 221-9330

Cost to family: transportation
beyond 75 miles
Prior enrollment: required
Over-enrollment: shared
Disposition: cremation/burial
of cremains in University
plot; return of cremains by
request
Body rejection: standard*,
major surgery, missing
body parts, emaciation,
obesity, under 18, previous
embalming, or other

Ohio State University
College of Medicine
Department of Anatomy
333 W. 10th Ave.
Columbus, OH 43210
614-292-4831
or University Hospital
Morgue

Cost to family: transportation outside Ohio/over $1 per mile
Prior enrollment: not required
Over-enrollment: has not occurred
Disposition: cremation/burial of cremains; return of cremains by request
Body rejection: standard*, under 18, prior embalming

Wright State University
North Dayton, OH 45431

Repeated requests for information have not been returned from this school.

Northeastern Ohio
Universities
College of Medicine
Rootstown, OH 44272
216-325-2511

Cost to family: transportation beyond 75-mile radius
Prior enrollment: not required
Over-enrollment: not shared
Disposition: cremation/ burial of cremains; return of cremains by request
Body rejection: standard*, missing body parts, major surgery, obesity, emacia-tion, over-enrollment

Medical College of Ohio
Toledo, OH 43614

Repeated requests for information have not been returned from this school.

*autopsy, decomposition, mutilation, severe burn victim, meningitis, hepatitis, AIDS

▶ **State Funeral Board**

The Board of Embalmers and Funeral Directors of Ohio has five members. There is one consumer representative.

(This section was reviewed by the Executive Director of the Ohio Board of Embalmers and Funeral Directors. A copy also was sent to the Ohio Department of Health.)

In Oklahoma

Please refer to Chapter 9 as you use this section.

Persons in Oklahoma may care for their own dead. The legal authority to do so is found in:

Title 59, Sec. 396.2 **Definitions - License required-Personal supervision of funeral director and embalmer:**
. . . Each funeral conducted within the State of Oklahoma must be under the personal supervision and presence of a duly-licensed funeral director. . . Nothing in this section regarding the conduct of funerals or personal supervision of a licensed director . . . shall apply to persons related to the deceased by blood or marriage.

Title 63, Sec. 1-317 . . . (b) The funeral director or person acting as such who first assumes custody of a dead body shall file the death certificate. . .

There are no other statutes or regulations which might require you to use a funeral director when embalming is not desired.

▸ **Death Certificate**

The family doctor or a local medical examiner will sign the death certificate within 48 hours, stating the cause of death. The remaining information must be supplied, typewritten or in black ink. The death certificate must be filed with the local registrar within three days and before final disposition.

▸ **Fetal Death**

A fetal death report is required for each fetal death. All other procedures apply if disposition is handled by the family.

▸ **Transporting and Disposition Permit**

The local registrar will issue the burial-transit permit. This authorization must be obtained within 72 hours of death and prior to final disposition of the body.

▸ **Burial**

Check with the county registrar for local zoning laws regarding home burial. There are no state burial statutes or regulations with regard to depth.

When burial is arranged, the family member acting as the funeral director must, within 10 days, sign the burial transit permit and file it with the registrar of the district where disposition takes place.

▸ **Cremation**

A permit for cremation must be obtained from the medical examiner. There may be a fee for this. Most crematories insist that a pacemaker be removed, and authorization by next-of-kin usually is required. The crematory will return the disposition authorization to the issuing registrar.

▸ **Other Requirements**

Oklahoma has no other requirements controlling the time schedule for the disposition of unembalmed bodies. Weather and reasonable planning should be considered.

If the person died of a contagious or communicable disease, the doctor in attendance should be consulted.

▸ **Crematories**

Oklahoma Cremation Service
6934 S. Western Ave.
P.O. Box 19267
Oklahoma City, OK 73144
405-634-4711 or 634-1439
Vondel Smith Mortuary
Available: 24 hours

Cost of cremation only: $175
Body container requirements:
  rigid combustible
Cardboard casket: $55
Cost of mailing cremains:
  included
Payment: at time of delivery

Cremation Society of
  Oklahoma
2103 E. 3rd St.
Tulsa, OK 74104
918-587-7000
Stumpff Funeral Home
Available: 24 hours

Cost of cremation only: $175
Body container requirements:
  rigid combustible
Plywood casket: available
Cost of mailing cremains: $25
Payment: at time of delivery,
  negotiable

Memorial Park
5111 S. Memorial Drive
Tulsa, OK 74145
918-627-0220
Independent
Available: 7:30-4 M-F,
  7:30-12 Sat.

Cost of cremation only: $175
Body container requirements:
  rigid combustible
Cardboard casket: not carried
Cost of mailing cremains:
  postage
Payment: at time of delivery

Tulsa Cremation Service
3959 E. 31st
Tulsa, OK 74135
918-743-6396
Stanleys Funeral Service
Available: 9-9 daily,
  24-hour phone

Cost of cremation only: $175
Body container requirements:
  rigid combustible
Cardboard casket: $55
Cost of mailing cremains: $35
Payment: at time of delivery

There may be additional crematories that are not on the lists
I used for this research.

▶ **Body Donation**

Oklahoma University
Health Sciences Center
P.O. Box 26901
Oklahoma City, OK 73190
405-271-2424
  or 271-6666

Cost to family: transportation
  beyond state
Prior enrollment: required
Over-enrollment: shared
Disposition: cremation/ burial
  or scattering of cremains;
  return of cremains by
  request
Body rejection: autopsy,
  meningitis, hepatitis, AIDS
  or other, under 18, cavity
  embalming

Oklahoma College of
Osteopathic Medicine
1111 W. 17th
Tulsa, OK 74107
918-582-1972

Cost to family: transportation
  outside of state
Prior enrollment: not required
Over-enrollment: shared
Disposition: cremation/
  scattering; return of
  cremains by request
Body rejection: autopsy,
  decomposition, AIDS

▶ **State Funeral Board**

The Oklahoma State Board of Embalmers and Funeral
Directors has seven members. There are two consumer

representatives.

(The Oklahoma section was sent to the Oklahoma Department of Health for review. No response was received by date of publication.)

In Oregon

Please refer to Chapter 9 as you use this section.

Persons in Oregon may care for their own dead. The legal authority to do so is found in:

> Title 432.307 (2): The funeral service practitioner or person acting as such who first assumes custody of the dead body shall file the death certificate.

> Title 97.130 (1). . . any of the following, in order of priority stated. . . shall have the right to control the disposition of the remains of a decedent: (a) the spouse (b) a son or daughter 18 years of age or older (c) either parent (d) a brother or sister 18 years of age or older (e) a guardian of the decedent at the time of his death (f) a person in the next degree of kindred

There are no other statutes or regulations which might require you to use a funeral director when embalming is not desired.

▶ **Death Certificate**

A report of the death must be filed with (or mailed to) the registrar within 24 hours by the person having custody of the body. The form will be supplied by the registrar (or a funeral director on weekends).

The family doctor or a local medical examiner will sign the death certificate within 48 hours, stating the cause of death. The remaining information must be supplied, typewritten or in black ink. Do not use a felt-tip pen; the information must carry through to the third copy. The death certificate must be filed with the district registrar within five days and (usually) prior to final disposition. There is a $5.00 charge for filing the death certificate.

▶ **Fetal Death**

A fetal death report is required after 20 weeks of gestation. If there is no family physician involved, the local medical examiner must sign the fetal death certificate. The certificate must be filed with the registrar within five days.

▶ **Transporting and Disposition Permit**

A body may be moved with the consent of a physician or medical examiner. The family member acting as the funeral director must fill in the parts under "disposition" which are a part of the death certificate on the first (white) page. The attached yellow page carbon serves as a burial-transit permit.

An identification tag, a round metal disc, must be obtained. The tag must be attached to the body receptacle, when death has occurred within the state, and remain with the body throughout final disposition. The identification number must be recorded on the death certificate in the upper left-hand corner. During working weekday hours the identification tag can be obtained from the county registrar. The person obtaining the tag must sign line 20a on the certificate of death. If death has occurred when it would be unwise to wait for the next working weekday, one of the tags assigned to a funeral home or crematory will be needed. In that case the funeral service licensee must sign line 20a and will be billed the $5.00 charge for filing the death certificate.

▶ **Burial**

Check with the county registrar for local zoning laws regarding home burial. There are no state burial statutes or regulations with regard to depth.

After burial, the person in charge must sign the burial-transit permit and return it within ten days to the registrar of the county in which death occurred.

▶ **Cremation**

No additional permit for cremation is needed. Most crematories insist that a pacemaker be removed, and authorization by next-of-kin usually is required. The crematory will sign the burial-transit permit which must be returned to the registrar of the county in which death occurred.

▶ **Other Requirements**

If a body will not reach its destination within 24 hours it must be embalmed or refrigerated.

If the person died of a contagious or communicable disease, the doctor in attendance should be consulted. Embalming may be required.

▶ **Crematories**

Littwiller-Simosen Funeral
  Home
1811 Ashland St.
Ashland, OR 97520
503-482-2816
Available: 9-5 M-F,
  24-hour phone

Cost of cremation only: $150
Body container requirements:
  rigid combustible
Cardboard casket: $15
Cost of mailing cremains: $25
Payment: at time of delivery,
  negotiable

Hughes Ransom Mortuary and
  Crematory
576 12th St.
Astoria, OR 97103
503-325-2535
Available: 24 hours

Cost of cremation only: $150
Body container requirements:
  rigid combustible
Cardboard casket: $50
Cost of mailing cremains: $20
Payment: negotiable

Niswonger & Reynolds, Inc.
105 N.W. Irving Ave, Box 229
Bend, OR 97709
503-382-2471
Funeral home affiliated
Available: 24 hours

Cost of cremation only: $100
Body container requirements:
  rigid combustible
Cardboard casket: $75
Cost of mailing cremains: $10
Payment: negotiable

Ocean View Memory Garden
1525 N.W. Ocean Blvd.
Coos Bay, OR 97420
503-888-4709
Independent
Available: 8-5 M-Sat.

Cost of cremation only: $140
Body container requirements:
  rigid combustible
Cardboard casket: not carried
Cost of mailing cremains: $25
Payment: negotiable

DeMoss-Durdan Crematory
815 N.W. Buchanan
Corvallis, OR 97330
503-754-6255
Funeral home affiliated
Available: 8-5 M-F,
  24-hour phone

Cost of cremation only: $150
Body container requirements:
  rigid combustible
Plywood casket: $85
Cost of mailing cremains:
  postage
Payment: negotiable

Chapel of Memories
Crematory
3745 W. 11th Ave.
Eugene, OR 97402
503-687-1431
Funeral home affiliated
Available: 24 hours

Cost of cremation only: $102
Body container requirements:
  none
Cardboard casket: $15
Cost of mailing cremains: $20
Payment: at time of delivery,
  negotiable

Lounsbury-Musgrove
1152 Olive St.
Eugene, OR 97401
503-686-2818
Funeral home affiliated
Available: 24 hours

Cost of cremation only: $125
Body container requirements:
  rigid combustible
Cardboard casket: $45
Cost of mailing cremains: $15
Payment: 30 days

Poole-Larsen Crematorium
1100 Charnelton St.
Eugene, OR 97401
503-484-1435
Funeral home affiliated
Available: 24 hours

Cost of cremation only: $100
Body container requirements:
  rigid combustible
Cardboard casket: available
Cost of mailing cremains: $25
Payment: negotiable

Hillcrest Crematory
141 N.W. "C" Street
Grants Pass, OR 97526
503-476-6868
Lundberg's L.B. Hall Funeral
  Home
Available: 9-5:30 M-Sat.,
  24-hour phone

Cost of cremation only: $125
Body container requirements:
  rigid combustible
Cardboard casket: $25
Cost of mailing cremains: $30
Payment: at time of delivery

Hull and Hull
612 N.W. "A" St.
P.O. Box 67
Grants Pass, OR 97526
503-476-4453
Funeral home affiliated
Available: 24 hours

Cost of cremation only: $125
Body container requirements:
  rigid combustible
Cardboard casket: $25
Cost of mailing cremains: $25
Payment: at time of delivery,
  negotiable

Bateman Funeral Chapel
520 W. Powell Blvd.
P.O. Box 407
Gresham, OR 97030
503-665-2128
Available: 24 hours

Cost of cremation only: $150
Body container requirements:
  rigid combustible
Cardboard casket: $15
Cost of mailing cremains: $12
Payment: at time of delivery

Eternal Hills Memorial
  Garden
4711 Highway 39
Klamath Falls, OR 97601
503-884-3668
Independent
Available: 8-4:30 M-F,
  24-hour phone

Cost of cremation only: $125
Body container requirements:
  rigid combustible
Cardboard casket: not carried
Cost of mailing cremains: $25
Payment: negotiable

Klamath Cremation Service
2680 Memorial Dr.
Klamath Falls, OR 97601
503-884-3456
O'Hair's Funeral Chapel
Available: 8-5 daily,
  24-hour phone

Cost of cremation only: $150
Body container requirements:
  rigid combustible
Particle board casket: $125
Cost of mailing cremains: $30
Payment: negotiable

Hillcrest Memorial Park
2201 N. Phoenix Rd.
Medford, OR 97501
503-773-6162
Funeral home affiliated
Available: 24 hours

Cost of cremation only: $150
Body container requirements:
  rigid combustible
Cardboard casket: $25
Cost of mailing cremains: $35
Payment: at time of delivery,
  negotiable

Siskiyou Memorial Park
605 Highland Drive
Medford, OR 97501
503-772-4013
Perl W. Siskiyou Funeral
  Service
Available: 9-5 M-F,
  24-hour phone

Cost of cremation only: $150
Body container requirements:
  rigid combustible
Cardboard casket: $35
Cost of mailing cremains: $25
Payment: negotiable

Blackmarr's Mt. View
  Crematory
428 N.E. Pacific Hwy.
Myrtle Creek, OR 97457
503-863-3148
Funeral home affiliated
Available: 24 hours

Cost of cremation only: $200
Body container requirements:
  rigid combustible
Cardboard casket: not carried
Cost of mailing cremains:
  postage
Payment: at time of delivery,
  negotiable

Central Coast Crematory
915 N.E. Yaquina Hts. Dr.
Newport, OR 97365
503-265-2751
Bateman Funeral Home
Available: 24 hours

Cost of cremation only: $185
Body container requirements:
  rigid combustible
Cardboard casket: $50
Cost of mailing cremains: $10
Payment: at time of delivery,
  negotiable

Lincoln Memorial Park
10500 S.E. Mt. Scott Blvd.
Portland, OR 97266
503-771-1117
Independent
Available: 8:30-5 M-Sat.,
  10-4 Sun.

Cost of cremation only: $105
Body container requirements:
  rigid 3/4-inch base,
  combustible
Cardboard casket: available
Cost of mailing cremains: $20
Payment: at time of delivery

Little Chapel of the Chimes
430 N. Killingsworth Avenue
Portland, OR 97217
503-283-1976
Funeral home affiliated
Available: 24 hours

Cost of cremation only: $140
Body container requirements:
  rigid combustible
Plywood casket: $85
Cost of mailing cremains: $25
Payment: at time of delivery,
  negotiable

Portland Memorial
6405 S.E. 14th Avenue, P.O.
  Box 02095
Portland, OR 97202
503-236-4141
Funeral home affiliated
Available: 24 hours

Cost of cremation only: $115
Body container requirements:
  rigid combustible
Cardboard casket: $40
Cost of mailing cremains: $25
Payment: at time of delivery

Riverview Cemetery Assn.
8421 S.W. Macadam Avenue
Portland, OR 97219
503-246-4251
Independent
Available: 9-5 M-Sat.,
  11-5 Sun. & holidays

Cost of cremation only: $125
Body container requirements:
  rigid combustible
Cardboard casket: not carried
Cost of mailing cremains: $25
Payment: negotiable

Rose City Cemetery Assn.
5625 N.E. Fremont Street
Portland, OR 97213
503-281-3821
Independent
Available: 9-5 M-F

Cost of cremation only: $115
Body container requirements:
  rigid combustible
Cardboard casket: not carried
Cost of mailing cremains: $25
Payment: at time of delivery

Ross Hollywood Chapel
4733 N.E. Thompson
Portland, OR 97213
503-281-1800
Funeral home affiliated
Available: 8-5:30 daily

Cost of cremation only: $125
Body container requirements:
   rigid combustible
Plywood casket: $85
Cost of mailing cremains: $25
Payment: at time of delivery

Sunset Hills Memorial Park
6801 S.W. Sunset Hwy.
Portland, OR 97225
503-292-6654
J.P. Finley & Sons
Available: 24 hours

Cost of cremation only: $175
Body container requirements:
   rigid combustible
Cardboard casket: not carried
Cost of mailing cremains: $15
Payment: negotiable

Buell Chapel
320 N. 6th St.
Springfield, OR 97477
503-747-1266
Funeral home affiliated
Available: 24 hours

Cost of cremation only: $150
Body container requirements:
   rigid combustible
Cardboard casket: $90
Cost of mailing cremains:
   postage
Payment: negotiable, 30 days

Young's Funeral Home and
   Crematory
11831 S.W. Pacific Hwy.
Tigard, OR 97223
503-639-1206
Available: 24 hours

Cost of cremation only: $125
Body container requirements:
   rigid combustible
Cardboard casket: $40
Cost of mailing cremains: $25
Payment: negotiable

One crematory in Portland had an answering machine and no response has been received. Another crematory in Portland said it would accept a body from a family but asked not to be listed in the book. One crematory in Salem declined to accept a body from other than a funeral director. Its concern was "no insurance. . . always the way we've done business."

There may be additional crematories that are not on the lists I used for this research.

▶ **Body Donation**

Oregon Health Science
  University
School of Medicine
3181 S.W. Sam Jackson Park
  Road
Portland, OR 97201
503-225-7811

Cost to family: embalming,
  transportation
Prior enrollment: not required
Over-enrollment: shared
Disposition: cremation; return
  of cremains
Body rejection: autopsy,
  decomposition, AIDS

Western State Chiropractic College receives its body donations through Oregon Health Sciences Center.

▶ **State Funeral Board**

The Oregon Mortuary Board has nine members. There are
three consumer representatives, one of which must be a
member of a senior citizen organization.

(This section was reviewed by the Oregon State Mortuary and
Cemetery Board.)

In Pennsylvania

Please refer to Chapter 9 as you use this section.

Persons in Pennsylvania may care for their own dead. The
legal authority to do so is found in:

> Title 450.501: The person in charge of interment or of
> removal of the dead body or fetal remains from the
> registration district shall file the certificate with any
> registrar who shall be authorized to issue certified copies
> of such death.

There are no other statutes or regulations which might
require you to use a funeral director when embalming is not
desired.

▶ **Death Certificate**

The family doctor or a local medical examiner will sign the death certificate stating the cause of death. The remaining information must be supplied, typewritten or in black ink. The death certificate must be filed with the local registrar within 96 hours and before final disposition.

▶ **Fetal Death**

A fetal death report is required for each fetal death. If there is no family physician involved, the local coroner must sign the fetal death certificate. All other procedures apply if disposition is handled by the family.

▶ **Transporting and Disposition Permit**

The local registrar will issue the authorization for disposition. The death certificate must be obtained first.

▶ **Burial**

Check with the county registrar for local zoning laws regarding home burial. The top of the coffin must be two feet below the natural surface of the earth.

When burial is arranged, the family member acting as the funeral director must sign the authorization for disposition and file the second copy with the Division of Vital Statistics within 10 days. The first copy is to be retained by the crematory, cemetery or the Humanity Gifts Registry. In the case of home burial, the local registrar may request the first copy for recording.

▶ **Cremation**

No additional permit is required for cremation. There is a 24-hour wait before cremation. Most crematories insist that a pacemaker be removed, and authorization by next-of-kin usually is required. The crematory will file the disposition authorization with the local registrar.

▶ **Other Requirements**

Pennsylvania has no other requirements controlling the time schedule for the disposition of unembalmed bodies. Weather and reasonable planning should be considered.

If the person died of a contagious or communicable disease, the doctor in attendance should be consulted.

▶ **Crematories**

Cedar Hill Memorial Park
R.D. 4, Airport,
P.O. Box 2284
Allentown, PA 18103
215-821-1100
Independent
Available: 8:30-5 M-F,
  8:30-1 Sat.

Cost of cremation only: $95
Body container requirements:
  rigid combustible
Cardboard casket: $45
Cost of mailing cremains:
  postage
Payment: negotiable

West Laurel Cemetery
215 Belmont
Bala-Cynwyd, PA 19004
215-483-1122
Independent
Available: 8-4 M-Sat.

Cost of cremation only: $120
Body container requirements:
  rigid combustible
Cardboard casket: not carried
Cost of mailing cremains:
  postage
Payment: at time of delivery

Cremation Services, Inc.
620 W. 10th St.
Erie, PA 16502
814-454-4551
Burton Funeral Home
Available: 24 hours

Cost of cremation only: $100
Body container requirements:
  rigid combustible
Cardboard casket: $50
Cost of mailing cremains:
  postage
Payment: at time of delivery,
  negotiable

Forest Lawn Memorial Park
  and Crematory
1530 Frankstown Rd.
Johnstown, PA 15902
814-535-8258
Independent
Available: 24 hours

Cost of cremation only: $160
Body container requirements:
  rigid combustible
Cardboard casket: $40
Cost of mailing cremains:
  included
Payment: at time of delivery

Greenwood Cemetery and
  Crematory
719 Highland Ave.
Lancaster, PA 17603
717-392-1224
Independent
Available: 24-hour phone

Cost of cremation only: $115
Body container requirements:
  rigid combustible
Cardboard casket: $20
Cost of mailing cremains:
  included
Payment: negotiable

Lansdale Crematory
Derstine & Cannon Aves.
Lansdale, PA 19446
215-855-3314
Funeral home affiliated
Available: 24 hours

Cost of cremation only: $65
Body container requirements:
  none
Cardboard casket: $25
Cost of mailing cremains:
  postage
Payment: at time of delivery

Chelten Hills Cemetery Co.
1701 E. Washington
Philadelphia, PA 19138
215-548-2400
Independent
Available: 9-5 M-F, 9-4 Sat.

Cost of cremation only: $90
Body container requirements:
  rigid combustible
Cardboard casket: $15
Cost of mailing cremains: $15
Payment: at time of delivery

Allegheny Cemetery
4734 Butler Street
Pittsburgh, PA 15201
412-682-1624
Independent
Available: 8-4, 24-hour phone

Cost of cremation only: $130
Body container requirements:
  rigid combustible
Cardboard casket:
  included
Cost of mailing cremains:
  postage
Payment: at time of delivery

Homewood Cemetery
Dallas & Aylesboro Avenues
Pittsburgh, PA 15217
412-421-1822
Independent
Available: 8:30-4:45 M-F,
  8:30-3:45 Sat.

Cost of cremation only: $140
Body container requirements:
  rigid combustible
Cardboard casket: $40
Cost of mailing cremains: $10
Payment: at time of delivery,
  negotiable

Tennessee Cremation Service
2630 W. Liberty Avenue
Pittsburgh, PA 15216
412-531-4000
Funeral home affiliated
Available: 24 hours

Cost of cremation only: $90
Body container requirements:
  rigid combustible
Cardboard casket: $35
Cost of mailing cremains:
  postage Payment: at time
of delivery

George Washington Memorial
  Park
Stenton & Butler
Plymouth Meeting, PA 19462
215-828-1417
Independent
Available: 9-5 M-F,
  11-4 weekends/holidays

Cost of cremation only: $125
Body container requirements:
  rigid combustible
Cardboard casket: $25
Cost of mailing cremains:
  postage
Payment: at time of delivery,
  negotiable

American Burial and
  Cremation Society
247 Penn St.
P.O. Box 431
Reading, PA 19603
215-374-4505 or
(in PA) 1-800-328-1307
Armand Funeral Home
Available: 24 hours

Cost of cremation only: $95
Body container requirements:
  rigid combustible
Cardboard casket: available
Cost of mailing cremains:
  postage
Payment: at time of delivery

Charles Evans Cemetery
1119 Centre
Reading, PA 19601
215-372-1563
Independent
Available: 8-5 M-F, 8-12 Sat.,
or by appointment

Cost of cremation only: $95
Body container requirements:
  rigid combustible
Cardboard casket: $20
Cost of mailing cremains:
  postage
Payment: negotiable

Henninger Crematory
229 N. 5th St.
Reading, PA 19601
215-373-4500
Funeral home affiliated
Available: 24 hours

Cost of cremation only: $95
Body container requirements:
  rigid combustible
Cardboard casket: $30
Cost of mailing cremains:
  postage
Payment: at time of delivery,
  negotiable

Sunset Memorial Park
County Line Road
P.O. Box 11508
Somerton, PA 19116
215-673-0572
Independent
Available: 9-5 M-F,
  10-4 Sat., 11-4 Sun.
  (extra charge)

Cost of cremation only: $85
Body container requirements:
  none
Cardboard casket: not carried
Cost of mailing cremains: to
  be arranged
Payment: at time of delivery

Delaware Valley Crematory
Street & 2nd
Southampton, PA 18966
215-357-1101
Funeral home affiliated
Available: 24 hours

Cost of cremation only: $80
Body container requirements:
  none
Cardboard casket: available
Cost of mailing cremains:
  included
Payment: at time of delivery,
  negotiable

Washington Cemetery Co.
498 Park Ave.
Washington, PA 15301
412-225-1040
Independent
Available: 24 hours

Cost of cremation only: $105
Body container requirements:
  rigid combustible
Cardboard casket: $15
Cost of mailing cremains:
  included
Payment: at time of delivery,
  negotiable

One crematory in Schaefferstown had an answering machine and no response has been received. Nine other crematories declined to accept a body from other than a funeral director: one each in Allentown, Clarion, Erie, Harrisburg, Sharon Hill, Upper Darby, York, and two in Pittsburgh. Their concerns were: "This business doesn't make sense to us," "I would be out of business in 30 days," "Employees not trained for this," "We do not run a check on permits," "If it's legal, it's news to me," "We're in an industrial area - it wouldn't be appropriate," "The State Board of Funeral Directors objects."

There may be additional crematories that are not on the lists I used for this research.

▸ **Body Donation**

One agency coordinates all body donations within the state.

Human Gifts Registry
130 S. 9th St.
Philadelphia, PA 19107
215-922-4440

Cost to family: transportation
  over $50, weekend refri-
  geration
Prior enrollment: not required
Over-enrollment: shared
Disposition: cremation; no
  return of cremains
Body rejection: standard*,
  embalmed, trauma, surgery,
  emaciation, obesity.
  Exceptions may be made.

*autopsy, decomposition, mutilation, severe burn victim, meningitis, hepatitis, AIDS

▸ **State Funeral Board**

The Pennsylvania State Board of Embalmers and Funeral Directors has seven members. There are two consumer representatives.

)

(The Pennsylvania section was reviewed by the Pennsylvania Department of Health, Vital Records.)

In Rhode Island

Please refer to Chapter 9 as you use this section.

Persons in Rhode Island may care for their own dead. The authority to do so is found in:

> Title 23-3-18. **Permits.** - The funeral director, his duly authorized agent or person acting as such, who first assumes custody of the dead body or fetus shall prepare a burial-transit permit prior to final disposition. . .

There are no other statutes or regulations which might require you to use a funeral director when embalming is not desired.

▶ Death Certificate

The family doctor will sign the death certificate "immediately," or a medical examiner within 48 hours, stating the cause of death. The remaining information must be supplied, typewritten or in black ink. The death certificate must be filed with the local registrar within seven days.

▶ Fetal Death

A fetal death report is required after 20 weeks of gestation. If there is no family physician involved, the local medical examiner must sign the fetal death certificate. All other procedures apply if disposition is handled by the family.

▶ Transporting and Disposition Permit

The funeral director or person acting as such prepares the burial-transit permit.

▶ Burial

Check with the local registrar for local zoning laws regarding home burial. There are no state burial statutes or regulations with regard to depth.

▶ **Cremation**

A permit for cremation must be obtained from the medical examiner. There may be a fee for this. There is a 24 hour wait before cremation unless the deceased died of a contagious or infectious disease. Most crematories insist that a pacemaker be removed, and authorization by next-of-kin usually is required.

▶ **Other Requirements**

Rhode Island has no other requirements controlling the time schedule for the disposition of unembalmed bodies. Weather and reasonable planning should be considered.

If the person died of a contagious or communicable disease, the doctor in attendance should be consulted.

▶ **Crematories**

Moshassuck Cemetery
978 Lonsdale Ave.
Central Falls, RI 02063
401-723-1087
Independent
Available: 8-3:30 M-F

Cost of cremation only: $125
Body container requirements:
  rigid combustible
Cardboard casket: not carried
Cost of mailing cremains:
  included
Payment: at time of delivery

Cremation Service
P.O. Box 216
No. Scituate, RI 02857
401-934-2276
Winfield Funeral Home
affiliated
Available: 24 hours

Cost of cremation only: $175
Body container requirements:
  rigid combustible
Cardboard casket: $88
Cost of mailing remains:
  postage
Payment: at time of delivery

Two crematories declined to accept a body from other than a funeral director, one in Providence and one in Wakefield. "The law is ambiguous. . . No one's been brave enough to test it." "We deal only with other funeral directors. . . I'd lose my business."

▸ **Body Donation**

Brown University
Division of Biology and
  Medicine
Providence, RI 02912
401-863-3355
  863-1000 after hours

Cost to family: no set policy;
  handled case-by-case
Prior enrollment: required
Over-enrollment: not shared
Disposition: cremation
Body rejection: handled on a
  case-by-case basis

▸ **State Funeral Board**

The Rhode Island State Board of Embalmers and Funeral
Directors has five members. There is one consumer representative.

(This section was reviewed by the Registrar of Vital
Statistics, Rhode Island Department of Health.)

In South Carolina

Please refer to Chapter 9 as you use this section.

Persons in South Carolina may care for their own dead. The
legal authority to do so is found in this and ensuing statutes:

> Regulation 61-19, sec. 18 (2b): The funeral director or
> person acting as such who first assumes custody of a
> dead body shall file the death certificate.

There are no other statutes or regulations which might
require you to use a funeral director when embalming is not
desired.

▸ **Death Certificate**

The family doctor will sign the death certificate within 48
hours, stating the cause of death. The remaining information
must be supplied, typewritten or in black ink. The death
certificate must be filed with the local registrar within five
days.

▸ **Fetal Death**

A fetal death report is required after 20 weeks of gestation or when the weight is 350 grams or more. If there is no family physician involved, the local medical examiner must sign the fetal death certificate. All other procedures apply if disposition is handled by the family.

▸ **Transporting and Disposition Permit**

A body may be moved with the consent of a physician or medical examiner. The local registrar, deputy, or sub-registrar will issue the authorization for disposition. When death has occurred in a hospital the subregistrar from whom to obtain the permit will be located there. If death occurred outside of an institution, the coroner of the county serves as subregistrar. This authorization must be obtained within 72 hours of death and prior to final disposition of the body.

▸ **Burial**

Check with municipal or county officials for local zoning laws regarding home burial. The casket must be at least ten inches below the earth's surface.

▸ **Cremation**

A permit for cremation must be obtained from the medical examiner in Charleston or Greenville County. A certified copy of the death certificate must accompany the burial-removal-transit permit when requesting this. There is no fee for the permit to cremate. Most crematories insist that a pacemaker be removed, and authorization by next-of-kin usually is required.

▸ **Other Requirements**

South Carolina has no other requirements controlling the time schedule for the disposition of unembalmed bodies. Weather and reasonable planning should be considered.

If the person died of a contagious or communicable disease, the doctor in attendance should be consulted.

A body to be shipped by common carrier must be embalmed.

▶ **Crematories**

John Liberatos Crematory
9 Cunnington Ave.
Charleston, SC 29405
803-722-2555
No funeral home, but licensed
for embalming
Available: 24 hours

Cost of cremation only: $150
Body container requirements:
none
Cardboard casket: $75
Cost of mailing cremains:
included
Payment: negotiable

Mackey Cremation Service
311 Century Dr., P.O. Box 55
Greenville, SC 29602
803-271-8604
Funeral home affiliated
Available: 24 hours

Cost of cremation only: $135
Body container requirements:
rigid combustible
Cardboard casket: $45
Cost of mailing cremains:
postage
Payment: at time of delivery

Island Funeral Home and
Crematory
4 Cardinal Rd.
Hilton Head, SC 29902
803-681-4400
Available: 24 hours

Cost of cremation only: $200
Body container requirements:
rigid combustible
Plywood casket: available
Cost of mailing cremains:
postage
Payment: negotiable

Caughman-Harmon Funeral
Home
503 N. Lake Dr.
Lexington, SC 29072
803-359-6118
Available: 9-5 M-F,
weekends by arrangement

Cost of cremation only: $220
Body container requirements:
rigid combustible
Cardboard casket: $25
Cost of mailing cremains:
included
Payment: 30 days

Bullard Funeral Home and
Crematory
701 65th St. & Somerset
P.O. Box 317
Myrtle Beach, SC 29578
803-449-3341
Available: 24 hours

Cost of cremation only: $150
Body container requirements:
rigid combustible
Cardboard casket: available
Cost of mailing cremains:
postage
Payment: at time of delivery,
negotiable

One crematory in North Charleston declined to accept a body
from other than a funeral director. Its concern: "I don't see
any reason to change." The crematory in Spartansburg had
only an answering service, and no calls were returned.

There may be additional crematories that are not on the lists I used for this research.

▶ **Body Donation**

Medical University of South
 Carolina
Department of Anatomy
171 Ashley Ave.
Charleston, SC 29425
803-792-3521, ext 211

Cost to family: none;
 transportation provided
 within state
Prior enrollment: required
Over-enrollment: not yet
 occurred
Disposition: cremation; return
 of cremains by request at
 expense of family
Body rejection: autopsy,
 decomposition, burn victim,
 AIDS, other at discretion
 of University

University of South Carolina
School of Medicine
Department of Anatomy
Columbia, SC 29208
803-733-3369
803-777-7000

Cost to family: none;
 transportation provided
 within state
Prior enrollment: usually
 required
Over-enrollment: not yet
 occurred
Disposition: cremation; burial
 of cremains
Body rejection: autopsy, burn
 victim, hepatitis, AIDS,
 over-enrollment, embalming
 (usually)

▶ **State Funeral Board**

The South Carolina State Board of Funeral Service has eleven members. There are two consumer representatives.

(This section was reviewed by the South Carolina Department of Health and Environmental Control, Office of Vital Records.)

In South Dakota

Please refer to Chapter 9 as you use this section.

Persons in South Dakota may care for their own dead. The legal authority to do so is found in these and ensuing statutes:

> Title 34-25-25: The funeral director or person acting as such who first assumes custody of a dead body shall file the death certificate.

> Title 34-26-14: The person charged by law with the duty of burying the body of a deceased person is entitled to the custody of such body. . .

> Title 34-26-16: The duty of burying the body of a deceased person. . . devolves upon the persons hereinafter specified: (1) . . . the husband or wife; (2) . . . person or persons in the same degree nearest of kin to the decedent, being of adult age. . .

There are no other statutes or regulations which might require you to use a funeral director when embalming is not desired.

▶ **Death Certificate**

The family doctor will sign the death certificate within 24 hours, stating the cause of death. The remaining information must be supplied, typewritten or in permanent ink. Use a ballpoint pen; there are two copies. The death certificate(s) must be filed with the local registrar within three days and before removal from the state.

▶ **Fetal Death**

A fetal death report is required after 20 weeks of gestation or when the weight is 500 grams or more. If there is no family physician involved, the local coroner must sign the fetal death certificate. All other procedures apply if disposition is handled by the family.

► **Transporting and Disposition Permit**

The local registrar will issue the burial-transit permit.

► **Burial**

Check with the county registrar for local zoning laws regarding home burial. There are no state burial statutes or regulations with regard to depth. The common practice in South Dakota is six feet deep.

When burial is arranged, the family member acting as the funeral director must sign the authorization for disposition and file the original with the local registrar within ten days. The third copy is retained by the cemetery. In the case of home burial, the county registrar may request this copy for recording.

► **Cremation**

No additional permit for cremation is required. Most crematories insist that a pacemaker be removed, and authorization by next-of-kin usually is required. The crematory will sign the permit for disposition which then must be filed with the local registrar within ten days.

► **Other Requirements**

South Dakota has no other requirements controlling the time schedule for the disposition of unembalmed bodies as long as it is within a "reasonable" time. Weather should be considered.

If the person died of a contagious or communicable disease, the doctor in attendance should be consulted.

► **Crematories**

Miller Funeral Home
507 So. Main St.
Sioux Falls, SD 57102
605-336-2640
Available: crematory day
   time, 24-hour phone

Cost of cremation only: $212
Body container requirements:
   rigid combustible
Cardboard casket: $65
Cost of mailing cremains:
   included
Payment: 30 days

Black Hill Crematory, Inc.
1440 Junction Ave.
Sturgis, SD 57785
605-347-3986
Jolley Funeral Home
Available: 24 hours

Cost of cremation only: $210
Body container requirements:
 rigid combustible
Cardboard casket: $35
Cost of mailing cremains:
 included
Payment: at time of delivery

These are the only crematories in South Dakota at the time
of this publication.

▶ **Body Donation**

University of South Dakota
Office of Dean
School of Medicine
Vermillion, SD 57069
605-677-5431 or
 677-5141
If no answer, call
 624-3932

Cost to family: transportation
 over 20 cents per mile
 South Dakota only or
 beyond 60-mile radius from
 Vermillion
Prior enrollment: not required
Over-enrollment: has not
 occurred
Disposition: cremation/ burial
 of cremains in local
 cemetery; return of
 cremains or remains by
 request and at expense of
 family
Body rejection: standard*
All prior donors accepted
 regardless of condition.

*autopsy, decomposition, mutilation, severe burn victim,
meningitis, hepatitis, AIDS

▶ **State Funeral Board**

The South Dakota State Board of Embalmers and Funeral
Directors has seven members. There are two consumer
representatives.

(This section was reviewed by the Office of Attorney General
for the state of South Dakota.)

In Tennessee

Please refer to Chapter 9 as you use this section.

Persons in Tennessee may care for their own dead. The legal authority to do so is found in this and ensuing statutes:

Title 68-3-502: (3b) The funeral director or person acting as such who first assumes custody of the dead body shall file the death certificate.

There are no other statutes or regulations which might require you to use a funeral director when embalming is not desired.

▶ **Death Certificate**

The family doctor or medical examiner will sign the death certificate within 48 hours, stating the cause of death. The remaining information must be supplied, typewritten or in black unfading ink. The death certificate must be filed with the local registrar of vital records within five days and usually before final disposition.

▶ **Fetal Death**

A fetal death report is required after 22 weeks of gestation or when the weight is 500 grams or more. If there is no family physician involved, the local medical examiner must sign the fetal death report. The report must be filed with the Department of Health within ten days. All other procedures apply if disposition is handled by the family.

▶ **Transporting and Disposition Permit**

A body may be moved with the consent of a physician or medical examiner. The registrar where the death certificate is to be filed can issue a burial-transit permit for cremation or removal from the state if the death certificate is not yet complete. However, persons handling death arrangements without the use of a funeral director should try to obtain the death certificate, if at all possible, before disposition.

▶ **Burial**

Family burial grounds are permitted. Check with the local registrar for local zoning laws regarding home burial. There are no state burial statutes or regulations regarding depth.

▶ **Cremation**

While no additional permit for cremation is mandated by state law, a crematory will require you to obtain a permit from the registrar in the local county Health Department. Most crematories insist that a pacemaker be removed, and authorization by next-of-kin usually is required.

▶ **Other Requirements**

Tennessee has no other requirements controlling the time schedule for the disposition of unembalmed bodies. Weather and reasonable planning should be considered.

If the person died of a contagious or communicable disease, the doctor in attendance should be consulted.

▶ **Crematories**

Highland Memorial Cemetery
P.O. Box 10106
Knoxville, TN 37939
615-588-0567
Funeral home affiliated
Available: 24 hours

Cost of cremation only: call
Body container requirements:
  cardboard only
Cardboard casket: $15
Payment: negotiable

East Tennessee Cremation Co.
Rte. 8, Box 431
Singleton Station Rd.
Maryville, TN 37801
615-970-2087
Funeral home affiliated
Available: 8-5 M-Sat.
  or by arrangement

Cost of cremation only: $200
Body container requirements:
  rigid combustible
Cardboard casket: not carried
Cost of mailing cremains: $10
Payment: at time of delivery

Memphis Memorial Park
5668 Poplar Avenue
P.O. Box 17338, White Sta.
Memphis, TN 38117
901-767-8930
Funeral home affiliated
Available: 24 hours

Cost of cremation only: $210
Body container requirements:
  rigid combustible
Cardboard casket: $45
Cost of mailing cremains: $25
Payment: negotiable

Two crematories, one in Gray and one in Nashville, declined to accept a body from other than a funeral director. Concerns were: "$600 isn't that much. . . I don't want to have to take them out of the back of station wagons," "I don't see any possibility of changing."

There may be additional crematories that are not on the lists I used for this research.

▸ **Body Donation**

East Tennessee State
  University
Department of Anatomy
Box 19960A
Johnson City, TN 38614
615-929-6241 8-5 M-F, or
  929-4480

Cost to family: transportation
  beyond 150 miles or if
  other than contract
  mortician
Prior enrollment: not required
Over-enrollment: occasionally
  shared by request
Disposition: cremation/burial
  or scattering; return of
  cremains by request
Body rejection: standard*,
  under 15, previous embalming, 300 lbs.

University of Tennessee
Department of Anatomy
875 Monroe Ave.
Memphis, TN 38163
901-528-5965 days, or
  528-5500

Cost to family: transportation
  and embalming if not prior
  enrolled
Prior enrollment: preferred
  but not required
Over-enrollment: not yet
  occurred
Disposition: burial in county
  cemetery; return of remains
  by request
Body rejection: standard*,
  infant, obesity

Meharry Medical College
Nashville, TN 37208

Repeated requests for
information have not been
returned by this school.

Vanderbilt University
School of Medicine
Nashville, TN 37203

Repeated requests for
information have not been
returned by this school.

*autopsy, decomposition, mutilation, severe burn victim, meningitis, hepatitis, AIDS

▸ **State Funeral Board**

The Tennessee State Board of Funeral Directors and Embalmers has five members. There is one consumer representative.

(This section was reviewed by the Assistant General Counsel for the Tennessee Department of Health and Environment.)

In Texas

Please refer to Chapter 9 as you use this section.

Persons in Texas may care for their own dead. The legal authority to do so is found in these and ensuing statutes:

Title 71-4477-40a: The person in charge of interment or of removal of the body from the district for disposition shall be responsible for obtaining and filing the certificate. . .

Title 71-4477-42a: That the undertaker, or person acting as undertaker, shall file the certificate of death with the local registrar of the district in which the death occurred; provided that any person who furnishes a casket, coffin or box in which to bury the dead and who renders service like or similar to that usually rendered by an undertaker, shall for the purposes of the Act be deemed an undertaker.

There are no other statutes or regulations which might require you to use a funeral director when embalming is not desired.

▶ **Death Certificate**

The family doctor or a local health officer will sign the death certificate stating the cause of death. The remaining information must be supplied, typewritten or in black ink. The death certificate must be filed with the local registrar within 10 days.

▶ **Fetal Death**

A fetal death report is required for each fetal death. If there is no family physician involved, the local health officer must sign the fetal death certificate. All other procedures apply if disposition is handled by the family.

▶ **Transporting and Disposition Permit**

The local registrar or deputy registrar will issue the burial-transit permit.

▶ **Burial**

Check with the county registrar for local zoning laws regarding home burial. The casket must not be less than two feet below the surface of the ground.

▶ **Cremation**

No additional permit for cremation is required. There is a 48-hour wait before cremation unless the person died of a contagious disease. The local medical examiner, or if none a justice of the peace, may waive the waiting period. Most crematories insist that a pacemaker be removed, and authorization by next-of-kin usually is required.

▶ **Other Requirements**

Texas has no other requirements controlling the time schedule for the disposition of unembalmed bodies. Weather and reasonable planning should be considered.

If the person died of a contagious or communicable disease, the doctor in attendance should be consulted.

▸ **Crematories**

Clifford Jackson Crematory
4200 Kostoryz
Corpus Christi, TX 78415
512-852-8233
Funeral home affiliated
Available: 24 hours

Cost of cremation only: $160
Body container requirements:
  rigid combustible
Cardboard casket: $58
Cost of mailing cremains:
  included
Payment: at time of delivery

Restland Memorial Park
Greenville Ave. & Restland
P.O. Box 31000
Dallas, TX 75231
214-235-7111
Restland Funeral Home
Available: 8-5 M-F,
  weekends by arrangement

Cost of cremation only: $135
Body container requirements:
  rigid combustible, not
  cardboard
Plywood casket: $65
Cost of mailing cremains: $25
Payment: negotiable

Evergreen East Cemetery
East Montana
El Paso, TX 79902
915-532-5511
Independent
Available: 8-5 M-F,
  weekends by arrangement

Cost of cremation only: $154
Body container requirements:
  rigid combustible
Cardboard casket: not carried
Cost of mailing cremains: $13
Payment: at time of delivery

Laurel Land Memorial Park
7100 Crowley Rd.
P.O. Box 6520
Ft. Worth, TX 76115
817-293-1350
Funeral home affiliated
Available: 9-5 M-Sat.,
  24-hour phone

Cost of cremation only: $155
Body container requirements:
  rigid combustible, not
  cardboard
Particle board casket: $125
Cost of mailing cremains: $15
Payment: at time of delivery,
  negotiable

Brookside Memorial Park
13401 Eastex Freeway
P.O. Box 11098
Houston, TX 77016
713-449-6511
Funeral home affiliated
Available: 8-5 M-F,
  8-1 Sat., 24-hour phone

Cost of cremation only: $130
Body container requirements:
  rigid combustible
Cardboard casket: $50
Cost of mailing cremains: $20
Payment: at time of delivery

Memorial Oaks Cemetery and
Crematory
13001 Katy Highwary
P.O. Box 19356
Houston, TX 77024
713-497-2210
Independent
Available: 8-4 M-F,
weekends by arrangement

Cost of cremation only: $140
Body container requirements:
rigid combustible
Cardboard casket: not carried
Cost of mailing cremains: $35
Payment: at time of delivery

Resthaven Memorial Garden
13102 N. Freeway
P.O. Box 16310
Houston, TX 77060
713-443-8666
Earthman-Resthaven Funeral
Home
Available: 7-4:30 M-Sat.,
24-hour phone

Cost of cremation only: $175
Body container requirements:
rigid combustible
Cardboard casket: $50
Cost of mailing cremains: $35
Payment: at time of delivery,
negotiable

South Park Crematory
12400 Telephone
P.O. Box 12655
Houston, TX 77017
713-485-2711
Niday-South Park Funeral
Home
Available: 8-5 M-Sat.,
24-hour phone

Cost of cremation only: $110
Body container requirements:
rigid combustible
Cardboard casket: $50
Cost of mailing cremains: $10
Payment: at time of delivery

Palm Valley Crematory
P.O. Box 644
Pharr, TX 78577
512-787-5222
Independent
Available: 24 hours

Cost of cremation only: $95
Body container requirements:
rigid combustible
Cardboard casket: not carried
Cost of mailing cremains: $10
Payment: at time of delivery

Mission Burial Park
1700 S.E. Military Drive
P.O. Box 2100
San Antonio, TX 78218
512-924-4242
Funeral home affiliated
Available: 8-4:30 M-Sat.

Cost of cremation only: $150
Body container requirements:
rigid combustible
Cardboard casket: $125
Cost of mailing cremains: $25
Payment: at time of delivery

Sunset Memorial Park
1701 Austin
San Antonio, TX 78218
512-828-2811
Sunset Funeral Home
Available: 9-5 M-Sat.,
24-hour phone

Cost of cremation only: $170
Body container requirements:
rigid combustible
Cardboard casket: $75
Cost of mailing cremains: $20
Payment: at time of delivery

Six crematories, one each in Amarillo, Austin, Big Spring, Brownsville, Corpus Christi and Dallas, declined to accept a body from other than a funeral director. Their concerns were: "I deal only with funeral directors," "Liability," "State law," "Too much paperwork," " We have a funeral home here," "We depend on income from funeral homes, not public."

There may be additional crematories that are not on the lists I used for this research.

▸ **Body Donation**

Texas A & M University
Department of Anatomy
Medical Science Building
Medical College
College Station, TX 77843
409-845-4914
822-1571

Cost to family: transportation
beyond 250 miles
Prior enrollment: preferred
but not required
Over-enrollment: shared
Disposition: cremation; return
of cremains if requested
Body rejection: autopsy, burn
victim, decomposition,
hepatitis, AIDS, under 15

University of Texas
Health Science Center
Southwestern Medical School
5323 Harry Hines Blvd.
Dallas, TX 75235
214-688-2232
688-2221

Cost to family: transportation
beyond 50 miles
Prior enrollment: preferred
but not always required
Over-enrollment: shared with
permission
Disposition: cremation; return
of cremains
Body rejection: All prior
enrolled are accepted
regardless of condition.

North Texas State University
College of Osteopathic
  Medicine
Camp Bowie at Montgomery
Fort Worth, TX 76107
817-735-2210

Cost to family: transportation
  beyond 50 miles
Prior enrollment: not required
Over-enrollment: shared
Disposition: cremation/ burial
  in University crypt; return
  of cremains by request
Body rejection: standard*,
  under 18, syphilis, suicide,
  missing body parts
  (sometimes)

University of Texas
Medical Branch at Galveston
Galveston, TX 77550
409-761-1293
409-761-1011

Cost to family: transportation
  beyond 300 miles
Prior enrollment: not required
Over-enrollment: shared
Disposition: cremation; return
  of cremains by request
Body rejection: AIDS,
  decomposition, hepatitis,
  meningitis, autopsy
  (usually)

Baylor College of Medicine
Department of Cell Biology
Texas Medical Center
Houston, TX 77030
713-799-4930
Brookside Funeral Home
713-449-6511

Cost to family: transportation
  beyond 100 miles/over $130
Prior enrollment: not required
Over-enrollment: shared
Disposition: cremation/
  scattered at Brookside
  Memorial Park; return of
  cremains by request
Body rejection: standard*,
  under 21, suicide, trauma,
  other communicable
  diseases

University of Texas Medical
  School
Health Science Center
Dept. of Neurobiology and
  Anatomy
P.O. Box 20708
Houston, TX 77225
713-792-5703
Brookside Funeral Home
713-449-6511

Cost to family: transportation
  beyond 250 miles
Prior enrollment: not required
Over-enrollment: shared
Disposition: cremation/
  scattered at Brookside
  Memorial Park
Body rejection: autopsy,
  meningitis, hepatitis, AIDS,
  under 14

Texas Tech University
School of Medicine
Lubbock, TX 79430
806-743-2700 weekdays, or
806-743-3111

Cost to family: transportation beyond 300 miles
Prior enrollment: required
Over-enrollment: shared
Disposition: cremation; return of cremains by request
Body rejection: standard*, under five years of age

Texas Chiropractic College
5912 Spencer Hwy.
Pasadena, TX 77505
713-487-1170 8-5 M-F

Cost to family: some transportation
Prior enrollment: not required
Over-enrollment: shared
Disposition: cremation
Body rejection: standard*, missing body parts

University of Texas
Health Science Center
7703 Floyd Curls Dr.
San Antonio, TX 78284-7762
512-691-6533

Cost to family: transportation beyond 100 miles
Prior enrollment: required
Over-enrollment: shared
Disposition: cremation/ burial of cremains in University plot; return of cremains by request
Body rejection: autopsy, burn victim, hepatitis, Jacob Creutzfeldt et al, herpes, drowning, homicide, suicide, trauma, obesity, emaciation

*autopsy, decomposition, mutilation, severe burn victim, meningitis, hepatitis, AIDS

▶ **State Funeral Board**

The Texas State Board of Morticians has five members. There is one consumer representative.

(This section was sent to the Texas Department of Health for review, but no response was received by publication date.)

In Utah

Please refer to Chapter 9 as you use this section.

Persons in Utah may care for their own dead. The legal authority to do so is found in these and ensuing statutes:

Title 26-2-13 (4): The funeral director or person acting as the funeral director who first assumes custody of the dead body shall file the certificate of death.

Title 26-2-17 (3): A burial-transit permit shall be issued by the registrar of the district where the certificate of death or fetal death is filed, for bodies to be transported out of the state for final disposition and when disposition is made by a person other than a licensed funeral director.

There are no other statutes or regulations which might require you to use a funeral director when embalming is not desired.

▶ **Death Certificate**

The attending physician will sign the death certificate within 72 hours, stating the cause of death. The remaining information must be supplied, typewritten or in black ink. The death certificate must be filed with the local registrar within five days and before final disposition.

▶ **Fetal Death**

A fetal death certificate is required for each fetal death. If there is no family physician involved, the local medical examiner must sign the fetal death certificate. All other procedures apply if disposition is handled by the family.

▶ **Transporting and Disposition Permit**

The local registrar will issue the burial-transit permit. This will be required before a body can be released from a hospital. After usual business hours, a law enforcement official or someone "on call" will supply the permit. Unless moved by a funeral director, a body must be encased in a container or plastic pouch.

▸ **Burial**

Check with the county registrar for local zoning laws regarding home burial. There are no state burial statutes or regulations regarding depth.

When burial is arranged, the family member acting as the funeral director must sign the burial-transit permit and file it with the registrar of the district where disposition takes place, by the 10th of the following month.

▸ **Cremation**

No additional permit is required for cremation. Most crematories insist that a pacemaker be removed, and authorization by next-of-kin usually is required. The crematory may offer to file the burial-transit permit.

▸ **Other Requirements**

After 24 hours a body must be embalmed or refrigerated.

If the person died of a contagious or communicable disease, the doctor in attendance should be consulted.

A body to be shipped by common carrier must be embalmed.

▸ **Crematories**

Aultorest Memorial Park
836 36th St.
Ogden, UT 84403
801-394-5556
Funeral home affiliated
Available: 24 hours

Cost of cremation only: $100
Body container requirements:
   rigid combustible
Cardboard casket: $65
Cost of mailing cremains: $10
Payment: negotiable, 30 days

Lindquist & Son
3408 Washington Blvd.
Ogden, UT 84401
801-394-6667
Funeral home
Available: 24 hours

Cost of cremation only: $125
Body container requirements:
   rigid combustible
Cardboard casket: $25
Payment: at time of delivery

Deseret Mortuary
36 East 700 South
Salt Lake City, UT 84111
801-566-1249
Available: 24 hours

Cost of cremation only:
$135 cardboard/cash-$108
$145 softwood/cash-$116
$165 hardwood/cash-$132
Body container requirements:
rigid combustible
Cardboard casket: available
Cost of mailing cremains: $10
Payment: at time of delivery,
negotiable

Neil O'Donnell & Son
372 East 100 South
Salt Lake City, UT 84111
801-363-6641
Funeral home
Available: 24 hours

Cost of cremation only: $125
Body container requirements:
rigid combustible
Cardboard casket: $22.50
Cost of mailing cremains: $25
Payment: negotiable

Larkin Sunset Lawn Mortuary
2350 East 1300 South
Salt Lake City, UT 84106
801-582-1582
Available: 9-6 M-Sat.,
1-5 Sun., 24-hour phone

Cost of cremation only: $125
Body container requirements:
rigid combustible
Cardboard casket: $55
Cost of mailing cremains: $35
Payment: at time of delivery,
negotiable

There may be additional crematories that are not on the lists
I used for this research.

▶ **Body Donation**

University of Utah
Department of Anatomy
50 N. Medical Dr.
Salt Lake City, UT 84132
801-581-6728 8-5 M-F
581-2121 other times

Cost to family: transportation
beyond 50-mile radius
Prior enrollment: not required
Over-enrollment: shared
Disposition: cremation; return
of cremains by request
Body rejection: standard*,
jaundice, obesity, young
child/infant

*autopsy, decomposition, mutilation, severe burn victim,
meningitis, hepatitis, AIDS

▶ **State Funeral Board**

The Utah State Board of Funeral Service has five members.
There is one consumer representative.

(The Utah section was reviewed by the Director of Vital Records, Utah Department of Health.)

In Vermont

Please refer to Chapter 9 as you use this section.

Persons in Vermont may care for their own dead. The legal authority to do so is found in this and ensuing statutes:

> Title 18, Section 5207. **Certificate furnished family; burial permit.** The physician or person filling out the certificate of death, within thirty-six hours after death, shall deliver the same to the family of the deceased, if any, or the undertaker or person who has charge of the body. Such certificate shall be filed with the person issuing the certificate of permission for burial, entombment or removal obtained by the person who has charge of the body before such dead body shall be buried, entombed or removed from the town. . .

There are no other statutes or regulations which might require you to use a funeral director when embalming is not desired.

▶ **Death Certificate**

The family doctor or a local medical examiner will sign the death certificate within 24 hours, stating the cause of death. The remaining information must be supplied, typewritten or in black ink. The death certificate must be delivered to the local town clerk where death occurred before final disposition in order to obtain a signature on the burial-transit permit. It must be returned to this town clerk after final disposition.

▶ **Fetal Death**

A fetal death report is required after 20 weeks of gestation or when the weight is 400 grams or more. All other procedures apply if disposition is handled by the family.

▸ **Transporting and Disposition Permit**

The local registrar or deputy registrar (funeral director) will sign the burial-transit permit. It is attached to the back of the death certificate. This permit must be filed with the registrar of the town in which disposition takes place by the first week of the following month.

▸ **Burial**

If burial is planned for private land set aside for the use of immediate family, the town clerk will need a map of the location to record in the land records. (A hand-drawn will usually suffice.) Check with the town clerk for local zoning laws regarding home burial. The bottom (not the top) of the casket must be five feet below the natural surface of the earth (three and one-half feet for infants). Burial must be at least 100 feet from a drilled well and 150 feet from shallow wells or streams. The burial site must be 25 feet from a power line.

When burial is arranged, the family member acting as the funeral director must sign the burial-transit permit and file it with the clerk of the town in which burial will occur.

▸ **Cremation**

A permit for cremation must be obtained from the medical examiner. The fee for this is $10. Most crematories insist that a pacemaker be removed, and authorization by next-of-kin usually is required. The crematory may offer to file the burial-transit permit.

▸ **Other Requirements**

Vermont has no other requirements controlling the time schedule for the disposition of unembalmed bodies. Weather and reasonable planning should be considered.

If the person died of a contagious or communicable disease, the doctor in attendance should be consulted. Disposition may be under the instructions of the local health officer.

▸ **Crematories**

Vermont Cremation Service
213 W. Main St.
Bennington, VT 05201
802-442-4329
Hanson-Walbridge Funeral
  Home
Available: 24 hours

Cost of cremation only: $125
Body container requirements:
  rigid combustible
Cardboard casket: $30
Cost of mailing cremains:
  postage
Payment: at time of delivery,
  negotiable

Mt. Pleasant Crematorium
39 Mt. Pleasant Ave.
St. Johnsbury, VT 05819
802-748-3063
Independent
Available: 24-hour phone

Cost of cremation only: $105
Body container requirements:
  rigid combustible
Cardboard casket: not carried
Cost of mailing cremains: $15
Payment: at time of delivery

One crematory, in South Burlington, declined to accept a body from other than a funeral director.

▸ **Body Donation**

University of Vermont
Department of Anatomy
Burlington, VT 05405
802-656-2230 8-5 M-F
  656-3131, other times

(This appears to be the only medical school that does not have a definite plan for body disposition if no return is requested by the family.)

Cost to family: transportation, even from Medical
  Center of Vermont
Prior enrollment: not required
Over-enrollment: shared
Disposition: Unless the family
  requests return of remains
  or cremation at its own
  expense, the body is stored
  at the medical school
  facility "indefinitely."
Body rejection: standard*

*autopsy, decomposition, mutilation, severe burn victim, meningitis, hepatitis, AIDS

▸ **State Funeral Board**

The Vermont State Board of Funeral Directors has three members. There are no consumer representatives.

(This section was reviewed by the Vermont Department of Health, Vital Records.)

In Virginia

Please refer to Chapter 9 as you use this section.

Persons in Virginia may care for their own dead. The legal authority to do so is found in:

> Title 32.1-263-B.: The funeral director or person who first assumes custody of a dead body shall file the certificate of death with the registrar.

There are no other statutes or regulations which might require you to use a funeral director when embalming is not desired.

▸ **Death Certificate**

The family doctor or a local medical examiner will sign the death certificate within 24 hours, stating the cause of death. The remaining information must be supplied, typewritten or in black, unfading ballpoint pen. The death certificate (two-copies) must be filed with the local registrar within three days and prior to disposition or removal from the state.

▸ **Fetal Death**

A fetal death report is required for each fetal death. If there is no family physician involved, the local medical examiner must sign the fetal death certificate. All other procedures apply if disposition is handled by the family.

▸ **Transporting and Disposition Permit**

A body may be moved with medical permission. If removal will be beyond the city or county, the registrar must be notified. A burial-transit permit is required only for out-of-state disposition. The death certificate must be obtained first. In all cases the local registrar must sign line 30 of the death certificate before disposition.

▶ **Burial**

The state requires no additional permit for disposition by burial. There are no state burial statutes or regulations with regard to depth. Check with the county registrar for local zoning laws regarding home burial.

Family graveyards, abandoned after 25 years, may be moved with the permission of the circuit court if there is no objection.

▶ **Cremation or Burial at Sea**

A permit for cremation or burial at sea must be obtained from the medical examiner. The usual fee for this is $50. There is a 24-hour wait before cremation or burial at sea unless visual identification and authorization are made by next-of-kin. Most crematories insist that a pacemaker be removed.

▶ **Other Requirements**

Virginia has no other requirements controlling the time schedule for the disposition of unembalmed bodies. Weather and reasonable planning should be considered.

If the person died of a contagious or communicable disease, the doctor in attendance should be consulted.

▶ **Crematories**

Blue Ridge Cremation Service
320 N. Bridge St.
Bedford, VA 24523
703-586-3443
Funeral home affiliated
Available: 24 hours

Cost of cremation only: $160
Body container requirements:
  none
Cardboard casket: $89
Cost of mailing cremains: $25
Payment: negotiable

Richlands Tazewell Crematory
210 Cedar Valley Drive
Cedar Bluffs, VA 24609
703-964-4011
Funeral home affiliated
Available: 24 hours

Cost of cremation only: $295
Body container requirements:
  none
Cardboard casket: $35
Cost of mailing cremains:
  postage
Payment: negotiable

Newport Crematory, Inc.
12746 Nettles Dr.
Newport News, VA 23606
804-596-2222
Funeral home affiliated
Available: 24 hours

Cost of cremation only: $125
Body container requirements:
  rigid combustible
Cardboard casket: $35
Cost of mailing cremains: $10
Payment: negotiable

Colonial Crematory, Inc.
1501 Colonial Ave.
Norfolk, VA 23517
804-623-9928
Funeral home affiliated
Available: 24 hours

Cost of cremation only: $100
Body container requirements:
  rigid combustible
Cardboard casket: $55
Cost of mailing cremains:
  postage
Payment: at time of delivery,
  negotiable

Forest Lawn
4000 Alma Ave.
Richmond, VA 23222
804-321-7655
Independent
Available: 8-4:30 M-F,
  24-hour phone

Cost of cremation only: $120
Body container requirements:
  rigid combustible
Cardboard casket: not carried
Cost of mailing cremains:
  included
Payment: at time of delivery

Greenwood Crematory
14101 Patterson Ave.
Richmond, VA 23233
804-784-5214
Independent
Available: 24 hours

Cost of cremation only: $135
Body container requirements:
  rigid combustible
Cardboard casket: available
Cost of mailing cremains:
  included
Payment: at time of delivery,
  negotiable, 30 days

Lynn Haven Crematory
3600 Virginia Blvd.
Virginia Beach, VA 23452
804-463-0150
Holloman-Brown F.H.
Available: 24 hours

Cost of cremation only: $120
Body container requirements:
  rigid combustible
Cardboard casket: not carried
Cost of mailing cremains:
  included
Payment: negotiable

Omps Crematory Service
1600 Amherst St.
Winchester, VA 22601
703-662-6633
Funeral home affiliated
Available: 24 hours

Cost of cremation only: $135
Body container requirements:
  rigid combustible
Cardboard casket: $50
Cost of mailing cremains:
  included
Payment: negotiable

Two crematories, one each in Harrisonburg and Salem, declined to accept a body from other than a funeral director. One said, "We just won't take them."

There may be additional crematories that are not on the lists I used for this research.

▶ **Body Donation**

State Anatomy Division
Department of Health
Richmond, VA 23219
804-786-2479 or
  786-2474 or
  786-3774

Cost to family: transportation
  over $25
Prior enrollment: not required
Over-enrollment: shared
state-wide
Disposition: cremation
Body rejection: standard*

*autopsy, decomposition, mutilation, severe burn victim, meningitis, hepatitis, AIDS

▶ **State Funeral Board**

The Virginia State Board of Funeral Directors and Embalmers has nine members. There are two consumer representatives.

(This section was reviewed by the Virginia Department of Health, Division of Vital Records.)

In Washington

Please refer to Chapter 9 as you use this section.

Persons in Washington may care for their own dead. The legal authority to do so is found in:

> 70.58.240: Each funeral director or person acting as such shall obtain a certificate of death and file the same with the local registrar, and secure a burial-transit permit, prior to any permanent disposition of the body.

There are no other statutes or regulations which might

require you to use a funeral director when embalming is not desired.

▸ **Death Certificate**

The family doctor or a local medical examiner will sign the death certificate within 48 hours, stating the cause of death. The remaining information must be supplied, typewritten or in black ink. The death certificate must be filed with the local registrar within 72 hours and before final disposition. The charge for filing the death certificate is $1 if it is filed in a county other than the county where death occurred.

▸ **Fetal Death**

A fetal death report is required after 20 weeks of gestation. If there is no family physician involved, the local medical examiner must sign the fetal death certificate. The fetal death certificate must be filed within five days. All other procedures apply if disposition is handled by the family.

▸ **Transporting and Disposition Permit**

The local registrar will issue the burial-transit permit. This authorization must be obtained within 72 hours of death and prior to final disposition of the body. After usual business hours, check with the medical examiner's office.

▸ **Burial**

Home burial is not permitted in Washington state. There are, however, (inexpensive) county cemeteries where a family might be allowed to handle the burial. The top of the casket must be three feet below the surface of the earth. The sexton will file the burial-transit permit.

▸ **Cremation**

The burial-transit permit serves as a permit for cremation. Most crematories insist that a pacemaker be removed, and authorization by next-of-kin usually is required. The crematory will return the disposition authorization to the issuing registrar.

▸ **Other Requirements**

Washington requires embalming or refrigeration if disposition has not been accomplished within 24 hours.

If the person died of a contagious or communicable disease, the doctor in attendance should be consulted. Death from cholera or plague requires embalming or cremation.

▶ **Crematories**

Fern Hill Cemetery
End of Roosevelt
Aberdeen, WA 98520
206-533-2930
Independent
Available: 8-4:30 M-F,
 9-12 Sat. or by
 arrangement

Cost of cremation only: $95
Body container requirements:
 rigid combustible
Cardboard casket: not carried
Cost of mailing cremains:
 postage
Payment: negotiable

Sunset Hills Memorial Park
1215 145th St. S.E.
Bellevue, WA 98009
206-747-6240
Green Funeral Home
Available: 9-5 M-F,
 24-hour phone

Cost of cremation only: $198
Body container requirements:
 rigid combustible
Cardboard casket: $35
Cost of mailing cremains: $30
plus postage
Payment: at time of delivery

Veroske-Jerns-Leveck
James & Sunset
Bellingham, WA 98225
206-734-0070
Funeral home affiliated
Available: 24 hours

Cost of cremation only: $130
Body container requirements:
 rigid combustible
Cardboard casket: $45
Cost of mailing cremains: $20
Payment: 30 days

Miller Woodlawn Memorial
 Park
5505 Kitsap Way
Bremerton, WA 98310
206-377-7648
Funeral home affiliated
Available: 8-5 M-F,
 8-1 Sat., 24-hour phone

Cost of cremation only: $175
Body container requirements:
 rigid combustible
Cardboard casket: $40
Cost of mailing cremains: $30
Payment: at time of delivery,
 negotiable

Cypress Lawn Memorial Park
1615 S.E. Everett Mall Way
Everett, WA 98204
206-353-7141
Independent
Available: 9-5 M-F,
 10-3 Sat.

Cost of cremation only: $85
Body container requirements:
 rigid combustible
Cardboard casket: included
Cost of mailing cremains: $25
Payment: negotiable

Purdy & Walters with Cassidy
P.O. Box 1320
Everett, WA 98206
206-252-2191
Funeral home affiliated
Available: 9-5 daily,
  24-hour phone

Cost of cremation only: $100
Body container requirements:
  rigid combustible
Plywood casket: $85
Cost of mailing cremains: $25
Payment: negotiable

Greenacres Memorial Park
5700 Northwest Rd.
Ferndale, WA 98248
206-384-3401
Greenacres Funeral Home
Available: 9-5 M-F,
  24-hour phone

Cost of cremation only: $155
Body container requirements:
  rigid combustible
Cardboard casket: not carried
Cost of mailing cremains: $20
Payment: negotiable

Green Hills Memorial Garden
1939 Mt. Brynion Rd.
Kelso, WA 98626
206-636-0540
Independent
Available: 6:30-4:30 M-F,
  Sat. by request

Cost of cremation only: $150
Body container requirements:
  rigid combustible
Cardboard casket: not carried
Cost of mailing cremains:
  postage
Payment: at time of delivery

Desert Lawn Memorial Park
1401 S. Union
Kennewick, WA 99336
509-783-9532
Funeral home affiliated
Available: 9-5 M-F

Cost of cremation only: $200
Body container requirements:
  rigid combustible
Cardboard casket: available
Cost of mailing cremains:
  postage
Payment: at time of delivery

Hawthorne Lawn Memorial
  Park
P.O. Box 398
Mt. Vernon, WA 98273
206-424-1154
Funeral home affiliated
Available: 24 hours

Cost of cremation only: $150
Body container requirements:
  rigid combustible
Cardboard casket: $35
Cost of mailing cremains: $25
Payment: at time of delivery

Mt. Vernon Cemetery
1200 E. Fir St.
Mt. Vernon, WA
206-336-6845
Kern Funeral Home
Available 8:30-4:30,
  24-hour phone

Cost of cremation only: $80
Body container requirements:
  rigid combustible
Cardboard casket: $50
Cost of mailing cremains: $15
Payment: negotiable

Forest Memorial Gardens
2501 Pacific Ave.
Olympia, WA 98506
206-943-6363
Forest Funeral Home
Available: 24 hours

Cost of cremation only: $320
Body container requirements:
  rigid combustible
Cardboard casket: $32
Cost of mailing cremains: $25
Payment: negotiable

Olympic Cremation
  Association
202 E. 9th
Olympia, WA 98501
206-357-4404
Olympic Funeral Home
Available: 8-5 daily

Cost of cremation only: $120
Body container requirements:
  rigid combustible
Cardboard casket: $30
Cost of mailing cremains: $25
Payment: at time of delivery,
  negotiable

Mt. Angeles Cemetery
Box 503
Port Angeles, WA 98362
206-452-6255
Independent
Available: 9-4:30 M-F, or
  by arrangement

Cost of cremation only: $125
Body container requirements:
  rigid combustible
Cardboard casket: available
Cost of mailing cremains: $25
Payment: at time of delivery,
  negotiable

Powers Funeral Home and
  Crematory
120 West Pioneer Ave.
Puyallup, WA 98371
206-845-0536
Available: 24 hours

Cost of cremation only: $165
Body container requirements:
  rigid combustible
Cardboard casket: $21
Cost of mailing cremains:
  included
Payment: at time of delivery

Mt. Olivet Cemetery
100 Blaine Ave. N.E., Box 547
Renton, WA 98057
206-255-0323
Independent
Available: 8-4:30,
  24-hour phone

Cost of cremation only: $153
Body container requirements:
  rigid combustible
Cardboard casket: not carried
Cost of mailing cremains:
  postage
Payment: at time of delivery

Einan's Funeral Home &
  Crematory
915 Bypass Hwy.
Richland, WA 99352
509-943-1114
Available: 24-hour phone

Cost of cremation only: $175
Body container requirements:
  rigid combustible
Cardboard casket: $25
Cost of mailing cremains:
  postage
Payment: at time of delivery

Acacia Memorial Park
15000 Bothwell Way, N.E.
Seattle, WA 98155
206-362-5525
Acacia Forkner & Home F.D.
206-364-7100
Available: 8:30-4:30,
  24-hour phone

Cost of cremation only: $100
Body container requirements:
  rigid combustible
Cardboard casket: not carried
Cost of mailing cremains: $50
Payment: negotiable

Arthur Wright Funeral Home
520 W. Raye St.
Seattle, WA 98133
206-282-5500
Available: 9-5 daily,
  24-hour phone

Cost of cremation only: $100
Body container requirements:
  rigid combustible, no
  cardboard
Plywood casket: $75
Cost of mailing cremains:
  postage
Payment: negotiable

Bleitz Funeral Home and
  Crematory
316 Florentia Street
Seattle, WA 98109
206-282-5220
Available: 24 hours

Cost of cremation only: $150
Body container requirements:
  rigid combustible, no
  particleboard, body wrapped
Cardboard casket: $35
Cost of mailing cremains: $40
Payment: negotiable

Bonney Watson
1732 Broadway
Seattle, WA 98122
206-322-0013
Funeral home affiliated
Available: 24 hours

Cost of cremation only: $175
Body container requirements:
  rigid combustible
Cardboard casket: $45
Cost of mailing cremains: $10
Payment: 30 days

Evergreen-Washelli Memorial
  Park
11111 Aurora Avenue N.
Seattle, WA 98133
206-362-5200
Funeral home affiliated
Available: 24 hours

Cost of cremation only: $145
Body container requirements:
  rigid combust. leakproof
Cardboard casket: $55
Cost of mailing cremains: $30
Payment: at time of delivery,
  negotiable

Forest Lawn Cemetery
6701 30th Avenue S.W.
Seattle, WA 98126
206-932-0050
Independent
Available: 9-5 M-Sat.

Cost of cremation only: $150
Body container requirements:
  rigid combustible
Cardboard casket: available
Cost of mailing cremains:
  postage
Payment: negotiable

Yarrington's White Center
10708 16th Avenue S.W.
Seattle, WA 98146
206-242-2771
Funeral home affiliated
Available: 8:30-5,
    24-hour phone

Cost of cremation only: $135
Body container requirements:
    rigid combustible
Cardboard casket: $40
Cost of mailing cremains: $35
Payment: at time of delivery,
    negotiable

McComb and Batstone
    Funeral Home
703 Railroad Ave.
P.O. Box 179
Shelton, WA 98584
206-426-4803
Available: 8-5,
    24-hour phone

Cost of cremation only: $190
Body container requirements:
    rigid combustible
Cardboard casket: $30
Cost of mailing cremains: $15
Payment: at time of delivery,
    negotiable

Hazen & Jaeger
1306 N. Monroe Street
Spokane, WA 99201
509-327-6666
Funeral home affiliated
Available: 24 hours

Cost of cremation only: $135
Body container requirements:
    rigid combustible
Cardboard casket: $40
Cost of mailing cremains: -
Payment: at time of delivery,
    negotiable

Hennessey-Smith Funeral
    Home and Crematory
N. 2203 Division St.
Spokane, WA 99207
509-328-2600
Available: 24 hours

Cost of cremation only: $175
$100 body examination
Body container requirements:
    rigid combustible
Cardboard casket: included
Cost of mailing cremains: $5
    plus postage
Payment: negotiable, 30 days

Riplinger Funeral Home
4305 N. Division Street
Spokane, WA 99207
509-483-8558
Available: 24 hours

Cost of cremation only: $220
Body container requirements:
    rigid combustible
Cardboard casket: $25
Cost of mailing cremains: $10
Payment: negotiable

Thornhill Valley Funeral
    Home and Crematory
1400 S. Pines
Spokane, WA 99206
509-924-2211
Available: 8-5 M-Sat.,
    Sun. by arrangement

Cost of cremation only: $135
Body container requirements:
    rigid combustible
Cardboard casket: $40
Cost of mailing cremains: $27
Payment: at time of delivery

Mountain View Memorial Park
4100 Steilacoom Blvd. S.W.
Tacoma, WA 98499
206-584-0252
Funeral home affiliated
Available: 8-5 M-Sat.,
  24-hour phone

Cost of cremation only: $179
Body container requirements:
  rigid combustible
Cardboard casket: $40
Cost of mailing cremains: $27
Payment: at time of delivery,
  negotiable

Oakwood Funeral Home and
  Crematory
5210 S. Alder Street
Tacoma, WA 98409
206-473-2900
Available: 9-5 M-F,
  24-hour phone

Cost of cremation only: $100
Body container requirements:
  rigid combustible
Cardboard casket: $40
Cost of mailing cremains: $35
Payment: 30 days

Tacoma Mausoleum Assn.
S. 53rd & Cedar Streets
Tacoma, WA 98409
206-474-9574
Funeral home affiliated
Available: 9-5 M-F,
  10-5 Sat./Sun.,
  24-hour phone

Cost of cremation only: $80
Body container requirements:
  rigid combustible
Cardboard casket: $50
Cost of mailing cremains:
  postage
Payment: at time of delivery,
  negotiable

Colonial-Dewitt Crematory
19 E. Birch Street
Walla Walla, WA 99362
509-529-4447
Funeral home affiliated
Available: 24 hours

Cost of cremation only: $125
Body container requirements:
  rigid combustible
Cardboard casket: $15
Cost of mailing cremains: $15
Payment: at time of delivery,
  negotiable

Professional Funeral Home
  and Crematory
2112 S. Second Avenue
Walla Walla, WA 99362
509-522-1625
Funeral home affiliated
Available: 24 hours

Cost of cremation only: $150
Body container requirements:
  rigid combustible
Cardboard casket: $30
Cost of mailing cremains: $10
Payment: negotiable

Jones and Jones
21 S. Chelan Avenue
Wenatche, WA 98801
509-662-2119
Funeral home affiliated
Available 8:30-5:30 M-Sat.,
   1-5:30 Sun., 24-hour phone

Cost of cremation only: $125
Body container requirements:
  rigid combustible
Cardboard casket: $24
Cost of mailing cremains: $15
plus postage
Payment: at time of delivery,
  negotiable

Terrace Heights Memorial
  Park
3001 Terrace Heights Rd.
Yakima, WA 98901
509-453-1961
Independent
Available: 9-5 M-F,
  9-12 Sat.

Cost of cremation only: $145
Body container requirements:
  rigid combustible
Cardboard casket: not carried
Cost of mailing cremains: $15
Payment: at time of delivery,
  negotiable

One crematory in Aberdeen agreed to accept a body from a
family or religious group but asked not to be listed in the
book. Three crematories, one each in Bremerton, Spokane and
Vancouver, declined to accept a body from other than a
funeral director. Their concerns were, "Too many loopholes,"
"I can't foresee any circumstances to change," and "This is
city-owned. . . we have a verbal agreement with the funeral
homes."

There may be additional crematories that are not on the lists
I used for this research.

▶ **Body Donation**

University of Washington
Department of Biological
Structure, SM-20
Seattle, WA 98195
206-543-1860
   548-3300 after hours

Cost to family: transportation
  beyond King County,
  University transports in
  county
Prior enrollment: preferred
  but not required
Over-enrollment: shared
Disposition: cremation/burial
  in University plot; return
  of cremains by request - to
  cemetery or funeral home
  only
Body rejection: autopsy,
  decomposition, meningitis,
  hepatitis, AIDS, cancer,
  trauma, obesity, previous
  embalming

▶ **State Funeral Board**

The Washington State Board of Funeral Directors and Embalmers has five members. There is one consumer representative.

(This section was reviewed by the Chairman of the Washington State Funeral Board and the Administrative Assistant to the State Cemetery Board.)

In West Virginia

Please refer to Chapter 9 as you use this section.

Members of a religious group in West Virginia may care for their own dead. The legal authority to do so is found in:

Title 30-6-9: (re embalmers and funeral directors) No provision of this article shall apply to or interfere with . . . the customs or rites of any religious sect in the burial of its dead.

There are no other statutes or regulations which might require you to use a funeral director when embalming is not desired.

▶ **Death Certificate**

The family doctor, local health officer or coroner will sign the death certificate within 24 hours, stating the cause of death. The remaining information must be supplied, typewritten or in black ball point ink; there are four copies. The death certificate must be filed with the local registrar within 72 hours and before final disposition.

▶ **Fetal Death**

A fetal death report is required after 20 weeks of gestation. All other procedures apply if disposition is handled by the family.

▶ **Transporting and Disposition Permit**

The local registrar must sign the death certificate within 72 hours of death and prior to final disposition of the body. The third page (blue) serves as the burial-transit permit.

▶ **Burial**

Check with the county registrar for local zoning laws regarding home burial. There are no state burial statutes or regulations with regard to depth.

When burial is arranged, the family member acting as the funeral director must sign the permit for disposition and file it with the local registrar within 10 days. When there is no person in charge of the burial ground, the words "No person in charge" shall be written across the face of the permit.

▶ **Cremation**

A permit for cremation must be obtained from the county medical examiner. The fee for this is $5. Most crematories insist that a pacemaker be removed, and authorization by next-of-kin usually is required. The crematory must sign the burial-transit permit before it is filed with the local registrar within 10 days.

▶ **Other Requirements**

West Virginia has no other requirements controlling the time schedule for the disposition of unembalmed bodies. Weather and reasonable planning should be considered.

If the person died of a contagious or communicable disease, the doctor in attendance should be consulted.

▶ **Crematories**

Keyser-Bryant Funeral Home and Crematory
1000 Johnstown
Beckley, WV 25801
304-252-8642
Available: 24 hours

Cost of cremation only: $200
Body container requirements: rigid combustible
Cardboard casket: $50
Cost of mailing cremains: included
Payment: negotiable

Barlow Bonsall Funeral Home
and Crematory
1118 Virginia St. E.
Charleston, WV 25301
304-342-8135
Available: 24 hours

Cost of cremation only: $200
Body container requirements:
rigid combustible
Cardboard casket: $50
Cost of mailing cremains: $10
Payment: at time of delivery,
negotiable

Rosedale Funeral Home and
Crematory
Rt.7, Box 210A
Martinsburg, WV 25401
304-263-4922
Available: 24 hours

Cost of cremation only: $120
Body container requirements:
rigid combustible
Cardboard casket: $45
Cost of mailing cremains:
postage
Payment: negotiable

There may be additional crematories that are not on the lists
I used for this research.

▶ **Body Donation**

Marshall University
School of Medicine
Department of Anatomy
Huntington, WV 25704
304-429-6788
525-8121 other times

Cost to family: transportation
outside of state, (state sets
transportation rate within)
Prior enrollment: not required
Over-enrollment: shared
Disposition: cremation/
interred in University
vault; return of cremains
by request
Body rejection: autopsy,
decomposition, AIDS, fetal
death, previous embalming

West Virginia School of
Osteopathic Medicine
400 N. Lee St.
Lewisburg, WV 24901
304-645-6270

Cost to family: transportation
beyond 150 miles
Prior enrollment: not required
Over-enrollment: shared
Disposition: cremation/
interred in cemetery vault;
return of cremains by
request
Body rejection: standard*

West Virginia University
School of Medicine
4052 BSB, WVU Medical
  Center
Department of Anatomy
Morgantown, WV 26506
304-293-6322
  293-0111 other times

Cost to family: transportation
  beyond 150 miles (state has
  transportation contract)
Prior enrollment: not required
Over-enrollment: shared
Disposition: cremation/
  interred in University
  vault; return of cremains
  by request
Body rejection: standard*,
  sepsis, under 18

*autopsy, decomposition, mutilation, severe burn victim,
meningitis, hepatitis, AIDS

West Virginia University coordinates the Human Gifts
Registry for all three schools although specific bequests may
be made.

▶ **State Funeral Board**

The West Virginia State Board of Embalmers and Funeral
Directors has seven members. There is one consumer representative.

(This section was reviewed by the Director of the West
Virginia Department of Health.)

In Wisconsin

Please refer to Chapter 9 as you use this section.

Persons in Wisconsin may care for their own dead. The legal
authority to do so is found in and ensuing statutes:

Title 69.37: The statement of facts relating to the
disposition of the body shall be signed by a funeral
director licensed in this state . . . except that such
statement of facts may be signed by any person who
personally prepares for burial and conducts the funeral
of any member of the immediate family.

There are no other statutes or regulations which might require you to use a funeral director when embalming is not desired.

A pamphlet, "Burial by Immediate Family Members," is available from the Wisconsin Center for Health Statistics, P.O. Box 309, Madison, WI 53701.

▶ **Transporting and Disposition Permit**

A body may be moved from a hospital or nursing home by the immediate family only if the family is conducting the burial. The "Notice of Removal of a Human Corpse from an Institution" must be signed. If the institution does not have this form, a funeral director or the Register of Deeds may be asked to supply one. The "Report for Final Disposition" also may be obtained from the Register of Deeds or a funeral director.

The "Report for Final Disposition" must be mailed to the local Register of Deeds within 24 hours (or in Kenosha, Manitowac, Milwaukee, Neenah, Oshkosh, Racine, Sheboygan, or West Allis to the City Health Officer). One copy must also be sent to the coroner or medical examiner, located through the office of the county Sheriff.

▶ **Death Certificate**

The attending doctor will sign the death certificate, in black ink, within 6 days, stating the cause of death. In some counties, the coroner must certify the cause when death occurred at home. The remaining information must be supplied, typewritten or in black ink. The death certificate must be filed by the family with the local registrar within two days of medical certification.

▶ **Fetal Death**

A fetal death report is required after 20 weeks of gestation or when the weight is 350 grams or more. The fetal death report must be filed with the registrar within five days. No forms or documents are required by law for fetal disposition unless transported out of state, in which case the Report of Final disposition must accompany the remains.

▶ **Burial**

Check with the registrar for local zoning laws regarding

home burial. There are no state burial statutes or regulations with regard to depth.

When burial is arranged, the family member acting as the funeral director must sign the Report for Final Disposition and retain one copy as a record for two years.

▸ Cremation

A permit for cremation must be obtained from the coroner or medical examiner in the county where death occurred. If a body is brought into the state for cremation, the coroner or medical examiner in the county where cremation will take place must sign the permit. There is a 48-hour wait before cremation unless death was caused by a contagious or infectious disease. Most crematories insist that a pacemaker be removed, and authorization by next-of-kin usually is required.

▸ Other Requirements

Wisconsin has no other requirements controlling the time schedule for the disposition of unembalmed bodies. Weather and reasonable planning should be considered.

The health department may regulate disposition when death was caused by a contagious or infectious disease. If the person died of a contagious or communicable disease, the doctor in attendance should be consulted.

A body to be shipped by common carrier must be embalmed.

▸ Crematories

Wichmann Funeral Home
537 N. Superior Street
Appleton, WI 54911
414-739-1231
Available:8-4:30 M-F,
   24-hour phone

Cost of cremation only: $125
Body container requirements:
   rigid combustible
Cardboard casket: $58
Cost of mailing cremains:
   included
Payment: at time of delivery

Wisconsin Memorial Park
13235 W. Capitol Drive
Brookfield, WI 53005
414-781-7474
Independent
Available: 8-4:30 M-Sat.

Cost of cremation only: $100
Body container requirements:
  rigid combustible
Cardboard casket: not carried
Cost of mailing cremains:
  postage
Payment: at time of delivery

Eau Claire Memorial
Cremation Service
2222 London Rd.
Eau Claire, WI 54701
715-832-6244
Funeral home affiliated
Available: 24 hours

Cost of cremation only: $175
Body container requirements:
  rigid combustible
Cardboard casket: $50
Cost of mailing cremains:
  included
Payment: negotiable

Memorial Crematory
701 N. Baird
Green Bay, WI 54302
414-432-5579
Funeral home affiliated
Available: 24 hours

Cost of cremation only: $135
Body container requirements:
  rigid combustible
Cardboard casket: $35
Cost of mailing cremains:
  included
Payment: negotiable

Milton Lawns Memorial Park
2200 Milton Ave.
Janesville, WI 53545
608-754-4222
Independent
Available: 8-5 M-F,
  8-12 Sat.

Cost of cremation only: $120
Body container requirements:
  rigid combustible
Cardboard casket: not carried
Cost of mailing cremains:
  postage
Payment: at time of delivery

Southport Crematory
1119 60th St.
Kenosha, WI 53140
414-654-3533
Funeral home affiliated
Available: 24 hours

Cost of cremation only: $120
Body container requirements:
  rigid combustible
Cardboard casket: $50
Cost of mailing cremains:
  included
Payment: negotiable, 30 days

Oak Grove Crematory
1081 Cedar Rd. P.O. Box 24
La Crosse, WI 54601
608-782-5244
Independent
Available: 24 hours

Cost of cremation only: $175
Body container requirements:
  rigid combustible
Cardboard casket:
  included
Cost of mailing cremains: $15
Payment: at time of delivery

Cress Funeral Service
3610 Speedway Rd.
Madison, WI 53705
608-238-3434
Funeral home affiliated
Available: 24 hours

Cost of cremation only: $100
Body container requirements:
 rigid combustible
Cardboard casket: $40
Cost of mailing cremains: $10
Payment: at time of delivery

Forest Hill Mausoleum and
 Crematory
One Speedway Road
Madison, WI 53705
608-233-5455
Independent
Available: 24-hour phone

Cost of cremation only: $125
Body container requirements:
 rigid combustible
Cardboard casket: $50
Cost of mailing cremains:
 postage
Payment: at time of delivery

Jens Funeral Home and
 Crematory
1122 S. 8th St.
Manitowoc, WI 54220
414-682-1568
Available: 24 hours

Cost of cremation only: $155
Body container requirements:
 rigid combustible
Cardboard casket: $80
Cost of mailing cremains:
 postage
Payment: negotiable

Forest Home Cemetery
2405 W. Forest Home Ave.
Milwaukee, WI 53215
414-645-2632
Independent
Available: 8-4:30 M-F,
 8-12 Sat.

Cost of cremation only: $115
Body container requirements:
 rigid combustible
Cardboard casket: not carried
Cost of mailing cremains: $14
Payment: at time of delivery

Cremation Service Unlimited
921 15th Ave., P.O. Box 404
Monroe, WI 53566
608-328-8376
Funeral home affiliated
Available: 24 hours

Cost of cremation only: $125
Body container requirements:
 rigid combustible
Cardboard casket: $15
Cost of mailing cremains:
 included
Payment: negotiable

Lakeview Memorial Park, Inc.
2786 Algoma
Oshkosh, WI 54901
414-235-5655
Independent
Available: 7:30-4:30 M-F,
 8-12 Sat., 24-hour phone

Cost of cremation only: $140
Body container requirements:
 rigid combustible
Cardboard casket: not carried
Cost of mailing cremains:
 included
Payment: negotiable

Ballhorn Crematory, Inc.
1201 N. 8th
Sheboygan, WI 53081
414-457-4455
Funeral home affiliated
Available: 8-8 daily,
  24-hour phone

Cost of cremation only: $175
Body container requirements:
  rigid combustible
Cardboard casket: $70
Cost of mailing cremains: $12
Payment: at time of delivery,
  negotiable 30 days

Brainard Funeral Home
522 Adams
Wausau, WI 54401
715-845-5525
Available: 24 hours

Cost of cremation only: $150
Body container requirements:
  rigid combustible
Cardboard casket: $50
Cost of mailing cremains:
  included
Payment: at time of delivery

John Borgward Funeral Home
  and Crematory
1603 S. 81st St.
West Allis, WI 53214
414-476-2010
Available: 24 hours

Cost of cremation only: $110
Body container requirements:
  rigid combustible
Cardboard casket: $85
Cost of mailing cremains: $15
Payment: negotiable

One crematory in Madison had an answering machine and no response has been received.

There may be additional crematories that are not on the lists I used for this research.

▶ **Body Donation**

University of Wisconsin
Medical School
Department of Anatomy
1300 University Ave.
Madison, WI 53706
608-262-2888 working days
  262-2800 other times or
  262-2122

Cost to family: none,
  University picks up body
  within state
Prior enrollment: usually
  required
Over-enrollment: will share,
  but has not occurred
Disposition: cremation/
  interred in University plot;
  return of cremains by
  request
Body rejection: standard*,
  jaundice, obesity, recent
  major surgery, under 18

Medical College of Wisconsin
Department of Anatomy
8701 Watertown Plank Rd.
P.O. Box 26509
Milwaukee, WI 53226
414-257-8261

Cost to family: transportation
to the medical school
Prior enrollment:
recommended but not
required
Over-enrollment: shared
Disposition: cremation/
scattering in school park;
no return of cremains
Body rejection: standard*

*autopsy, decomposition, mutilation, severe burn victim, meningitis, hepatitis, AIDS

▶ **State Funeral Board**

The Wisconsin State Board of Funeral Directors and Embalmers has five members. There is one consumer representative.

(This section was reviewed by the Wisconsin Center for Health Statistics.)

In Wyoming

Please refer to Chapter 9 as you use this section.

Persons in Wyoming may care for their own dead. The legal authority to do so is found in this and ensuing statutes:

Title 35-1-418 (b): The funeral director or person acting as such who first assumes custody of a dead body shall file the death certificate.

There are no other statutes or regulations which might require you to use a funeral director when embalming is not desired.

▶ **Death Certificate**

The family doctor or local health officer will sign the death certificate within 24 hours, stating the cause of death. The remaining information must be supplied, typewritten or in permanent ink. Do not use a felt-tip pen; there are four copies. The third copy (pink) is for the records of the person acting as the funeral director. The remaining portions of the death certificate must be filed with the local registrar within three days and before removal from the state.

▸ Fetal Death

A fetal death report is required after 20 weeks of gestation. If there is no family physician involved, the local coroner must sign the fetal death certificate. All other procedures apply if disposition is handled by the family.

▸ Transporting and Disposition Permit

A body may be moved with the consent of a physician, medical examiner or county coroner. The fourth page of the death certificate (green) serves as the burial-transit permit and must be signed by the registrar in the district where death occurred before accompanying the body to its final disposition.

▸ Burial

Check with the local registrar for zoning laws regarding home burial. There are no state burial statutes or regulations with regard to depth. The burial-transit permit must be filed with the registrar in the district of disposition within ten days.

▸ Cremation

There is a 24-hour wait before cremation unless a coroner's permit has been obtained. Most crematories insist that a pacemaker be removed, and authorization by next-of-kin usually is required.

▸ Other Requirements

Wyoming has no other requirements controlling the time schedule for the disposition of unembalmed bodies. Weather and reasonable planning should be considered.

The Board of Health may regulate disposition when death has occurred because of a contagious or communicable disease. The doctor in attendance should be consulted.

▶ **Crematories**

Cheyenne Memorial Services
2015 Warren Ave.
Cheyenne, WY 82001
307-632-2462
Weiderspahn Chapel of the
    Chimes Funeral Home
    632-1900
Available: 24 hours

Cost of cremation only: $125
Body container requirements:
    rigid combustible
Cardboard casket: $75
Cost of mailing cremains:
    postage
Payment: negotiable

Sunset Park Crematory
2323 Carey Ave.
Cheyenne, WY 82001-3697
307-634-1568
Schrader Funeral Home
Available: 24 hours

Cost of cremation only: $100
Body container requirements:
    rigid combust.,no plastic
Cardboard casket: $70
Cost of mailing cremains: $15
Payment: at time of delivery

These are the only crematories in Wyoming at the time of this publication.

▶ **Body Donation**

There are no medical schools in Wyoming. Persons wishing to consider body donation should check the nearest neighboring state.

▶ **State Funeral Board**

The Wyoming State Board of Embalming has five members including the Secretary of the State Board of Health. There are no consumer representatives.

(This section was reviewed by the Secretary, Wyoming State Board of Embalming.)

SUMMARY KEY

For specific details consult the individual state chapters.

F   =   A family may manage all usual death arrangements in this state.

R   =   A religious group may manage all usual death arrangements in this state.

P   =   A funeral director is required to sign the death certificate/obtain permits.

T   =   A family may only transport a body. A funeral director is required for all other arrangements.

FD   =   A funeral director must manage all death arrangements.

MS   =   Medical schools in this state.

   AB =   Anatomy Board (or its equivalent) which receives and distributes all body donations for this state.

CR   =   The number of crematories contacted.

Y   =   The number of those crematories that will accept a body from a family.

FB   =   The number of total members on the state funeral board, most usually made up of licensed funeral directors and embalmers.

   [   ] =   The health department regulates the funeral business in this state Advisory board to state agency.

   (   ) =   Professional mortuary commission without state authority. No state board exists.

PM   =   The number of consumer representatives (public or lay members) on this board.

E   =   Embalming required by statute in some circumstances such as for communicable diseases, transportation out-ot-state, delayed disposition.

@   =   Riverside County. In other California counties and in all states, the medical examiner may have the authority to order embalming.

STATE SUMMARY	F	R	P	T	FD	MS	CR	Y	FB	PM	E
Alabama	□					AB	2	1	7	0	□
Alaska	□					0	5	5	[0]	[0]	□
Arizona	□					1	16	15	7	3	□
Arkansas	□					1	6	3	7	2	□
California	□					11	96	81	5	3	□
Colorado		□				1	15	14	(5)	(2)	□
Connecticut			□			2	6	6	5	2	□
Delaware	□					0	3	1	7	2	□
District of Columbia	□					3	2	1	4	0	
Florida	□					AB	47	40	7	2	
Georgia	□					4	5	3	6	0	
Hawaii	□					1	3	3	[0]	[0]	
Idaho	□					0	7	7	3	0	□
Illinois		□				AB	11	8	5	0	□
Indiana		□				AB	9	8	6	0	
Iowa	□					3	8	6	5	2	
Kansas	□					1	5	5	5	2	□
Kentucky	□					2	5	2	5	1	
Louisiana				□		AB	5	3	7	0	
Maine	□					1	4	3	7	1	
Maryland	□					AB	8	7	12	2	
Massachusetts					□	4	0	0	5	1	
Michigan					□	3	0	0	9	3	□
Minnesota		□				3	12	11	5	1	□
Mississippi	□					1	2	2	9	2	
Missouri	□					7	10	6	6	1	
Montana	□					0	8	7	5	1	□
Nebraska					□	AB	0	0	4	1	
Nevada	□					1	4	3	3	1	□
New Hampshire					□	1	0	0	4	1	
New Jersey					□	2	0	0	5	0	
New Mexico	□					1	6	4	5	1	
New York				□		14	21	6	[10]	[4]	
North Carolina	□					4	13	11	9	1	
North Dakota	□					1	1	1	3	0	□
Ohio		□				7	27	20	5	1	
Oklahoma	□					2	4	4	7	2	
Oregon	□					2	29	27	9	3	□
Pennsylvania	□					AB	27	17	7	2	
Rhode Island	□					1	4	2	5	1	
South Carolina	□					2	7	5	11	2	□
South Dakota	□					1	2	2	7	2	
Tennessee	□					4	5	3	5	1	
Texas	□					9	17	11	5	1	
Utah	□					1	5	5	5	1	□
Vermont	□					1	3	2	3	0	
Virginia	□					AB	10	8	9	2	
Washington	□					1	40	37	5	1	
West Virginia		□				3	3	3	7	1	
Wisconsin	□					2	17	16	5	1	□
Wyoming	□					0	2	2	5	0	

@

Part Three:
Caring For Your
Own Dead

APPENDICES, REFERENCES, AND AFTERWORD

How to Fill Out
a Death Certificate

If you assume responsibility for death arrangements without the use of a funeral director, it will be up to you to be certain that a death certificate is properly completed and filed in the appropriate municipal or state office.

All death certificates are based on the U.S. Standard Certificate of Death, although there may be slight variations in some states. The 1978 revision of the certificate is current as of this writing.

The death certificate will be provided, and partially filled out, by medical authorities. In most cases, the person doing this will be the attending physician, the family doctor, or the coroner or medical examiner. In some states, under specific circumstances when a death is expected, the death certificate may be filled out ahead of time and signed by a registered nurse when the patient dies. If you have any question about this, check with your family doctor.

Medical authorities will fill out only the portion of the certificate having to do with medical information, including the cause of death. The remainder is filled out by the "funeral director or person acting as such." If you fill it out, you are the "person acting as such."

The personal (non-medical) information must be provided by a specific family member or friend, who is referred to on the form as the "informant." Even if the form is filled out by a funeral director, the "informant" should be certain that the information is accurate and complete. When there is no funeral director, the "person acting as such" is often also the "informant."

The form is not complex. However, it must be completed in a careful, conscientious manner. Any error or omission, **even in the portion that is filled out by a doctor,** can delay your plans for disposition of the body or subject family members to questioning at a later date.

The following general and line-by-line instructions are condensed from the guidelines provided to funeral directors and doctors by the U.S. Department of Health and Human Services. Please do not be deterred by the length of the instructions; the form is much shorter. But since every death is different, it seems important to list the rules covering as many contingencies as possible.

General Instructions

▸ The persons responsible for providing the information are (a) the attending physician or medical examiner or coroner, and (b) the "informant." In designating an "informant," the following order of preference should be used, if possible: the spouse, one of the parents, one of the children of the decedent, another relative, or another person who has knowledge of the facts.

▸ Type all entries whenever possible. If a typewriter cannot be used, print legibly in black ink.

▸ Complete each item, following the specific instructions for that item.

▸ **Do not make alterations or erasures or use "white out."**

▸ All signatures must be obtained. Rubber stamp or other facsimile signatures are not acceptable.

▸ The original certificate must be filed with the registrar. Reproductions or duplicates are not acceptable. Certified copies may be obtained from the registrar, for a fee, for use in probate, Social Security notifications, and any other purpose for which proof of death is necessary.

▸ Avoid abbreviations except those recommended in the specific item instructions.

▸ Verify with the informant the spelling of names, especially those that have different spellings for the same sound (Smith or Smyth, Gail or Gayle, Wolf or Wolfe, etc.).

▸ If problems arise that are not covered by these instructions, check with the state office of vital statistics or with the local registrar.

Line-By-Line Instructions

The items below will be included on any death certificate, although the sequence may vary in some cases. The only significant exception is that a different form is used for fetal death reports. Included are instructions for the sections which must be completed by the physician or coroner. A common complaint by registrars is that doctors - whose priority is keeping people alive and healthy - sometimes make hasty errors on death certificates. Since an error, even a simple one such as a signature on the wrong line, can delay body disposition, it may be worthwhile to double check the medical portions of the form. The numbers on the form may vary slightly, depending on the state and on whether it originated with an attending physician or a coroner.

1. **Decedent - Name: First, Middle, Last.** Do not abbreviate.

2. **Sex.** Enter "male" or "female." Do not leave blank.

3. **Date of Death (Month, Day, Year).** Enter the full or abbreviated name of the month (Jan., Feb., March, etc.). Do not use a number for a month. If the person died at midnight, the date of death is considered to be at the end of one day, rather than the beginning of the next.

4. **Race - White, Black, American Indian, Etc. (Specify).** For groups other than those listed in the question, the national origin of the decedent should be listed (Chinese, Japanese, Korean, etc.). The information provided on this line is used for studies of health characteristics of minority groups, planning and evaluation of health programs, and in making population estimates.

5. **Age.** There are three lines, only one of which should be filled out. **5a** is used if the decedent was over a year old. The person's age in years, as of the last birthday, should be entered. **5b** is used for infants who died between one day and one year of age. Enter the age in completed months, or if less than one month, completed days. **5c** is used when an infant dies within the first day after birth. Enter the age in hours, or if less than one hour, in minutes.

6. **Date of Birth (Month, Day, Year).** Use the full or abbreviated name of the month, rather than a number.

7. **Place of Death.** In **7a** and **7b**, indicate the county and city or town where death occurred. In **7c**, indicate the hospital or other institution where the person died. If death occurred at home or at another location, indicate the street address. **7d** should be filled out if the person was pronounced dead at a hospital or other institution. It indicates whether the person was dead on arrival, or whether the person was being treated as an inpatient,

outpatient, emergency room patient, etc. If death occurred
in a moving conveyance other than en route to a hospital,
enter as the place of death the address where the body
was first removed from the conveyance. If death occurred
in international waters or airspace, or in a foreign country,
contact the State office of vital statistics for instructions.

8.   State of Birth (If Not in U.S.A., Name Country). If you
know the person was born in the U.S. but don't know
which state, enter "U.S. - unknown." If no information is
available regarding place of birth, enter "Unknown." Do not
leave this space blank.

9.   Citizen of What Country. If the decedent was born or
naturalized as a U.S. citizen, simply enter U.S.A. If the
person was a citizen of another country, filling out this
item will allow notification of officials of that country.

10. Married, Never Married, Widowed, Divorced (Specify).
Enter the marital status at the time of death. A person is
legally married even if separated. If marital status cannot
be determined, enter "Unknown." Do not leave this space
blank.

11. Surviving Spouse (If Wife, Give Maiden Name). If the
person was married, this information is necessary for
insurance and other survivor benefits.

**12. Was Decedent Ever in U.S. Armed Forces? (Specify Yes
or No).** If veteran status cannot be determined, enter
"Unknown." Do not leave blank.

13. Social Security Number. This is useful for identification
and facilitates any Social Security claims.

14. Occupation and Industry of Decedent. This information
should be filled in if the person was 14 or more years of
age - even if he or she was retired, disabled, or institu-
tionalized at time of death. Line **14a** lists the person's
"usual occupation." This does not necessarily mean the
person's last occupation before death. Enter the kind of
work the person did during most of his or her working
life, such as claim adjuster, farmhand, coal miner, house-
wife, civil engineer, etc. "Retired" is not an acceptable
entry. "Student" is an appropriate entry if the person was
a student at the time of death and was never regularly
employed. Line **14b** lists the kind of business or industry to
which the usual occupation was related, such as insurance,

farming, hardware store, government, etc. Do not enter the name of the firm or organization.

15. Residence of Decedent. This is where the person actually resided, and may be different from the "home state," "voting residence," "legal residence," or "mailing address."

Never enter a temporary residence such as one used during a visit, business trip, or vacation. However, the place of residence during a tour of military duty or attendance at college is not considered temporary, and should be entered as the residence on the death certificate. Also, persons who at the time of death were living in institutions where individuals usually stay for long periods of time, such as nursing homes, mental institutions, penitentiaries, or hospitals for the chronically ill, are residents of the location of the institution.

If the decedent is a child, residence is the same as that of the parents (or custodial parent) or legal guardian, unless the child was living in an institution where individuals usually stay for long periods of time, as indicated above.

The residence information is divided into lines **15a** through **15e**. The individual lines are for the state; the county; the city or town; the street and number (if no number and street name, enter RFD number or post office box number); and whether the person resided within the municipal boundaries of the city or town.

16-17. Parentage. Enter the full names - first, middle, and last, of the decedent's father and mother. The mother's maiden name is requested. The justification for this is that the information is useful in tracing of family trees.

18. Identity of Informant. Enter the name and full mailing address of the person who furnished the personal facts about the decedent and his or her family. If you are the principal source of information, enter your own name and mailing address. The "informant" may be contacted if there are inquiries to correct or to complete any items on the death certificate.

19. Type and Place of Disposition. Line **19a** asks whether the type of disposition was burial, cremation, entombment, removal, or other specified disposition. If a body is to be used by a hospital or medical school for scientific or educational purposes, enter "Removal-Donation", and specify the name and location of the institution in the later lines.

Line **19b** asks the name of cemetery, crematory, or institution, and **19c** asks the location (city, town, and state).

20. Funeral Service Licensee Information. Line **20a** is signed by the "funeral service licensee or person acting as such." If no funeral director is involved and you are completing the death certificate, your signature should appear here. Line **20b** asks the "name of facility." If no funeral director is involved, you may avoid confusion by entering your relationship to the deceased, or if you are working with a church group, the name of the church group. Similarly, on line **20c**, which asks the "address of facility," you may wish to enter your home address or the address of the church group. Please note that at this writing, ten states require the signature of a funeral director, rather than a family member or church group spokesperson "acting as such." To be sure that you may sign here, please refer to the state-by-state chapters. To be sure no statutory changes have been enacted in the meantime, you may want to double check with the local registrar or your family lawyer.

21. Certification: Physician. This should be filled out by the attending physician or family doctor. If certification is required by the medical examiner or coroner, this space should be left blank. As the "person acting as funeral director," your only role is to be sure the lines are filled in correctly to avoid later inconvenience for you or family members. Line **21a** asks for the signature of the doctor who certifies the death. Line **21b** asks the date (month, day, and year) the certificate was signed. The full or abbreviated name of the month, rather than a number, must be used. Line **21c** asks the exact time of death (hours and minutes), according to local time. If daylight savings time is the prevailing time where death occurs, it should be used. "12 noon" or "12 midnight" should be entered as such; otherwise "A.M." or "P.M." should be noted. Line **21d** asks the "name of attending physician if other than certifier." If the certifier is the attending physician, that space should be left blank.

22. Certification: Medical Examiner or Coroner. This should be filled out instead of 21 if a medical examiner or coroner is involved. Lines **22a** through **22c** are identical to their counterparts in **21**. Lines **22d** and **22e** ask the month, day, year, hour, and minute the person was pronounced dead.

23. Name and Address or Certifier. The name and address of the person whose signature appears in items **21a** or **22a** should be typed or printed in this space.

24. Registrar - Signature and Date Received. The local official (registrar) will sign and date the form here at the time it is filed.

25. Cause of Death. This section must be filled out by the physician, coroner, or medical examiner whose signature appeared on lines **22a** or **22a**. It is extremely important that the section be filled out properly, so the "person acting as funeral director" can review it to be sure there are no hasty errors. The section is divided into two parts.

Part I. Only one cause of death is to be entered on each line of Part I. The mode of dying (e.g., heart failure, respiratory failure, senility, or old age) should not be stated at all since it is no more than a symptom of the fact that death occurred.

Line **a** asks the immediate cause of death. This is the disease, injury, or complication that directly preceded death. It can be the sole entry in the cause of death statement if only one condition was present at death. There must always be an entry on line **a**. In the case of violent death, enter the result of the external cause (e.g. fracture of vault of skull, crushed chest, etc.). In the case of a specific cancer or injury, the site should be noted as well (e.g. pancreas, left lung, etc.).

Line **b** asks what disease, injury, or complication, if any, gave rise to the direct or immediate cause of death reported above. This condition must be considered to have been antecedent to the immediate cause. If it is believed to have prepared the way for the immediate cause, it can be considered as antecedent even if a long interval of time has elapsed since its onset. In case of injury, the form of external violence or accident is antecedent to an injury entered on line **a** and should be entered on line **b** although the two events are almost simultaneous (e.g., automobile accident, fallen on by tree, etc.).

Line **c** asks what condition, if any, gave rise to the antecedent condition on line **b**. If the decedent had more than three causally related conditions leading to death, the person should add lines **d**, **e**, etc. The final line should state the condition which the physician feels is the underlying cause of death: i.e. the condition that started the sequence of events between normal health and the immediate cause of death. Health departments complain that this section is often in default by the medical persons completing the certificate. If the attending physician is other than the usual family doctor, your help may be invaluable in giving the medical history needed here.

Space is provided at the end of lines **a, b,** and **c,** for recording the interval between onset and death for the immediate cause, antecedent condition, if any, and underlying cause. These intervals usually are established by the physician on the basis of information available. The time of onset may be obscure or entirely unknown, in which case the physician can state that the interval is "unknown." This space should not be left blank.

Part II. Any other important disease or condition that was present at the time of death which may have contributed to death but which was not related to the immediate cause of death should be recorded on this line. For example, a patient who died of metastasis from carcinoma of the breast may also have had a hypertensive heart disease that contributed to the death. In this case, the hypertensive heart disease would be entered in Part II as a contributory cause of death.

26. Autopsy. Enter "Yes" if a partial or complete autopsy was performed. Otherwise, enter "No." Do not leave this space blank.

27. Was Case Referred to Medical Examiner or Coroner? This item is to be completed when the cause of death is certified by an attending physician. Enter "Yes" if the medical examiner or coroner was contacted in reference to the case; otherwise enter "No."

28. Accident or Injury. This section must be filled out if death resulted from an accident or injury. In most instances, such deaths are certified by a medical examiner or coroner, who will complete this section. Otherwise, it should be completed by the attending physician. In line **28a,** specify whether cause of death was caused by accident, suicide, homicide, undetermined, or pending investigation. In lines **28b** and **28c,** enter the year, month, day, and exact time of the injury. (As always, use the full or abbreviated name of the month, not a number.) Line **28d** asks for a description of how the injury occurred. This should be a concise statement, such as, "fell off ladder while painting house." Line **28e** asks whether the injury occurred at work. Enter "Yes," "No," or "Unknown." In line **28f** enter the type of place where the injury occurred (home, farm, street, factory, office building, etc.). In line **28g**, enter the complete address of the location of the injury.

Origin or Descent. An additional question regarding origin or descent is asked on the death certificates of many, but not all, states. The question takes two forms. The first is: "Was the decedent of Spanish origin? (Specify 'Yes' or 'No'.) If 'Yes,' specify Mexican, Cuban, Puerto Rican, etc." The second form of the question is: "Origin or descent (e.g. Italian, Mexican, Puerto Rican, English, Cuban, etc.). (Specify)."

For the purposes of this question, origin or descent refers to the nationality group of decedents or their ancestors before their arrival in the United States (except for American Indians and Alaskan natives). There is no set rule as to how many generations are to be taken into account in determining ethnic origin. A person's origin may be reported based on the origin of a parent, grandparent, or some far-removed ancestor. The response is to reflect what the person considered himself or herself to be, and is not based on percentages of ancestry.

Multiple origins (e.g. English-German) may be entered if the person identified with both or all. If the person did not particularly identify with a foreign birthplace or nationality group, it is entirely appropriate to enter "American."

It is **not** appropriate to enter the name of a religious group (Jewish, Moslem, Protestant, etc.). The question refers only to country of origin or nationality group.

It should also be noted that this question is entirely separate from the racial question **(4)**. In some cases (e.g. Japanese, Chinese, Hawaiian, etc.) the answers may be the same, but responses to both questions are requested.

Federal Consumer Protection

(The following is reprinted, in its entirety, from the "Consumer Guide to the FTC Funeral Rule" published by the Federal Trade Commission. If you wish to review the entire "Funeral Rule," it is published in the **Federal Register** of September 24, 1982, and in the **Code of Federal Regulations,** 16 CFR Ch. 1, Part 453 - Funeral Industry Practices.)

CONSUMER GUIDE TO THE FTC FUNERAL RULE

Each year, Americans arrange more than two million funerals for family and friends. When arranging a funeral, consumers may not be initially concerned about cost. Still, many consumers may spend more for a funeral than for almost anything else they buy. In fact, at an average cost of $2,400, a funeral may be the third most expensive consumer purchase after a home and a car.

The Federal Trade Commission developed a trade regulation rule concerning funeral industry practices, which went into effect on April 30, 1984. It is called the Funeral Rule, and its purpose is to enable consumers to obtain information about funeral arrangements.

In general, the rule makes it easier for you to select only those goods and services you want or need and to pay for only those you select. Now, for example, you can find out the cost of individual items over the telephone. Also, when you inquire in person about funeral arrangements, the funeral home will give you a written price list of the goods and services available. When arranging a funeral, you can purchase individual items or buy an entire package of goods and services. If you want to purchase a casket, the funeral provider will supply a list that describes all the available selections and their prices. Thus, as described in greater detail in the following sections, the FTC's Funeral Rule helps you obtain information about the cost and availability of individual funeral goods and services.

Telephone Price Disclosures

When you call a funeral provider and ask about terms, conditions, or prices of funeral goods or services, the funeral provider will:

- tell you that price information over the telephone
- give you prices and any other information from the price lists to reasonably answer your questions
- give you any other information about prices or offerings that is readily available and reasonably answers your questions.

By using the telephone, you can compare prices among funeral providers. Getting price information over the telephone may thus help you select a funeral home and the arrangements you want.

General Price List

If you inquire in person about funeral arrangements, the funeral provider will give you a general price list. This list, which you can keep, contains the cost of each individual funeral item and service offered. As with telephone inquiries, you can use this information to help select the funeral provider and funeral items you want, need, and are able to afford.

The price list also discloses important legal rights and requirements regarding funeral arrangements. It must include information on embalming, cash advance sales (such as newspaper notices or flowers), caskets for cremation, and required purchases.

Embalming Information

The Funeral Rule requires funeral providers to give consumers information about embalming that can help them decide whether to purchase this service. Under the rule, the funeral provider:

- may not falsely state that embalming is required by law
- must disclose in writing that, except in certain special cases, embalming is **not** required by law
- may not charge a fee for unauthorized embalming unless it is required by state law
- will disclose in writing that you usually have the right to choose a disposition such as direct cremation or immediate burial if you do not want embalming

▸ will disclose to you in writing that certain funeral arrangements, such as a funeral with a viewing, may make embalming a practical necessity and, thus, a required purchase.

Cash-Advance Sales

The Funeral Rule requires funeral providers to disclose to you in writing if they charge a fee for buying cash-advance items. Cash-advance items are goods or services that are paid for by the funeral provider on your behalf. Some examples of cash-advance items are flowers, obituary notices, pallbearers, and clergy honoraria. Some funeral providers charge you their cost for these items. Others add a service fee to their cost. The Funeral Rule requires the funeral provider to inform you when a service fee is added to the price of cash-advance items, or if the provider gets a refund, discount, or rebate from the supplier of any cash advance item.

Caskets for Cremation

Some consumers may want to select direct cremation, which is cremation of the deceased without a viewing or other ceremony at which the body is present. If you choose a direct cremation, the funeral provider will offer you either an inexpensive alternative container or an unfinished wood box. An alternative container is a non-metal enclosure used to hold the deceased. These containers may be made of pressboard, cardboard, or canvas.

Because any container you buy will be destroyed during the cremation, you may wish to use an alternative container or an unfinished wood box for a direct cremation. These could lower your funeral cost since they are less expensive than traditional burial caskets.

Under the Funeral Rule, funeral directors who offer direct cremations:

▸ may not tell you that state or local law requires a casket for direct cremations
▸ must disclose in writing your right to buy an unfinished wood box (a type of casket) or an alternative container for direct cremation
▸ must make an unfinished wood box or alternative container available for direct cremation.

Required Purchase

You do not have to purchase unwanted goods or services as

a condition of obtaining those you do want unless you are required to do so by state law. Under the Funeral Rule:

- ▸ You have the right to choose only the funeral goods or services you want, with some disclosed exceptions.
- ▸ The funeral provider must disclose this right in writing on the general price list.
- ▸ The funeral provider must disclose on the statement of goods and services selected the specific law that requires you to purchase any particular item.

Statement of Funeral Goods and Services Selected

The funeral provider will give you an itemized statement with the total cost of the funeral goods and services you select. This statement also will disclose any legal, cemetery, or crematory requirements that compel you to purchase any specific funeral goods or services.

The funeral provider must give you this statement after you select the funeral goods and services that you would like. The statement combines in one place the prices of the individual items you are considering for purchase, as well as the total price. Thus, you can decide whether to add or subtract items to get what you want. If the cost of cash advance items is not known at that time, the funeral provider must write down a 'good faith estimate' of their cost. The Rule does not require any specific form for this information. Therefore, funeral providers may include this information in any document they give you at the end of your discussion about funeral arrangements.

Preservative and Protective Claims

Under the Funeral Rule, funeral providers are prohibited from telling you that a particular funeral item or service can indefinitely preserve the body of the deceased in the grave. The information gathered during the FTC's investigation indicated that these claims are not true. For example, funeral providers may not claim that embalming or a particular type of casket will indefinitely preserve the deceased's body.

The Rule also prohibits funeral providers from making claims that funeral goods, such as caskets or vaults, will keep out water, dirt, and other gravesite substances when that is not true.

Other Considerations

Most decisions about purchasing funeral goods and services are made by people when they are grieving and under time constraints. Thinking ahead may help you make informed and thoughtful decisions about funeral arrangements. In this way, you can carefully choose the specific items you want and need and can compare prices offered by one or more funeral providers.

If you decide to make advance plans about funeral arrangements either for yourself or a loved one, you can choose among several types of dispositions and ceremonies. The type of disposition you choose may affect the cost. Some people prefer a ceremonial service, religious or secular, with the body present. Others choose an immediate burial and hold a memorial or other ceremony with no body present. Another service is cremation which may be performed either directly or after a ceremony. In addition, the deceased body may be donated (either directly or after a ceremony) to a medical or educational institution. To help ensure that your wishes are carried out, you may want to write down your preferences. It may also be helpful to tell relatives and other responsible persons what you have decided.

For More Information

Most states have a licensing board that regulates the funeral industry. You may contact the licensing board in your state for information or help. You may also contact the **Conference of Funeral Service Examining Boards**, 520 E. Van Trees Street, P.O. Box 497, Washington, Indiana 47501, (812)254-7887. This association, which represents the licensing boards of 47 states, will provide information on the laws of the various states and will accept and respond to consumer inquiries or complaints about funeral providers.

If you want additional information on how to make funeral arrangements or the options available, you may also want to contact interested business, professional, and consumer groups. Some of the largest include:

▸ **Continental Association of Funeral and Memorial Societies,** 2001 S Street, N.W., Suite 530, Washington, D.C. 20009, (202)745-0634. CAFMS is a consumer organization that disseminates information about alternatives for funeral or non-funeral dispositions. It encourages advance planning and cost efficiency.

▶ **Cremation Association of North America,** 111 East Wacker Drive, Chicago, Illinois 60601, (312)644-6610. CANA is an association of crematories, cemeteries, and funeral homes that offer cremation. More than 600 members belong who own and operate crematories and who encourage the concept of memorialization.

▶ **International Order of the Golden Rule,** P.O. Box 3586, Springfield, Illinois 62708, (217)544-7428. OGR is an international association of independent funeral homes in which membership is by invitation only. More than 1200 funeral homes are members of OGR.

▶ **Jewish Funeral Directors of America, Inc.,** 122 East 42nd Street, New York, New York 10168, (212)370-0024. JFDA is a national trade association of funeral directors serving the Jewish community. It has approximately 200 members.

▶ **National Funeral Directors Association,** 135 West Wells Street, Suite 600, Milwaukee, Wisconsin 53203, (414)276-2500. NFDA is the largest educational and professional association of funeral directors. Established in 1882, it has 14,000 members throughout the United States.

▶ **National Funeral Directors and Morticians Association,** 5723 South Indiana Avenue, Chicago, Illinois 60620, (312)752-7419. NFDMA is a national association primarily of black funeral providers. It has 2,000 members.

▶ **National Selected Morticians,** 1616 Central Street, Evanston, Illinois 60201, (312)475-3414. NSM is a national association of funeral firms in which membership is by invitation only and is conditioned upon the commitment of each firm to comply with the association's Code of Good Funeral Practice. Consumers may request a variety of publications through NSM's affiliate, the Consumer Information Bureau, Inc.

▶ **Pre-Arrangement Interment Association of America,** 1133 15th Street, N.W., Washington, D.C. 20005, (202)429-9440. PIAA is a national association with more than 600 members in the cemetery and funeral home business. The primary purpose of the organization is to provide pre-arrangement purchases of funeral and cemetery goods and services.

▶ **ThanaCAP,** 135 West Wells Street, Suite 600, Milwaukee, Wisconsin 53203, (414)276-9788. ThanaCAP is an independent organization sponsored by the National Funeral Directors Association (listed above) that channels and arbitrates consumer complaints involving funeral directors. It will handle complaints whether or not the funeral director is a member of NFDA.

For Further Help

If you have a problem concerning funeral matters, first attempt to resolve it with your funeral director. If you are dissatisfied, contact your federal, state, or local consumer protection agencies, the Conference of Funeral Service Examining Boards, or ThanaCAP (both listed). While the Federal Trade Commission does not resolve individual consumer or private disputes, information about your experience may show a pattern of conduct or practice that the Commission may investigate to determine if any action is warranted. Write or call: Federal Trade Commission, Bureau of Consumer Protection, Division of Enforcement, Washington, D.C. 20580, (202)376-2891.

Pre-Need Spending

(The following article first appeared in the **Wall Street Journal** May 3, 1985. It is reprinted here in its entirety.*)

Prepaid Funerals May Bring the Unwary
A Lot More Grief Than Peace of Mind

By Mark Zieman
Staff Reporter of The Wall Street Journal

Prepaid funerals are becoming more popular, but unwary consumers are being buried by bad deals.

These plans, which allow people to pay funeral homes now for their eventual burial or cremation, are tempting for anyone who wants to spare survivors the task of making and paying for arrangements during a time of grief. The funeral industry has responded by setting up a variety of trusts and insurance programs to finance the plans.

The concept is simple and appealing: Money paid today fixes the cost of the funeral for the consumer and enables the funeral home to buy insurance or securities that will cover any cost increases.

In only a few years deposits in funeral trusts alone have reached at least $4 billion, industry officials estimate. A fund in New Jersey is growing by nearly $40,000 a week. Last year almost a half-million Texans were enrolled in such programs.

But while the theory may be simple and the plans popular, they aren't always safe - as 80-year-old Pauline Bagley of Lincoln City, Ore., discovered. Three years ago she paid a local mortician, Dale Omsberg, $2,039 for her funeral arrangements. The money was supposed to earn 8% interest in a trust.

Pocketed Check

But Mr. Omsberg pocketed her check, according to local authorities. And instead of performing 50 prepaid cremations, they found that he had stacked some of the remains in the basement of his mortuary and buried others in mass graves.

Mr. Omsberg pleaded guilty in January to 60 counts of theft and abuse of a corpse, was sentenced to 30 days in jail and was ordered to leave the county for five years. Mrs. Bagley got back half her money after threatening to sue him.

"Oh, it was a bitter, bitter experience," she says today. "I would like to have the assurance that my funeral expenses would be taken care of, but I would not do it that way again."

Such atrocities are the work of crooks, not the vast majority of undertakers. Yet funerals have always been expensive, and the industry has suffered repeated allegations of abuse. After decades of controversy, the federal government a year ago began regulating certain funeral costs and sales practices.

Funeral operators, including a few big, image-conscious companies, laud and defend prepayment programs as a way to protect survivors when they are grieving and most vulnerable to abuse. "People have a great desire to have their funeral arrangements taken care of," says Donald Campbell, in charge of pre-arranged funerals for Houston-based Service Corp. International, the country's largest funeral home operator. Adds David Bohardt, executive director of the National Funeral Directors Association: "You have to assume that a goodly portion of these people are probably taking money from CDs, money-markets and other accounts" to fund their funeral plans. "They must understand what's involved," he says.

But many people, particularly the elderly, don't always understand. Although most prepaid funeral trusts, insurance programs and installment plans are legal and safe, consumer groups note that hundreds of programs like the one that victimized Mrs. Bagley aren't controlled by state trust and insurance laws, creating the potential for fraud and abuse. And they say that subtle contract clauses and vague stipulations in prepaid funeral programs can shortchange the unwary as much as the basest scam.

Many plans, for instance, leave buyers in the lurch if the sponsoring funeral home is sold or closed. Other agreements aren't honored if the buyer dies before completing payments. Still others are cancelled if the buyer relocates, which can result in big losses for the consumer. Even plans that promise a "good-faith effort" to transfer the accounts of relocated buyers to other morticians have a hitch: Undertakers in the new locations might not assume the accounts, since the original funeral homes usually retain the interest earned on them as "administrative fees."

And when the survivors don't know the terms of the plan, their loved one may wind up in a pine box instead of the oak casket that was paid for.

State trust and insurance laws governing these plans also don't adequately cover potential abuse, according to some state officials. For example, the Texas Banking Department is advocating a move to strengthen the state's laws on prepaid funerals, claiming they have encouraged undertakers to switch money from trust funds into less-beneficial insurance policies. Through this maneuver, the department has found, some operators are pocketing interest accumulated in trust funds and putting customers into policies subject to cancellation penalties often as high as 60%.

The department is also pursuing several lawsuits, including one against a mortician in Amarillo, who used prepaid funeral funds as collateral for a personal loan, then defaulted and lost his customers' money to the bank.

State laws also vary greatly in what they allow. Some states, such as New York and New Jersey, permit buyers to withdraw 100% of their payments and interest if they cancel their contracts. These states also force operators to return any unspent funds following the burial or cremation. But other states let funeral homes write irrevocable contracts, or let them keep a huge share of the payments - up to 20% in Missouri and 50% in Mississippi, for instance - if the contract is cancelled.

Even in states with strong regulations, consumers pay in other ways. In states with the 100%-refund provision, for example, funeral operators tend to charge much higher rates for prepaid services.

Lower Rates

Because of the confusion, the American Association of Retired Persons urges members to get advice from an attorney before signing any prepaid plan. But some other consumer groups advocate staying away from the plans. The contracts often accumulate value at much lower rates than certificates of deposit or money-market funds, and for decades can tie up money that may be needed elsewhere, says Carol Coile, director of the Continental Association of Funeral & Memorial Societies, a Washington-based watchdog and consumer-information group. Most people, she says, are better off opening their own interest-bearing accounts or buying more life-insurance.

Meanwhile, the new federal rules make planning for funerals easier. For instance, undertakers must disclose prices over the phone, making it easier for consumers to avoid strong-arm sales tactics.

Despite the new federal laws, critics contend that some

operators don't provide the required itemized account of a funeral's expense, and other morticians have used itemization to raise prices on products and services that formerly cost consumers less when they were included in package deals.

"The rules were enacted for the benefit of consumers," Ms. Coile says, "but really and truly it remains to be seen."

Living Will and Durable Power of Attorney

Appendix IV

Living Will and Durable Power of Attorney are two forms of written documents which, in many states, allow you to express in advance your desires on health care if you later become too ill to express those decisions. The following are typical examples. However, laws on these issues are different from state to state. Therefore, **before drawing up such a document, you should become familiar with the provisions for your state.** This information may be obtained from a lawyer or from the Society for the Right to Die; 250 West 57th Street; New York, New York 10107.

▶ **Example of Living Will:**

To my family, my physician, my lawyer, my clergyman. To any medical facility in whose care I happen to be. To any individual who may become responsible for my health, welfare, or affairs.

Death is as much a reality as birth, growth, maturity, and old age - it is the one certainty of life. If the time comes when I, _____, can no longer take part in decisions of my own future, let this statement stand as an expression of my wishes, while I am still of sound mind.

If the situation should arise in which I am in a terminal state and there is no reasonable expectation of my recovery, I direct that I be allowed to die a natural death and that my life not be prolonged by extraordinary measures. I do, however, ask that medication be mercifully administered to me to alleviate suffering even though this may shorten my remaining life.

This statement is made after careful consideration and is in accordance with my strong convictions and beliefs. I want the wishes and directions here expressed carried out to the extent permitted by law. Insofar as they are not legally enforceable, I hope that those to whom this will is addressed will regard themselves as morally bound by these provisions.

Signed: _____ Date: _____

Witness:_____
Witness:_____
Copies of this request have been given to:

_____
_____
_____

▸ **Example of Durable Power of Attorney:**

(Please note that in most states where Durable Power of Attorney is allowed, the document is far more flexible than a Living Will. You may include any specific directions or conditions allowed by law. The following is meant only as a representative example.)

Know all men by these presents that I,_____, the undersigned, being of sound mind, do hereby make, constitute and appoint my __(wife, son, etc.)__ , __(name)__ , of___(address)___ , as my true and lawful attorney-in-fact for me and in my name, place, and stead for the purpose of making decisions regarding my health care at any time that I may be, by reason of physical or mental disability, incapable of making decisions on my own behalf.

If he or she is unable or unwilling to serve as my attorney at the time decisions regarding my health care must be made, I designate my __(daughter, close friend, etc.)__ , __(name)__ , of ___(address)___ , as alternate attorney-in-fact for me and in my name, place and stead for the purpose of making decisions regarding my health care.

1. I grant to said attorney-in-fact full power and authority to do and perform all and every act and thing whatsoever requisite, proper, or necessary to be done, in the exercise of the rights herein granted, as fully to all intents and purposes as I might or could do if personally present and able, with full power of substitution or revocation, hereby ratifying and confirming all that said attorney-in-fact shall lawfully do or cause to be done by virtue of this power of attorney and the rights and powers granted herein.

2. If, at any time, I am unable or unwilling to make decisions concerning my medical care or treatment, by virtue of physical, mental or emotional disability, illness or otherwise, my said attorney-in-fact shall have the authority to make all health care decisions for me and on my behalf, including consenting, refusing to consent or withdrawing consent to any care, treatment, service or procedure to

maintain, diagnose or treat my mental or physical condition, subject to the provisions of paragraphs 3 and 4 hereof if I am suffering from a terminal condition.

3. If, at any time, I should have an incurable injury, disease, illness or disability, certified to be a terminal condition, and two physicians who have personally examined me (one of whom shall be my attending physician), have determined that my death will occur from such condition whether or not life-sustaining procedures are utilized, and that application of life-sustaining procedures would serve only to prolong the dying process, I specifically direct my said attorney-in-fact to authorize the withholding or withdrawal of such procedures. It is my intention that I be permitted to die naturally, with only the medication and nursing procedures necessary to alleviate pain and to provide me with comfort, dignity, and supportive care.

4. I also direct my said attorney-in-fact to make arrangements for the treatment of my terminal illness under the auspices of a hospice, if I should qualify for such care. I understand that acceptance into hospice care entails foregoing curative treatment and life-sustaining procedures that might otherwise be performed, such as resuscitation in case of cardiac arrest, and that foregoing such procedures might hasten my dying. I hereby consent to hospice care under such conditions, and direct my attorney-in-fact to make any and all necessary arrangements for me to receive such care, including the signing of such consent forms as may be required by the hospice, any third party payor, and the federal government.

5. In the absence of my ability to give directions regarding my health care, it is my intention that my said attorney-in-fact shall exercise this specific grant of authority and that such exercise shall be honored by my family, physicians, nurses, and any health care facilities in which I may be treated (including ambulances by which I may be conveyed between my residence and a health care facility), as the final expression of my legal right to refuse medical or surgical treatment. I understand and accept the consequences of such refusal.

6. This instrument is to be construed and interpreted as a limited power of attorney.
7. This power of attorney shall not terminate on my disability or incompetence.

The rights, powers, and authority of said attorney-in-fact herein granted shall commence and be in full force and effect on this _____ day of _____, 19___, and such rights, powers and authority shall remain in full force and effect thereafter until this power of attorney or any part thereof is revoked by means sufficient under applicable state law to cause revocation.

Dated _____, 19____.

_____
Signature

_____
Address

_____

The undersigned hereby attest to their belief that _____ _____ was of sound mind this _____ day of _____, 19___, at _____ am/pm when said principal signed this power of attorney.

We further attest that we are not related to the principal by blood or marriage, neither are we financially or professionally responsible for his/her care, or employed by any institution so responsible. To the best of our knowledge, we are not entitled to any portion of the principal's estate either under the laws of intestate succession of this jurisdiction or under the terms of any will or codicil thereto.

_____   _____
Name   Name

_____   _____
Address   Address

_____   _____
Signature   Signature

(Please note that some states require signing before a judge or a notary. It is important to confirm witnessing requirements of your state.)

A Good Neighbor's List
For A Time Of Death

These things helped me the most:

▸ One friend came in right away and cleaned my house. She knew me well enough to know where little things went and never asked a thing as she silently and efficiently put things in order or made coffee. Thank you, Donna.

▸ A canned ham and frozen food were among the many gifts my neighbors brought. Sometimes it was weeks or months later that I needed the break, and it was with loving gratitude that I relished those thoughtful items long after the time of death. One neighbor who doesn't smoke brought me cigarettes (bless you, Nancy), and others even thought to bring ordinary staples - rice, raisins, tea, a casserole.

▸ Flowers made me feel better. The ones I appreciated most were not the big fancy arrangements, but those which had been picked out flower by flower, like the favorites in John's garden.

▸ I will always be grateful for the money I was given. Our families were scattered all over the U. S., and my telephone bill was exorbitant for months.

▸ Don't ask for mementos right away. I needed to cling for a bit. After losing my husband, I resented people asking for his things. If something is special, there is always a tactful way to let a person know how you feel.

▸ Even if you don't know what to say, the calls and the cards do count. I had never been one to send cards or call because, after all, what can anyone possibly say at a time like that? But the personal notes from those who shared their thoughts were the ones I kept. And it did help to know that others cared even a little.

▸ My neighbors took my kids long and often. I needed that, and my children did, too.

▸ My friends let me talk. And they listened - in my case, for months!

▸ One of the most special gestures came from my white-haired friend, Faire Edwards, a widow of many years and now living modestly on her Social Security income. I met her on the street one day not long after John's death. She threw an arm around me with a quick hug, then started pawing through her pocketbook. Out came a five-dollar bill. "Spend it on yourself," she said. "Spoil yourself with some indulgence. Don't you dare spend it on peanut butter." It was not so much the money, though with Faire's income that was a lot, but she understood and encouraged me to take the time I needed to heal my grieving.

Afterword: Mourning

by Clayton Hewitt

The concept of "caring for your own dead" dates back to the dawn of civilization. Archeologists and anthropologists have shown similar reactions to death in all cultures for thousands of years. Over time, however, especially in the now prevailing funeral practices in American society, "we have given up the rituals which sanctioned the full expression of grief," and thus denied "mourners the opportunity for catharsis of their grief."[1]

The therapeutic value of ritualized funeral mourning is acknowledged today with the recognition that it is time-limited and only the first step in the mourning process.

The thesis expressed in this book is that the funeral should again become the focus of the beginning mourning process, and the way in which we relate to the body of our loved one before and during the funeral ritual can either facilitate or inhibit the mourning process.

The author suggests that we should become "more actively involved in funeral preparations," a practice that has diminished as professionals have more and more assumed this role in American society. By avoiding "custom-made funerals" and dealing with death in a more personal way, the author says that mourners can fulfill "emotional needs that probably cannot be met in any other way."

Most would agree that the contemporary American funeral is for the living, not the dead. It has evolved as a ritual response acknowledging death, usually in a religious context, and a commemoration of a life lived. It is a ritual of disposal necessary to the social group to insure its continuity and equilibrium in the face of loss.

What we do from the moment of death of our loved one to the final goodbye has profound implications for our future physical and psychological adjustment to loss. Confronting the "physical aspects of death" says the author, will make it possible for us to handle our "emotional needs as well."

---

1 Weizman, Savine Gross and Kamm, Phyllis. About Mourning (New York: Human Sciences Press, 1987), p.24.

John, Raphael, and Mary Jane

It is at the point of death that we must begin to make choices. Convention, circumstances, and values dictate what these are. We do have some options, however, which if taken, help facilitate the mourning process.

For example, in the first three chapters of this book we see a variety of possible responses, which helped the participants through the initial phase of the mourning process.

When John died, perhaps driven more by economic necessity than plan, the author was forced to take an active role in the final disposition of her husband's body.

At the moment of her greatest sorrow, she had to acknowledge the reality of her husband's death through active involvement in the funeral plans. What could she do with limited funds? She was forced to make inquiries about the costs of the traditional services offered by local funeral homes, and to make decisions about alternatives to reduce those costs.

In choosing cremation, buying a "box," and personally transporting John to the crematory, she was unknowingly beginning the first phase of the mourning process. That phase concluded when she held an open house for community mourning two days later, buried the remains in her home garden, and inscribed John's slate memorial with a Boy Scout jackknife.

The author had the rare opportunity of acting out her grief, an opportunity which may have been lost if money had been available for a conventional funeral.

The experience of the author's children shows how important it is for children to participate in the mourning process. Because they did not apparently share as best they could in the personal involvement of their mother when the funeral plans were made, their grief was inhibited and "It was months later that their grief and questions finally spilled and continued to flow."

Weizman and Kamm have said that "Seeing the deceased may be helpful for a child, just as with adults, in verifying the reality and finality of death." Under no conditions, however, should adults insist that children "view the body," but "they can encourage, give the child permission, and stand by with proper preparation and support."[2]

---

2 Weizman and Kamm, p. 163.

In Chapter 2, describing the death of Raphael, the advantages of the home funeral and burial are discussed. In this instance, both children and adults were permitted to view Raphael in his small pine box at his "rustic country home." The reality of death was directly experienced by the family, and members of the bereaved community came to offer comfort and share their sorrow with Raphael's parents. One version of the positive impact of their presence could be summed up in the statement, "Grief shared is grief diminished."

The committal service of Raphael reflected the need of his parents to say goodbye in a manner that was significant for them. There were no funeral professionals carefully orchestrating the burial ritual. Instead, we see a spontaneous expression of shared sorrow and active participation, culminating with all the participants dropping shovels of earth on Raphael's "box" and flowers.

The death of Mary Jane in Chapter 3, another example of a home burial, was, for the brothers involved, an example and extension of anticipatory grief. They began their mourning process by caring for their dying mother with love, compassion, and sensitivity.

After her death, said Steve Carlson, "It didn't occur to us to delegate our final acts of love to an outsider . . . When it came time for burial and tribute, the qualities of thoughtfulness, consideration, and love seemed far more important than professional expertise."

The common theme running through the three deaths described at the beginning of this book relates to the power of "acting out" in rituals which permitted the individuals involved to actively do something. As Therese Rando has put it, active participation "cuts through intellectualization, providing an objective focus in the present for the expression of feelings and reaching emotions on unconscious levels more effectively than mere verbalization. It allows emotions to be interpreted and channeled more easily . . . ."[3]

Holding and Viewing the Body

Active involvement in the death process compels us to consider how we react to the body of our loved one after death occurs. In advice to new funeral professionals, one

---

3 Rando, Therese A. Grief, Dying, and Death (Champaign, Ill.: Research Press Co., 1984), p. 182.

expert says, "Give the bereaved adequate private time to be with, touch, caress, and hold the body . . . Do not rush the survivors, as time with the deceased may be very critical in helping them finish unfinished business, accommodate the changed relationship they must have with the deceased, and accept the reality of loss."4

Being with our loved one after death is part of the first step of our mourning and helps us to accept the reality of our loss on both an emotional and intellectual level. For most people "it is a special time, and reassuring, although very sad. For most people it is not frightening or aversive. Even though one might think it would be more difficult to take in the fact of the death when touching and caressing the warm body, that is not actually so. It is a way of taking your leave and beginning to absorb the reality."5

There are conflicting opinions regarding viewing the body after death. Just as holding the body affirms the reality of death, so too does seeing the body. What part the visible evidence of death has in the mourning process is primarily a subjective judgment based on many variables.

One author has concluded that, "Those who did not view the body or had arranged for immediate disposition of the remains (excluding the normal Jewish custom of not viewing the body) reported the greatest hostility following the death; the greatest increase in consumption of alcohol, tranquilizers, and sedatives; the greatest increase in tension and anxiety; the lowest positive recall of the deceased; and greater problems in adjustment to the death, particularly among male respondents."6

Those who refuse to view the body usually say something like, "I want to remember her alive." Some object to cosmetic restoration of the body as an attempt to avoid death by recreating a lifelike appearance of the deceased.

The way in which the body is displayed in the funeral home may indeed discourage the closeness survivors would like to feel. Stephen Levine describes it in this manner: "The deceased lies in a metal box two or three feet off the floor so that, as you pass, you don't have the feeling that you

---

4 Rando, p. 192.

5 Weizman, p. 26.

6 Rando, p. 191.

may touch, hug, kiss, cry, pray. The separation seems unconquerable."7

Holding and viewing are, generally, to be encouraged so that family members can share the reality of death as part of the initial phase of the mourning process. Otherwise, mourning will be delayed because death has not been accepted on an emotional level. As Levine puts it, to be around the body of one who has just died gives us an "unparalleled" opportunity through the pain of holding "to let go gently into the light, for ourselves and for others."8

By extension, caring for your own dead, in the ways described in this book, may help in confronting the reality of death, in "acting out" one's grief, and in helping one through the first phase of mourning.

◉

Clayton Hewitt is Professor of Sociology and chairperson of the Social Science Division at Middlesex Community College in Middletown, Connecticut. He is also a psychotherapist specializing in death-related issues.

In 1983, Hewitt researched and developed a Death and Dying course which he has taught at the college for four years. A member of the American Association of Suicidology, he is facilitator of a Survivors of Suicide group which he founded in 1984.

In 1985 Hewitt was certified as a Death Educator and as a Death Related Counselor by the Association for Death Education and Counseling.

---

7 Levine, Stephen. Who Dies (Garden City, New York: Anchor Press/Doubleday, 1982), pp. 221,222.

8 Levine, p. 224.

References

Some of the volumes listed below have been quoted or otherwise acknowledged in the text pages of **Caring For Your Own Dead,** with full permission of the copyright holders. All are recommended to readers who desire additional information on the specific issues covered.

Congressional Hearings on the FTC Funeral Rule before the Subcommittee on Oversight and Investigations of the House Committee on Interstate and Foreign Commerce, February 13 and 21, 1980 (Serial No. 96-174) and before the Subcommittee on Commerce, Transportation, and Tourism of the House Committee on Energy And Commerce, May 4, 1983 (Serial No. 98-18), printed by the U.S. Government Printing Office, Washington, D.C.

You might have to hunt through the archives of your local library, or solicit the help of your local congressional office to track down copies of these hearing records, but they are fascinating reading. They include extensive testimony which ultimately led to congressional approval of the FTC Funeral Rule, the most sweeping reform of funeral practices in the U.S. in recent decades. As stuffy as "government documents" might sound, some of this reads like a "dime novel" and is well worth the time to examine.

Continental Association Bulletin, 2001 S. St. NW, Suite 530, Washington, DC 20009. Yearly subscription $15.

This is a monthly publication of the national Memorial Societies organization. It tends to focus most on those death-related issues which might be of national interest but which daily local papers may overlook. It especially maintains a consumer-oriented viewpoint, and keeps track of what is going on in each state on a current basis.

Cremation by Paul E. Irion. Copyright 1968. Published by Fortress Press, Philadelphia, PA 19129.

There has been relatively little popular literature written

on the subject of cremation. Irion's book is excellent reading for those who desire to know more about the subject, especially from a religious point of view.

Dealing Creatively with Death: A Manual of Death Education and Simple Burial by Ernest Morgan. Copyright 1984 by Celo Press, 1901 Hannah Branch Road, Burnsville, NC 28714. Also may be ordered from Upper Access Publishers, Box 457, Hinesburg, VT 05461. (A new edition is due soon.) $6.50.

Ernest Morgan's classic book, in its tenth edition at the time of this writing, is essential reading. It covers a wide range of subjects, including death education, living with dying, bereavement, the right to die, simple burial and cremation, Memorial Societies, death ceremonies, and how the dead can help the living. It contains a large appendix of additional useful information. Mr. Morgan's writing is characterized by personal honesty and depth of feeling which make reading it a moving as well as informative experience.

Funerals - Consumers' Last Rights by the editors of **Consumer Reports.** Copyright 1977 by Consumers Union of United States, Inc., published by Pantheon Books, New York, NY. All excerpts in this book are reprinted by permission of Consumers Union of United States, Inc.

This book compiles in extensive detail information on practices and prices of the funeral industry in the United States from the vantage point of the consumer. What it may lack in personal expression it counters with detailed and practical research. Highly recommended, even in 1987.

How To Avoid Probate - Updated by Norman F. Dacey. Copyright 1980. Crown Publishers, Inc., New York, NY.

This book has helped hundreds of thousands of families to reduce the dollar drain of legal costs following death. The first 35 pages take the mystery out of probate. The remaining several hundred pages contain forms for filing an "inter vivos" trust on almost anything one owns. This book is helpful only if it is used before death!

Inventing the American Way of Death, 1830-1920 by James J. Farrell. Copyright 1980 by Temple University Press, Philadelphia, PA 19122. All excerpts in this book reprinted by permission of Temple University Press.

Farrell's book is a rare combination of thorough academic research and compelling reading for anybody interested in the evolution of the modern funeral industry/profession.

It's Your Funeral by William L. Coleman. First published by Tyndale House, Wheaton, Illinois. Copyright 1979, reserved by author. Available from William L. Coleman, 1115 9th St., Aurora, Nebraska 68818. $3.95 plus .50 mailing. All excerpts in this book reprinted by permission of William L. Coleman.

Written from the perspective of a Christian pastor, Coleman encourages advance planning of death arrangements, and provides a general overview of some of the available options.

On Death and Dying by Elisabeth Kubler-Ross. Copyright 1969. MacMillan Publishing Co., Inc., 866 Third Ave., New York, NY 10022.

This book, now a classic on the subject, will be helpful for those who need to explore their feelings at a time of death. . . the anger is not only explained and understood, the process of grief becomes more clear and natural.

PDA *Personal Death Awareness by J. William Worden, Ph.D. and William Proctor. Copyright 1976 by the authors. Published by Prentice-Hall, Inc., Englewood Cliffs, NJ Excerpts in this book reprinted by permission of J. William Worden and William Proctor.

Through this popular self-help book, Dr. Worden has provided inspiration and guidance for thousands of people in coming to terms with their own mortality and preparing for death.

The American Way of Death by Jessica Mitford. Copyright 1963. Simon and Schuster, Inc., Rockefeller Center, 630 Fifth Avenue, New York, NY

Despite the passage of decades, this best-seller is still relevant in exposing the funeral industry excesses and identifying the commonly uninformed or misinformed public choices. The author's research appears thorough, but the book is written in a down-to-earth way with the reader in mind. It continues to be widely read and discussed today.

Glossary

===

air tray: an uncovered container used for placing a body into a cremation chamber, generally made from cardboard or cardboard and plywood.

alternative container: an inexpensive body container; funeral directors often use the term "minimum" container. This can be a box of cardboard or plywood; some are covered with cloth.

arrangements: a word used to cover all preparations for a funeral and for the disposition of a dead body.

ashes: a misused term for what is left after cremation; the residue is bone fragments which resemble broken sea shells when not pulverized. See **cremains**.

attending physician: the doctor who is present at the time of death; sometimes this can be the family doctor responsible for a person's care even if not actually present at the moment of death.

autopsy: examination or dissection of a body to determine the cause of death, sometimes requiring lengthy chemical analysis or laboratory procedures.

body donation: the bequest of a human body to a medical school for the purpose of anatomical study necessary in training doctors, including osteopaths, chiropractors, and dentists. In addition to the teaching of basic anatomy courses, scientific research may be a part of the medical school program; in many cases this amounts to a loan since the body or cremains may be returned to the family by request when study is complete. See Chapter 8.

burial-transit permit: the form which usually accompanies a body to its final disposition; sometimes it is attached to a death certificate and sometimes it is a separate document. This permit may indicate that the death either has been investigated by a medical examiner or does not need to be; it is also a way for a state to record where final disposition takes place. See Chapter 9.

cadaver: a dead body. The term is used most often in reference to a body donated for medical study.

casket/coffin: the box used for containing a body after death. The least expensive ones are cardboard or simple, unfinished wood; the most expensive may be copper or bronze with ornate handles, elaborate cloth lining, and an adjustable inner-spring mattress. Regardless of how well sealed a coffin may be, decomposition is to be expected even when a body is embalmed.

coffin vault: a large one-piece tank, usually concrete but sometimes metal or fiberglass, which is lowered by machine into a grave-site excavation; after the coffin is placed inside, a lid is added. The purpose in using such an item is to keep the ground from settling after decomposition. Extra soil is carted away, and grounds maintenance is simplified. There is no significant effect on body preservation. Coffin vaults usually cost twice the price of a grave liner. No state law requires a coffin vault, but cemetery policy may, even when a metal casket is used. See Chapter 7.

columbarium: a building, usually adorned with stained glass windows and other aesthetic embellishments, containing probably several hundred small chambers for cremated remains. The door behind which an urn is placed may be marked with a bronze plaque bearing the name of the deceased. See Chapter 5.

common carrier: public transportation such as railroad or airplane. Shipping of a body by common carrier usually requires embalming or a hermetically sealed container.

coroner: usually an elected official who must investigate the circumstances surrounding the cause of death when other than natural cause is suspected. The coroners in some states are not required to have medical training and may refer the case to a state pathologist or medical examiner for study. See Chapter 9.

corpse: a dead body.

cremains: the bone fragments remaining after the cremation process, a more accurate term than ashes. Most crematories now pulverize these fragments into small granular particles.

cremation: reduction of body mass by the use of heat or fire; only mineral content remains. See Chapter 5.

crypt: part of a vaulted chamber into which a casket is placed. Originally, a crypt was below ground, but in current cemetery practices, an above-ground space in a mausoleum is referred to as a crypt.

decomposition: the natural process of disintegration of any once-living matter.

disposition/final disposition: the last resting place of a dead human body. Since few states have statutes governing the final plans for cremains, the cremation itself is considered disposition. Body donation is usually considered final disposition even if the remains or cremains are to be returned to a family. Burial is the most common form of disposition in the U. S. at this time.

embalm: to inject with chemicals to retard decay. Routine embalming is not required by law in any state. However, death from a communicable/contagious disease or transportation by a common carrier requires embalming in a few states. The type of embalming used to delay funeral arrangements for several days does not preserve a body much beyond that time. See Chapter 6. Chapter 8 describes medical embalming.

embalmer: a person who has received training in body preservation. In some states, an embalmer's license is additional to or separate from the license required to operate as a funeral director. A medical school might need an embalmer on its staff, but it would not need a funeral director.

FTC: Federal Trade Commission. See Appendix II for a description of the FTC "Funeral Rule."

fetal death: a miscarriage or spontaneous termination of pregnancy before birth. In some states an abortion must be reported as a fetal death. A fetal death report is used primarily for statistical purposes. See Chapter 9.

funeral: the ceremony held at a time of death. Usually a funeral is planned within a religious context and with the body present. It also is considered an occasion for family and friends to share in the grieving process and to acknowledge regard for the deceased.

funeral board: a state-authorized board which licenses funeral directors and embalmers. The state funeral board will often be instrumental in writing legislation for that state regarding the practice of funeral directing. The board is generally in charge of regulating those practices.

funeral director: a person whose services may be hired to make all the arrangements at a time of death. In some states, a funeral director is not necessarily an embalmer.

grave liner: see **coffin vault**. A grave liner is usually assembled at the grave-site from several pieces. It costs about half the amount of a coffin vault. See Chapter 7.

hermetically sealed: airtight; the primary purpose of such a casket is to prevent the escape of noxious odors which may develop during decomposition. An embalmed body will continue to decay even inside an air-tight container.

hospice: originally a shelter for travellers, later for the sick and poor. In current U.S. practice, a hospice organization functions as a support group and can assist the family in caring for a terminally ill person at home and in preparation for death.

interment: burial.

inurnment: placement in an urn.

mausoleum: once synonymous with tomb. This structure may contain only those crypts of a family or it may be a building large enough to contain several hundred crypts.

medical examiner: a physician trained for medical investigation.

memorial society: an organization which can assist a person in making pre-death funeral plans or arrangements. The emphasis tends to be toward a funeral of simplicity. Memorial societies also make an effort to educate the public in a wide variety of matters regarding death and funeral arrangements.

memorial service: a funeral service without a body present.

morgue: a place for the temporary storage of a dead body, usually refrigerated.

mortician: a funeral director/embalmer.

mortuary: a funeral home.

mortuary arts: the ability to restore a dead body to a life-like pose. Mortuary science deals especially with body preservation.

next-of-kin: the relative(s) in nearest blood or marriage relationship; the exact order may vary somewhat from state to state. See Chapter 9 for one common listing.

niche: a small wall-chamber for cremains, usually side-by-side with many others. See **columbarium** and Chapter 5.

obituary: the written notice of a death published by a newspaper. See Chapter 9.

organ donation: the removal after death of a body part which can be transplanted to a living person in need. See Chapter 8.

over-enrollment: more body donations than are needed at a given time. Because a person who has signed a body bequest may have had strong feelings about favoring a particular school, some schools are reluctant to offer surplus donations to others. However, the need for body donations varies greatly and is far from adequate in all colleges. See Chapter 8. Also check Ernest Morgan's book.

pacemaker: an electronic device which is surgically implanted beneath the skin to regulate heartbeat. The batteries which power a pacemaker can explode during cremation. See Chapter 9.

perpetual care: maintenance of a cemetery forever. Town or city cemeteries may be taken care of by tax money, especially small rural ones. Large for-profit cemeteries usually charge an additional sum for this; the money is invested, with the investment income applied to maintenance costs.

prior enrollment: the bequest or "will" signed before death when you wish to donate your body to medical science. Some medical schools require this. Other medical schools will accept a donation by next-of-kin after death. See Chapter 8.

pre-need: funeral arrangements made and often paid for before death. See Appendix III.

pyre: a pile of wood on which a body is placed for burning, a common funeral rite in India. See Chapter 5.

remains: a dead body or its collected parts (after a disaster).

shroud: the clothing or cloth used to wrap a dead body.

undertaker: funeral director; the term undertaker is no longer in vogue, although many statutes still include this word.

unattended death: a death without a physician present. In some states, this is interpreted more liberally: i.e., the death of a person who has been regularly under a physician's care and whose death was anticipated need not be investigated.

urn: a covered container for cremains. An elaborate urn may be somewhat like a vase, and many are made of metal. If the family has not chosen such a purchase, the "urn" used to deliver cremains is a simple box. See Chapter 5.

vault: see **coffin vault.** This word is also used to describe the chamber a cemetery uses to hold a body until spring burial. See Chapter 7.

viewing: a common funeral ritual which allows friends and relatives to see the dead person. Close family members who may not have been present at the time of death often feel the need to see a body in accepting the reality of death. See Afterword.

vital statistics: the record of births, deaths, and marriages which every state is required to keep.

Notes

CARING FOR YOUR OWN DEAD

To Order By Mail

Write to: Upper Access Publishers
One Upper Access Road
P.O. Box 457
Hinesburg, Vermont 05461

Include: • Your full name;
• Mailing address (including zip code);
• Number of copies requested;
• Specify hard cover or soft cover;
• Check or money order, made out to
Upper Access Publishers.

Price (includes $2.00 postage and handling):
Hard Cover, $19.95 per copy;
Soft Cover, $14.95 per copy.

Discounts are available for quantity orders. For details, please write to Upper Access Publishers at the above address, or telephone (802) 482-2988.